Queen's Rangers

Queen's Rangers

John Simcoe and his Rangers During
the Revolutionary War for America

John Simcoe

LEONAUR

Queen's Rangers: John Simcoe and his Rangers During
the Revolutionary War for America
by John Simcoe

Published by Leonaur Ltd

Text in this form copyright © 2007 Leonaur Ltd

Originally published in 1787 under the title:
Simcoe's Military Journal: a History of the Operations of
a Partisan Corps, called The Queen's Rangers,
Commanded by Lieutenant-Colonel J. G. Simcoe,
During the War of the American Revolution

ISBN: 978-1-84677-255-9 (hardcover)
ISBN: 978-1-84677-256-6 (softcover)

http://www.leonaur.com

Publisher's Note

The opinions expressed in this book are those of the author
and are not necessarily those of the publisher.

Contents

Introduction

The writer of these Memoirs has been induced to print them by a variety of reasons, among which the following are included. Actions erroneously attributed to others may be restored to those who really performed them: His own memory may be renewed, and preserved in their bosoms, whose patronage and confidence he acknowledges with pride and gratitude; while, at the same time, he bears testimony to the merits of those excellent officers and soldiers whom it was his good fortune to command, during the late war in America: a war which he always considered as forced upon Great Britain, and in which he served from principle. Events, however unfortunate, can neither alter its nature nor cancel his opinion. Had he supposed it to have been unjust, he would have resigned his commission; for no true soldier and servant of his country will ever admit that a British officer can divest himself of the duties of a citizen, or in a civil contest is bound to support the cause his conscience rejects.

The command of a light corps, or, as it is termed, the service of a partisan, is generally esteemed the best mode of instruction for those who aim at higher stations; as it gives an opportunity of exemplifying professional acquisitions, fixes the habit of self-dependence for resources, and obliges to that prompt decision which in the common rotation of duty subordinate officers can seldom exhibit, yet without which none can be qualified for any trust of importance. To attain this employment was therefore an early object with the author; nor could he be diverted from his purpose by the shameful character of dishonesty, rapine, and falsehood, supposed to attend it; at least by those who formed their judgment on the conversation of such officers as had been witnesses to the campaigns in Germany. He had fairer examples to profit from; as the page of military history scarcely details more spirited exertions in this kind of service, than what distinguishingly marked the last civil commotions in England; and Massey's well known saying, "that he could not look upon the goods of any Englishman as those of an enemy," delineated the integrity of the citizen, and the honourable policy of the soldier.

His intimate connection with that most upright and zealous officer the late Admiral Graves, who commanded at Boston in the year 1775, and some services which he was pleased to entrust him with, brought him acquainted with many of the American loyalists: from them he soon learned the practicability of raising troops in the country whenever it should be opened to the King's forces; and the propriety of such a measure appeared to be self-evident. He therefore importuned Admiral Graves to ask of General Gage that he might enlist such negroes as were in Boston, and with them put himself under the direction of Sir James Wallace, who was then actively engaged at Rhode Island, and to whom that colony had opposed negroes; adding to the Admiral, who seemed surprised at his request, " that he entertained "no doubt he should soon exchange them for whites:" Gen. Gage, on the Admiral's application, informed him that the negroes were not sufficiently numerous to be serviceable, and that he had other employment for those who were in Boston.

When the army sailed from Halifax for Staten Island, the author was Captain of the grenadier company of the 40th regiment, and during the time of winter quarters at Brunswick, in 1776, went purposely to New York to solicit the command of the Queen's Rangers, then vacant The boat he was in, being driven from the place of its destination, he was exceedingly chagrined to find that he had arrived some hours too late: but he desired that Col. Cuyler, Sir William Howe's Aid-de-Camp, would mention his coining thither to him, as well as his design. On the army's embarking for the Chesapeake, he wrote to General Grant, under whom he had served, requesting his good offices in procuring him a command like that of the Queen's Rangers, if any other corps intended for similar employment should be raised in the country, to which the expedition was destined.

These circumstances are related, not only as introductory to the subsequent journal, but to show how very early his thoughts were bent on attaining the command of a corps raised in America, for the active duty of light troops.

The journal, as it is, in its own nature, not generally interesting, and guarded from any observations foreign to the subject, he by no means wishes to obtrude upon the public; but hopes it will be favourably received by those to whom he shall offer it as a testimony of respect, and with whom it may claim some indulgence, as the particular nature and event of the American war gives a degree of consequence to operations however minute: for it terminated not in the loss of some petty fortress, or trivial island, but in the divulsion of a continent from a continent; of a world from a world.

The officer who conducts a light corps properly, will in his small sphere make use of the same principles which Generals apply to the regulation of armies. He will naturally imitate the commanders under whom he serves; while the individuals of his corps (for in such a service *only* individuals become of importance) will manifest a spirit which probably the whole army may possess without having similar opportunities of calling it into action.

History cannot produce examples of more ardent zeal in the service of their country, than that which characterised the British officers and soldiers in America. They despised all those conveniences without which it would be thought impracticable for European armies to move. They did not tamely wait for the moment of exertion in the precise line of their duty, but boldly sought out danger and death; and no sooner was one officer lost on any hazardous service than many competitors appeared to succeed in the post of honour. It was this spirit which, among uncommon difficulties, so frequently triumphed over numbers of brave, skilful, and enterprising opponents. The British soldier who thought himself superior, actually became so; and the ascendancy which he claimed was in many instances importantly admitted by his antagonists. Nor was this spirit, the result of principle; confined to the operations of the field: it was shown in the hour of civil persecution and rigorous imprisonment; in situations where coolness supplies the place of activity, and thought precedes execution. General Gage in a celebrated letter to Washington at the commencement of the war, had said, "that such trials would be met with the fortitude of martyrs;" and the behaviour of the loyalists amply confirmed his prophesy.

The British Generals were commonly obliged to hazard their armies without any possibility of retreat in case of misadventure: they trusted to the spirit and discipline of their troops; and the decision, with which they risked themselves, forms the most striking and singular feature of the American war. Nor was this only done when the armies were in their full force; by Sir William Howe in his

campaigns, particularly in the glorious battle of the Brandywine; by Sir Henry Clinton in his celebrated march
through the Jersies; by Earl Cornwallis in a latter period at
Guildford, when the war was transferred to the Carolinas;
and eminently by Lord Rawdon, who was:

Left to bide the disadvantage of a field
Where nothing but the sound of Britain's name
Did seem defensible?

but the same spirit was infused into the smallest operations;
and the light troops in their enterprises, confident in the
superiority of their composition, scarcely admitted the idea
of retreat, or calculated against the contingency of a repulse.
An account of the Queen's Rangers, and their operations,
will elucidate the preceding positions; show in such a point
of view their similitude to the British army, and contain, as
it were, an epitome of its history.

This Journal alleges no fact but what the author believes
to be true; the frequent introduction of his own name may
appear redundant, but is absolutely necessary to the perspi-
cuity of the work. He never valued himself so highly on
the actions which it was his good fortune to perform to
the satisfaction of his superiors, as voluntarily to prescribe
them for the boundaries of his professional ambition. Yet,
as a British officer, should he live to double the number
of years which he has already devoted to the service of his
country, it is scarcely possible that he shall ever be appointed to so important a trust as that which he solicited, when
he offered to fortify and maintain Billingsport: and as an
European soldier, and an European subject, what field for
honourable enterprise can ever be so wide, as that which
he would have expatiated in, had he according to his own
plan, joined the Indians; directed them to collateral exertion; and associating the loyalists of the back countries zeal-

ous in the British cause, united them with the enemies of Congress; set before them the Queen's Rangers as their most necessary guides and examples; led the whole combination to incessant and adventurous action during the war; and if victorious, had remained at their head in that hour when America was declared independent by a critical and unexpected peace.

Preface

The military journal of Lt. Col. Simcoe, was privately printed by the author in 1787, for distribution among a few of his personal friends. The production has hitherto, it would seem, entirely escaped the attention of those who are curious in the history of our Revolutionary War. As a record of some interesting particulars and local occurrences of that memorable struggle, and as a well written documentary illustration of the times and the circumstances of the American Rebellion, it deserves circulation and favour. The fortunate procurement of a copy of the work in London enables the publishers to present it in an edition securing its preservation and facilitating a general knowledge of its contents.

A memoir of so much of the author's life as is not exhibited in his journal, it is thought, will interest the reader and increase the permanent value of the volume. Accordingly such a memoir has been prepared from available and authentic materials, and, by way of introduction, may serve to fill out the history of the commander of the Queen's Rangers, presenting also a few facts concerning the corps not otherwise appearing. Not to extend that portion of the publication too far, however, various relevant quotations from different sources, interesting essen-

tially, and expletive in their character, are thrown into the
appendix in addition to what the journalist has given in
that form himself.

New York
December, 1843

CHAPTER 1

The Rangers are Formed

On the 15th of October, 1777, Sir William Howe was pleased to appoint Captain Simcoe of the Grenadiers, with the Provincial rank of Major, to the command of the Queen's Rangers; the next day he joined the regiment, which was encamped with the army in the vicinity of Germantown.

On the 19th the army marched to Philadelphia, the Queen's Rangers formed the rear guard of the left column, and, in the encampment, their post was on the right of the line, in front of the village of Kensington; the army extending from the Delaware to the Schuylkill

On the 20th the regiment was augmented with nearly an hundred men, who had been enlisted by Captain Smyth during the various marches from the landing of the army in the Chesapeake to this period.

This was a very seasonable recruit to the regiment; it had suffered materially in the action at Brandywine, and was too much reduced in numbers to be of any efficient service; but if the loss of a great number of gallant officers and soldiers had been severely felt, the impression which that action had left upon their minds was of the highest advantage to the regiment; officers and soldiers became known to each other; they had been engaged in a more serious manner, and with greater disadvantages than they were likely again to meet with in the common chance of war; and having extricated themselves most gallantly from such a situation, they felt themselves invincible.

This spirit vibrated among them at the time Major Simcoe joined them; and it was obvious, that he had nothing to do but to cherish and preserve it. Sir William Howe, in consequence of their behaviour at Brandywine, had promised that all promotions should go in the regiment, and accordingly they now took place.

The Queen's Rangers had been originally raised in Connecticut, and the vicinity of New York, by Colonel Rogers, for the duties which their name implies, and which were detailed in his commission; at one period they mustered above four hundred men, all Americans, and all loyalists. Hardships and neglect had much reduced their numbers, when the command of them was given to Colonel French, and afterwards to Major Weymess, to whom Major Simcoe succeeded; their officers also had undergone a material change; many gentlemen of the Southern colonies who had joined Lord Dunmore, and distinguished themselves under his orders, were appointed to supersede those who were not thought competent to the commissions they had hitherto borne; to these were added some volunteers from the army, the whole consisting of young men, active, full of love of the service, emulous to distinguish themselves in it, and looking forward to obtain, through their actions, the honour of being enrolled with the British army.

The Provincial corps, now forming, were raised on the supposed influence which their officers had among their loyal countrymen, and were understood to be native American loyalists; added to an equal chance among these, a greater resource was opened to the Queen's Rangers, in the exclusive privilege of enlisting old countrymen (as Europeans were termed in America) and deserters from the rebel army; so that could the officers to whom the Commander in Chief delegated the inspection of the Provincial corps have executed their orders, the Queen's Rangers, however dangerously and incessantly employed, would never have been in want of recruits. At the same time, the original loyalists, and those of this description, who were from time to time enlisted, forming the gross of the corps, were the source from whence it derived its value and its discipline; they were men who had already been exiled for their attachment to the British government, and who now acted upon the firmest principles in its defence. On the contrary, the people they had to oppose, however characterised by the enemies of Great Britain, had never been considered by them as engaged in an honourable cause, or fighting for the freedom of their country; they estimated them not by their words, but by an intimate observance of their actions, and to civil desecration, experience had taught them to add military contempt. Such was the composition of the Queen's Rangers, and the spirit that animated it

The junction of Captain Smyth's company augmented the regiment into eleven companies, the number of which was equalised, and the eleventh was formed of Highlanders. Several of those brave men, who had been defeated in an attempt to join the army in North Carolina, were now in the corps; to those others were added, and the command was given to Captain M'Kay; they were furnished with the Highland dress, and their national piper, and were posted on the left flank of the regiment, which consisted of eight battalions, a grenadier, and light infantry company. Upon the march from German Town to Kensington, Sir William Erskine, in directing what duties Major Simcoe should do, had told him to call upon him for dragoons, whenever he wanted them; upon this, Major Simcoe took the liberty of observing, "that the clothing and habiliments of the dragoons were so different from those of the Queen's Rangers (the one being in red, and with white belts, easily seen at a distance, and the other in green, and accoutred for concealment) that he thought it would be more useful to mount a dozen soldiers of the regiment" Sir William Erskine highly approved of the idea, and sent a suitable number of horses, saddles, and swords; such men were selected for the service as the officers recommended for spirit and presence of mind; they were put under the direction of Kelly, a Sergeant of distinguished gallantry.

A light corps, augmented as that of the Queen's Rangers was, and employed on the duties of an outpost, had no opportunity of being instructed in the general discipline of the army, nor indeed was it very necessary: the most important duties, those of vigilance, activity, and patience of fatigue, were best learnt in the field; a few motions of the manual exercise were thought sufficient; they were carefully instructed in those of firing, but above all, attention was paid to inculcate the use of the bayonet, and a total reliance on that weapon. The divisions being fully officered, and weak in numbers, was of the greatest utility, and in many trying situations was the preservation of the corps; two files in the centre, and two on each flank, were directed to be composed of trained soldiers, without regard to their size or appearance. It was explained, that no rotation, except in ordinary duties, should take place among light troops, but that those officers would be selected for any service who appeared to be most capable of executing it: it was also enforced by example, that no service was to be measured by the numbers employed on it, but by its own importance, and that five men, in critical situations or employment, was a more honourable command than an hundred on common duties. Sergeant's guards were in a manner abolished, a circumstance to which in a great measure may be attributed, that no sentinel or guard of the Queen's Rangers was ever surprised; the vigilance of a gentleman and an officer being transcendently superior to that of any non-commissioned officer whatsoever. An attention to the interior economy of a company, indispensable as it is, by no means forms the most pleasing military duty upon service, where the officer looks up to something more essentially useful, and values himself upon its execution.

A young corps raised in the midst of active service, and without the habits of discipline, which are learnt in time of peace, required the strictest attention in this point It was observed, that regularity in messing, and cleanliness in every respect, conduced to the health of the soldier; and from the numbers that each regiment brought into the field, superior officers would in general form the best estimate of the attention of a corps to its interior economy; and to enforce the performance of these duties in the strongest manner, it was declared in public orders, "that to such only when in the field, the commanding officer would entrust the duties of it, who should execute with spirit what belongs to the interior economy of the regiment when in quarters." To avoid written orders as much as possible, after the morning parade, the officers attended, as the German custom is, and received verbally whatever could be so delivered to them, and they were declared answerable that every written order was read to the men on their separate parades.

CHAPTER 2

Action Around Frankfort

Near the end of October the Queen's Rangers were directed to patrol beyond Frankfort, four miles from Philadelphia; it was the day that Colonel Dunlop made his unfortunate attempt on Red Bank; they advanced as far as the Red Lion, which several of the rebel officers had left a few minutes before.

The country in front of Philadelphia, where the Queen's Rangers were employed, was in general cleared ground, but intersected with many woods; the fields were fenced out with very high railing: the main road led straight from Philadelphia to Bristol Ferry on the Delaware; about five miles from Philadelphia, on this road, was Frankfort Creek which fell into the Delaware nearly at that distance, and the angle that it formed was called Point-no-Point, within which were many good houses and plantations.

Beyond the bridge over the creek, on a height, was the village of Frankfort; below the bridge it was not fordable, but it was easily passed in many places above it The rebels frequently patrolled as far as Frankfort, and to a place called the Rocks, about a mile beyond it. Four miles farther was Pennypack Creek, over which was a bridge; three miles beyond this was the Red Lion tavern, and two miles further was Bristol, a small town opposite Burlington: this road was the nearest to the river Delaware; nearly parallel to it was the road to York, which was attended to by the light infantry, of the guards, and the army; there were many cross roads that intersected the country between these main roads, a most perfect knowledge of which was endeavoured to be acquired by maps, drawn from the information of the country people, and by ocular observation.

The village of Kensington was several times attacked by the rebel patrolling parties; they could come by means of the woods very near to it undiscovered; there was a road over a small creek to Point-no-Point; to defend this a house was made musket proof, and the bridge taken up; cavalry only approached to this post, for it lying, as has been mentioned, in an angle between the Delaware and the Frank-fort road, infantry were liable to be cut off; on the left there was a knoll that overlooked the country; this was the post of the piquet in the daytime, but corn fields high enough to conceal the approach of an enemy reached to its basis; sentinels from hence inclined to the left and joined those of Colonel Twistleton's (now Lord Say and Sele) light infantry of the guards, so that this hill projected forward, and on that account was ordered by Sir William Erskine not to be defended if attacked in force, and it was withdrawn at night.

It was usual, if the enemy approached, to quit this post till such time as the corps could get under arms, and the light infantry of the guards were informed of it; when, marching up the road, the enemy fearing to be shut up within the creek that has been mentioned, abandoned their ground and generally suffered in their retreat to the woods. At night the corps was drawn back to the houses nearer Philadelphia, and guards were placed behind breastworks, made by heaping up the fences in such points as commanded the avenues to the village; (which was laid out and enclosed in right angles;) these were themselves overlooked by others that constituted the alarm post of the different companies. Fires also were made in particular places before the piquet, to discover whatsoever should approach.

Before day the whole corps was under arms, and remained so till the piquets returned to their day post, which they resumed, taking every precaution against ambuscades; the light infantry of the guards advanced their piquets at the same time, and Colonel Twistleton was an admirable pattern for attention and spirit, to all who served with him. He was constantly with the piquets, which generally found out the enemy's patrols, and interchanged shot with them: his horse was one morning wounded by a rifle shot. The mounted men of the Queen's Ranger's were found very serviceable on these occasions.

The woods in the front were every day diminishing, being cut down for the uses of the army, and the enemy kept at a greater distance. An attempt was made to surprise the rebel post at Frankfort; by orders from headquarters the Queen's Rangers were to march near to the bridge at Frankfort, and to lay there in ambuscade till such time as Major Gwyn, who made a circuit with a detachment of cavalry, should fall into the rear of the town. Accordingly the corps marched through bye paths, and attained its position: some dragoons at the appointed time passed the bridge from Frankfort. The light was not sufficient to enable the Rangers to discover whether they were friends or enemies, till upon their turning back and hearing a shot, the corps rushed into the town; unfortunately, either by accident or from information, the rebel post had been withdrawn.

Some days after the Queen's Rangers, with thirty dragoons of the 16th, under Lieutenant Pidcock, marched at midnight to attempt the same post; after making a circuit, and nearly attaining the rear of the Jolly Post, the public house where the guard was kept, the party fell in with a

A Rifleman of the Queen's Rangers

patrol; this was cut off from the house; it luckily did not fire, but ran towards the wood: the detachment was carefully prevented from firing. No time was lost in the pursuit of the enemy, but the infantry crossed the fields immediately in the rear of the house, and a disposition was formed for attacking it, in case, as it well might have been, it should be defended: the cavalry made a circuit to the road in the rear, and the post was completely surprised.

An officer and twenty men were taken prisoners, two or three of whom were slightly wounded in an attempt to escape; they were militia, and what is very remarkable, they had the word " Richmond" chalked in their hats; the officer said "Richmond was the countersign, and that he chalked it there that his men might not forget it" Sergeant Kelly dismounted an officer, and in pursuit of another man, left him; the officer gave his watch to another dragoon; it was however adjudged to the sergeant, as he was the person who dismounted him, spared his life, and pursued his duty.

It is not improper here to observe, that formerly Major Simcoe had forbidden the soldiers to take watches, and indeed did so after this, 'till he accidentally overheard a man say it was not worth while to bring in a prisoner; he therefore made it a rule, that anyone who took a prisoner, if he publicly declared he had his watch, should keep it; so that no soldier was interested to kill any man. This spirit of taking as many prisoners as possible was most earnestly attempted to be inculcated, and not without success.

Soon after, as a strong patrol of cavalry, under Major Gwyn, was out, some of its men returned in great confusion, saying, "that they were attacked by a superior body, both in front and rear:" at the same time Colonel Twistleton and Major Simcoe, who were on the Knoll, occupied by the piquet of the Rangers, could perceive by the glittering of arms, a large body of foot in a wood, near which

Major Gwyn was to return, they immediately took their respective piquets, about twenty men, and marched to mask the wood. The soldiers in camp were ordered to run to the Knoll, without waiting, and the officer of the piquet was directed to form them as fast as they came up, by twelves, and to forward them under the first officer or Sergeant who should arrive.

The whole regiment and the light infantry of the guards were soon on the march; the enemy in the wood retreated; and gaining better intelligence, Colonel Twisleton halted on the verge of it, till Major Gwyn, who had beaten back the enemy, returned. The next day it was known that Pulaski had commanded the enemy: a skirmish had happened the day before, between smaller parties, and he, supposing that a large patrol would be sent out from Philadelphia, obtained the command of a very strong one to ambuscade it; but, however able and spirited he might be, he was soon convinced that his irregulars could not withstand the promptitude and strength of the British cavalry.

Parties of the Rangers every day went to Frankfort, where the enemy no longer kept a fixed post, though they frequently sent a patrol to stop the market people. A patrolling party of the Rangers approached undiscovered so close to a rebel sentinel, posted upon the bridge, that it would have been easy to have killed him. A boy, whom he had just examined, was sent back to inform him of this, and to direct him immediately to quit his post or that he should be shot; he ran off, and the whole party, on his arrival at the guard, fled with equal precipitation; nor were there any more sentinels placed there: a matter of some consequence to the poor people of Philadelphia, as they were not prevented from getting their flour ground at Frankfort mills.

It was the object, to instil into the men, that their superiority lay in close fight, and in the use of the bayonet, in which the individual courage, and personal activity that characterise the British soldier can best display themselves. The whole corps being together on the Frankfort road, information was received that Pulaski with his cavalry was approaching; on each side of the road, for some distance, there was wood, and very high rails fenced it from the road; the march was not interrupted, and the following disposition was made to attack him. The light infantry in front were loaded, and occupied the whole space of the road; Captain Stephenson, who commanded it, was directed not to fire at one or two men, who might advance, but, either on their firing or turning back, to give notice of his approach, to follow at a brisk and steady rate, and to fire only on the main body when he came close to them. The eight battalion companies were formed about thirty feet from the light infantry, in close column by companies, their bayonets fixed, and not loaded; they were instructed not to heed the enemy's horses, but to bayonet the men. The grenadiers and Highland company were in the rear, loaded; and the directions given to Captain Armstrong were, that the grenadiers should cross the fences on the right, and the Highlanders those on the left, and secure the flanks; the men were so prepared and so cheerful, that if an opportunity of rushing on Pulaski's cavalry had offered, which by the winding of the road was probable, before they could be put into career, there remains no doubt upon the minds of those who were present, but that it would have been a very honourable day for the Rangers.

CHAPTER 3

The Huzzars are Formed

On the 3rd of November the news of the surrender of General Burgoyne's army was communicated in general orders. It was read to the Rangers on their parade; and amidst the distress that such an event must naturally occasion to Englishmen and soldiers, never did Major Simcoe feel himself more elevated, or augur better of the officers and men he had the honour to command, than when he came to the rejection of one of the proposed articles, in the following terms: "Sooner than this army will consent to ground their arms in their encampment, they will rush on the enemy, determined to take no quarter;" the whole corps thrilled with animation, and resentment against the enemy, and with sympathy for their fellow soldiers; it would have been the most favourable moment, had the enemy appeared, to have attacked them.

Major Grymes, a Virginia gentleman of loyalty, education, and fortune, who was second Major of the Queen's Rangers, at this time resigned his commission, to the great regret of Major Simcoe and of the corps, whose confidence he had won by extricating them from a very disadvantageous situation, by a decisive and bold exertion at Brandywine: he was succeeded in duties, with the rank of Captain Commandant, by Lieutenant Ross of the 35th regiment, with whose intrepidity, and zeal for the service, Major Simcoe was well acquainted.

The redoubts in front of Philadelphia being finished, the advance piquets were withdrawn and posted in them, that of the Queen's Rangers excepted; it remained without the redoubt, though it had fallen back much nearer to it: it was liable to insult, but it would have been difficult to have surprised it. The Knoll was still the outpost, and the general place to which many of the officers of the line rode, in order to laugh at the mounted men and their habiliments; but other troops of cavalry were now raising, and the utility of them, through all the ridicule of bad horses and want of appointments, became very obvious.

On General Washington's occupying the camp at Whitemarsh, Sir William Howe thought proper to move towards him, and the army marched accordingly on the 5th of December; the Queen's Rangers were ordered to flank the right of the baggage. The army encamped on Chesnut Hill and its vicinity; and the piquet of the Rangers made fires on the road that led to it, so that the approach of any parties of the enemy could easily be seen.

The army remained the next day in the same position. On the 7th, at night, Major Simcoe with the Queen's Rangers, and a party of dragoons under Captain Lord Cathcart, took up the position of some of the troops who had retired; this post was sometime afterwards quitted in great silence, and he joined the column that was marching under General Gray.

The General marched all night, and on approaching the enemy's outpost, he formed his column into three divisions; the advanced guard of the centre consisted of the Hessian Yagers, who marched with their cannon up the road that led through the wood in which the enemy's light troops were posted; the light infantry of the guards advanced upon the right, and the Queen's Rangers on the left; the enemy were outflanked on each wing, and were turned in attempting to escape by the unparalleled swiftness of the light infantry of the guards, and driven across the fire of the Yagers, and the Queen's Rangers. The loss of the rebels was computed at near an hundred, with little or none on the part of the King's troops; a mounted man of the Queen's Rangers, in the pursuit, was killed by a Yager, through mistake: he wore a helmet that had been taken from a rebel patrol a few days before. General Grey was pleased to express himself highly satisfied with the order and rapidity with which the Rangers advanced.

The night was passed in a wood not far from the enemy's camp. The next day Major Simcoe patrolled in the vicinity: he left the infantry of his party at the edge of the wood, and approached a house; the owner of it, who supposed that all the British soldiers wore red, was easily imposed upon to believe him a rebel officer, and a cow-bell being, as preconcerted, rang in the wood, and an officer galloping to Major Simcoe and telling him that the British were marauding and hunting the cattle, the man had no doubt of the matter, and instantly acquiesced in a proposal to fetch some more cavalry to seize the British; he accordingly mounted his horse and galloped off.

The ambuscade was properly laid for whomsoever he should bring, when Captain Andre came with orders to retreat, the column being already in motion; the infantry were scarce sent off and the mounted men following, when about thirty of the rebel dragoons appeared in sight and on the gallop; they fired several carbine shot, to no purpose. The army returned to Philadelphia.

The disaster that happened to the mounted Ranger determined Major Simcoe to provide high caps, which might at once distinguish them both from the rebel army and their own; the mounted men were termed Huzzars, were armed with a sword, and such pistols as could be bought, or taken from the enemy; Major Simcoe's wish was to add a dagger to these arms, not only as useful in close action, but to lead the minds of the soldier to expect that decisive mode of combat. Several good horses had been taken from the rebels, so that the Huzzars were now well mounted, on hardy serviceable horses, which bore a very unusual share of fatigue. Lieutenant Wickham, an officer of quickness, and courage, was appointed to command them, and a sergeant of the 16th regiment of light dragoons attended their parade, to give them regularity in its duties.

Several men having deserted, Major Simcoe directed that the countersign should not be given to the sentinels; they were ordered to stop any persons at a distance, more than one, until the guard turned out; and in posting of sentinels, the rule was, to place them so that, if possible, they could see and not be seen, and in different posts in the night from those of the day. Near high-roads, double sentinels, without being loaded, were advanced beyond the front of the chain; these were composed of old soldiers who, with all others, were sedulously instructed to challenge very loud. The sentinels were relieved every hour. The subaltern frequently patrolled, as did the captain of the day, and the field officers: the consequence was, that the Queen's Rangers never gave a false alarm, or had a sentinel surprised, during the war. It is remarkable that a man deserted at this time who left all his necessaries, regimentals excepted: he had lately come from Europe, and, to all appearance, had enlisted merely to facilitate his joining the rebel army.

It may be here a proper place to describe the country in front of Philadelphia; and the general duties on which the Queen's Rangers were employed, during the winter.

The road on the right, and nearest the Delaware, has been

already mentioned by the name of the Frankfort road: from the centre of Philadelphia, the main road led up the country, and about two miles off, at the Rising Sun, it branched into the Old York road on the right, and that of the Germantown on the left. The light infantry of the guards patrolled up the York-town road, as that of the line did the German-town; those that ran on the side of the Schuylkill, were in front of the Yagers, and patrolled by them.

The Queen's Rangers, by their position, were at the greatest distance from Mr. Washington's camp, which was now at Valley Forge, beyond the Schuylkill, and as the course of the Delaware inclined away from the Schuylkill, the distance was considerably increased; so that no detachment from his camp could have been made without extreme hazard; from the York-town road, therefore, on the left, and the Delaware river on the right, Major Simcoe felt no apprehensions; when he passed Frankfort creek in front he was to be guided by circumstances. The general directions he received were to secure the country, and facilitate the inhabitants bringing in their produce to market

To prevent this intercourse, the enemy added, to the severe exertions of their civil powers, their militia. The roads, the creeks, and the general inclination of the inhabitants to the British government, and to their own profit, aided the endeavour of the Queen's Rangers. The redoubt on the right had been garrisoned by the corps till, on Major Simcoe's representation that the duty was too severe, it was given to the line: within this redoubt the corps fitted up their barracks. The 4th of January was the first day since their landing at the head of Elk, that any man could be permitted to unaccoutre.

There is not an officer in the world who is ignorant, that permitting the soldier to plunder, or maraud, must inevitably destroy him; that, in a civil war, it must alienate the large body of people who, in such a contest, are desirous of neutrality, and sour their minds into dissatisfaction: but, however obvious the necessity may be, there is nothing more difficult than for a commander in chief to prevent marauding. The numerous orders that are extant in King Charles' and the Parliament's army, prove it in those dreadful times; and the Duke of Argyle, in his description of the Dutch auxiliaries, in the year 1715, who, he says, "were mighty apt to mistake friend for foe," exemplifies the additional difficulty where foreign troops are combined with natives.

No officer could possibly feel the attention that was necessary to this duty more strongly than Major Simcoe, and he thought himself warranted to declare, when a general order was given out to enforce it, "that it is with the utmost satisfaction Major Simcoe believes there would have been no necessity for the general orders of this day, had every corps of the army been as regular, in respect to their abstaining from plunder and marauding, as the Rangers. He trusts, that so truly a military behaviour will be continued; and that the officer and soldier of the corps will consider it as honourable to him as the most distinguished bravery."

Major Simcoe took care to prevent the possibility of plunder, as much as lay in his power: he never halted, if he could avoid it, but in a wood; sent safeguards to every house; allowed no man, in marching, to quit his ranks; and was, in general, successful in instilling into the minds of the men, that while they protected the country, the inhabitants would give every information of the enemy's movements and ambuscades. The officers were vigilant in their attention to this duty, and the soldiers had admirable examples of discipline and good order, from the native loyalists of the corps, who were mostly non-commissioned officers. On the contrary, the rebel patrols, who came to stop the markets, were considered by the country people as robbers; and private signals were everywhere established, by which the smallest party of the Rangers would have been safe in the patrolling the country.

The general mode that Major Simcoe adopted was, to keep perfectly secret the hour, the road, and the manner of his march; to penetrate, in one body, about ten miles into the country. This body generally marched in three divisions, one hundred yards from each other, so that it would have required a large force to have embraced the whole in an ambuscade, and either division, being upon the flank, it would have been hazardous for an enemy so inferior in every respect, but numbers, as the rebels were, to have encountered it; at ten or twelve miles the corps divided, and ambuscaded different roads; and at the appointed time returned home. There was not a bye path or ford unknown, and the Huzzars would generally patrol some miles in front of the infantry. The market people, who over night would get into the woods, came out on the appearance of the corps, and proceeded uninterruptedly, and from market they had an escort, whenever it was presumed that the enemy was on the Philadelphia side of Frankfort to intercept them on their return into the woods.

The infantry, however inclement the weather, seldom marched less than ninety miles a week; the flank companies, Highlanders, and Huzzars, frequently more: these marches were, by many people, deemed adventurous, and the destruction of the corps was frequently prophesied. The detail that has been exhibited, and experience, takes away all appearance of improper temerity; and, by these patrols, the corps was formed to that tolerance of fatigue, and marching, which excelled that of the chosen light troops of the army, as will hereafter be shown.

These matters have been dwelt upon, not only as they exhibit what is conceived to have been the drilling of the

Queen's Rangers for more important services, but, as it proves that the protection of Philadelphia and the opening a way to its markets, were provided for by Sir William Howe, and that his orders were systematically and industriously obeyed.

The Huzzars, by this time, were increased to thirty, mounted on such horses as they had taken from the enemy; and Ensign Proctor was added to them. The country in front of Philadelphia was foraged, and the Queen's Rangers formed the advance guard of the parties which made it; but it was with great reluctance that Major Simcoe saw Point-no-Point included in the general forage, as he had taken particular care to preserve it from plunder; it is impossible to protect any country from the depredations of foraging parties.

The clothing of the Provincials was served by contract; the duties of the Queen's Rangers would have worn out much better; they were obliged, by the inclemency of the weather, to wear the new ones, without altering. It being determined, for the next year, to cloth the Provincials in red, Major Simcoe exerted himself to preserve the Rangers in green, and to procure for them green waistcoats: his purpose was to wear the waistcoats with their sleeves during the campaign, and to add sleeves to the shell, or outer coat, to be worn over the waistcoats in winter: green is without comparison the best colour for light troops with dark accoutrements; and if put on in the spring, by autumn it nearly fades with the leaves, preserving its characteristic of being scarcely discernable at a distance.

CHAPTER 4

Fighting Wayne

At the end of February, General Wayne having been detached from Washington's army to collect such cattle as were in the lower Jersies, Sir William Howe sent Lieutenant-Colonel Abercrombie down the Delaware, to land and attack him, while Colonel Stirling with the 42nd regiment and the Queen's Rangers, crossed that river opposite to Philadelphia, and marched to Haddonfield, to intercept him; at the same time, a detachment under Colonel Markham passed over, and took post at Cooper's ferry, to collect forage in its vicinity.

Colonel Stirling reached Haddonfield early in the morning; some stragglers of Wayne's corps had just left it as he arrived there. The ground in front of the village was immediately occupied: the Queen's Rangers on the left, with their left flank to a creek which nearly extended the whole length of their front.

A circumstance happened here, which, though not unusual in America and in the rebel mode of warfare, it is presumed is singular elsewhere. As Major Simcoe was on horseback, in conversation with Lieutenant Whitlock, and near the out sentinels, a rifle was fired, and the ball grazed between them; the ground they were on being higher than the opposite bank, the man who had fired was plainly seen, running off: Lieutenant Whitlock, with the sentinels, pursued him, and the guard followed in case of necessity, the piquets occupying their place; the man was turned by Mr. Whitlock, and intercepted and taken by the sentinels. On being questioned, "how he presumed to fire in such a manner?" he answered, "that he had frequently fired at the Hessians, (who a few weeks before had been there,) and thought he might as well do so again." As he lived within half a mile of the spot, had he not been taken and the patrols pushed there the next day, they would have found him, it is probable, employed in his household matters, and strenuously denying that he either possessed, or had fired a gun: he was sent prisoner to Philadelphia.

Upon posting the guards, at night, they were augmented so as to have the rounds every fifteen minutes, and Major Simcoe recommended to the officer to be particularly alert, as it was reasonable to presume that Wayne, who had been surprised by General Grey, could have but two ideas: the one of being surprised himself, which the distance prevented; and the other of retaliation; which, having secured his convoy and being master of the country, there was every reason to apprehend and guard against.

Early the next morning Major Simcoe was detached to destroy such boats and stores as were upon Timber creek, and which had been conveyed thither when the naval armaments on the Delaware were burnt. As the boats appeared valuable, and some refugees offered to carry them to Philadelphia, they were accordingly directed to fall down the creek; when fortunately one hundred and fifty barrels of tar, of which the fleet was in want, were discovered, and with this the boats were laden, and sent to Captain Hammond, who commanded the navy in the Delaware. The party returned in the evening with some few militia as prisoners, who, from their green clothing, had mistaken the Rangers for what they attempted to appear—Wayne's rear guard.

At midnight, Colonel Stirling sent for Major Simcoe, who found at his quarters one of those Refugees to whom the boats had been entrusted: he related, that during their progress down the creek, they had been attacked by the militia of the country, and that amidst the confusion he got ashore, and escaped. Major Simcoe was directed to march as early as possible, and to quell any of the militia who might be there, and to give an opportunity for the refugees, who most probably had concealed themselves in the marshes, to escape.

Before day-break Major Simcoe surrounded the house of Tew, a militia lieutenant, with the Huzzars, and in perfect secrecy and silence lay there until the arrival of the infantry. Tew was supposed to have headed some of his neighbours in arms, as it was well known there was no body of men in the country, and only a few inhabitants who could possibly be collected. Captain Saunders, with the cavalry and some infantry, was sent further down the creek, to procure information. There was nobody in Tew's house but his wife and other females; she was informed, that if her husband, as was supposed, appeared to be at the head of the party, who, contrary to common prudence and the rules of war, had fired upon the boats the preceding night, his house should be burnt, as an example to deter others; at the same time she might have assistance to remove her furniture, and to save it in an outhouse, for which purpose some refugees, her former neighbours, offered to assist her; and preparations were accordingly making, when Captain Saunders returned with certain information, that a predatory party from the shipping at Philadelphia, imagining themselves secure from the troops being at Haddonfield, had rowed up the creek, and meeting the Refugees, they fired upon each other, but the mistake being soon discovered, they returned together to the Delaware.

Tew's house, of course, remained uninjured, and the troops marched back to Haddonfield, and early the next morning made an excursion on the road to Egg-harbour, to get what cattle and rum (of which there was intelligence) might be found on it. The advanced part of the corps, and the Huzzars, marched about twenty miles from Haddonfield; a few hogsheads of rum and some cattle were procured, and some tobacco destroyed.

On the return, and about two miles from Haddonfield, Major Simcoe was observing to some officers a peculiar strong ground, when, looking back, he saw a house that he had passed in flames; it was too far gone for all his endeavours to save it; he was exceedingly hurt at the circumstance, but neither threats of punishment, nor offers of reward, could induce a discovery: this was the only instance of a disorder of this nature that ever happened under his command, and he afterwards knew it was not perpetrated by any of the Queen's Rangers.

At night, a man arrived at the outpost, furnished with such credentials as made it proper to believe his information: his account was, that Wayne was on his march from Mount Holly, to attack the troops at Haddonfield, and that he intended to make a circuit to fall in upon the right; the man was immediately forwarded to Colonel Stirling; and Major Simcoe remarked to Captain Saunders, his confidential friend, "that probably Colonel Stirling would send for him, and, if any room should be left for consultation, his advice would be, that the whole corps should move forward and ambuscade Wayne's march on the strong ground which Major Simcoe had remarked a few hours before; that every inhabitant of the town should be secured, and the Huzzars left to take post at the direct roads; that, upon information being forwarded to Sir William Howe, Colonel Markham would probably be sent to Haddonfield, and possibly a strong corps embarked, and passed up the Delaware, above Wayne."

Major Simcoe accordingly was sent for, but it was to receive directions for an immediate retreat: Colonel Stirling understanding that the force under Wayne had been so considerably augmented, that it would be imprudent to remain at Haddonfield; his business there being completed, and his intentions, otherwise, being to return the next morning; the rum was staved, and the whole detachment prepared to march immediately.

In consideration of the fatigue of the Queen's Rangers, and that there was no probability of any action, Major Simcoe solicited to lead the march. In the mean time, some of the enemy fired upon the advanced posts of the Rangers, and made great noise to draw their attention that way: this was a frequent mode of the rebels; it might have been proper at the moment of attack, but anticipating it for some hours, in general it gave a knowledge of their designs, and increased a just and military contempt for this mode of conducting them.

The night was uncommonly severe, and a cold sleet fell the whole way from Haddonfield to Cooper's Ferry, where the troops arrived late, and the ground being occupied by barns and forage, they were necessitated to pass the coldest night that they ever felt, without fire. As dawn arrived, the weather cleared up; about three miles and a half from Cooper's Ferry, and half a mile within the direct road to Haddonfield, there was some forage remaining; fifty of the 42nd and Rangers, under the command of Captain Kerr, were sent as an escort to the wagons that went for it.

Lieutenant Wickham, with ten Huzzars, was directed by

Colonel Stirling to patrol in his front towards Haddonfield. A few miles off, Lieutenant Wickham met the enemy; he sent information to Captain Kerr, and to Colonel Stirling, and, with six Huzzars, attended their front. As the road led through thick woods, the enemy were apprehensive of ambuscades, and were intimidated by Lieutenant Wickham's frequently calling out, as to the infantry, "to halt, not to march so fast," &c. &c., so that the enemy's cavalry, though more than two hundred, did not rush on him. He gave time to Captain Kerr to retreat, then joined and returned to camp with him, ushering the enemy to the very outpost.

The line was formed; the 42nd regiment on the right, Colonel Markham's detachment in the centre, and the Queen's Rangers on the left. The embarkation still proceeded; the horses were now sent off, and, as the enemy did not advance, Colonel Markham's detachment followed them.

It was scarce half way over the Delaware, when the piquets were attacked. The enemy were probably induced to attack earlier than they intended, by a barn having been accidentally set on fire, and which it was reasonable for them to suppose might have been done by some lurking person, after the troops in general had embarked. Upon the appearance of the enemy, the 42nd regiment marched forward in line, and orders were sent to the Queen's Rangers to advance, which it did, in column, by companies; Cooper's Creek secured its left flank; the artillery horses of the three pounders being embarked, the seamen, with their accustomed alacrity, offered to draw on the cannon; the artillery followed the light infantry company, and preceded the battalion.

Some of the enemy appearing on the opposite bank of the Cooper Creek, Captain Armstrong, with the grenadiers, was directed to march and line a dyke on this side: an advantage the enemy had not; and to keep off any stragglers who might be posted there.

41

A heavy fire was kept up on the right, by the 42nd; there was nothing opposed to the Rangers but some cavalry, watching their motions, and as Major Simcoe advanced rapidly to gain an eminence in front, which he conceived to be a strong advantageous position, they fled into the wood, an officer excepted, who, reining back his horse, and fronting the Rangers as they advanced, slowly waved with his scimitar for his attendants to retire; the fight infantry being within fifty yards of him, he was called out to, "You are a brave fellow, but you must go away," to which not paying so much attention as he ought, M'Gill, afterwards quartermaster, was directed to fire at him, on which he retired into the woods.

A few straggling shot were fired in the front; the light infantry company was detached there, and supported by the Highlanders, who soon cleared the front; the battalion halted on the advantageous ground it had moved towards, and, at the entreaties of the sailors, a few cannon shot were fired at a party of the enemy, who were near the bridge over Cooper's Creek, till perceiving they were busy in destroying it, they were no longer interrupted: the firing totally ceased, and the enemy retreated. Some few of the Rangers were wounded, among whom, Sergeant M'Pherson of the grenadiers died; in every respect he was much to be lamented.

The person whom M'Gill fired at, proved to be Pulaski; his horse was wounded; and had not the Huzzars been sent over the Delaware previous to the attack, he would have been taken, or killed.

The embarkation took place without any interruption; and On the 2nd of March the Queen's Rangers returned to their old quarters, and former duties. Colonel Stirling made the most handsome and favourable report of the behaviour of the corps, to Sir William Howe.

CHAPTER 5

Expedition Down the Delaware

An expedition was formed under the command of the late Colonel Mawhood, consisting of the 27th and 46th regiments, the Queen's Rangers, and New Jersey Volunteers; they embarked the 12th of March, and fell down the Delaware.

On the 17th, the Queen's Rangers landed, at three o'clock in the morning, about six miles from Salem, the Huzzars carrying their accoutrements and swords. Major Simcoe was directed to seize horses, to mount the cavalry, and the staff, and to join Colonel Mawhood at Salem; this was accordingly executed.

Major Simcoe, making a circuit and passing over Lambstone's bridge, arrived at Salem, near which Colonel Mawhood landed. The Huzzars were tolerably well mounted, and sufficient horses procured for the other exigencies of the service: Colonel Mawhood had given the strictest charge against plundering; and Major Simcoe, in taking the horses, had assured the inhabitants that they should be returned, or paid for, if they did not appear in arms, in a very few days; and, none but officers entering the houses, they received no other injury.

The Queen's Rangers' infantry were about two hundred and seventy, rank and file, and thirty cavalry; Colonel Mawhood gave directions for the forage to take place on the 18th.

The town of Salem lies upon a creek of that name which falls into the Delaware nearly opposite Reedy Island; the Aloes, or Alewas creek, runs almost parallel to the Salem creek, and falls into the Delaware to the southward of it; over this creek there were three bridges: Hancock's was the lower one, Quintin's that in the centre, and Thompson's the upper one; between these creeks the foraging was to commence; the neck, or peninsula, formed by them was at its greatest distance seven, and at its least four miles wide.

The rebel militia was posted at Hancock's and Quintin's, the nearest bridges, which they had taken up, and defended by breast-works. Colonel Mawhood made detachments to mask these bridges; and foraged in their rear: the officer who commanded the detachment, consisting of seventy of the 17th infantry, at Quintin's bridge, sent information that the enemy were assembled in great numbers at the bridge, and indicated as if they meant to pass over whenever he should quit it, in which case his party would be in great danger.

Colonel Mawhood marched with the Queen's Rangers to his assistance: he made a circuit, so as to fall in upon the road that led from Thompson's to Quintin's bridge, to deceive any patrol which he might meet on his march, and to make them believe that he directed it to Thompson's, not Quintin's bridge. Approaching the bridge, the Rangers halted in the wood, and Colonel Mawhood and Major Simcoe went to the party of the 17th, but in such a manner as to give no suspicion that they were part of a reinforcement; the ground was high, till within two hundred yards of the bridge, where it became marshy; immediately beyond the bridge, the banks were steep, and on them the enemy had thrown up breast-works; there was a public house very near the road, at the edge of its declivity into the marsh, on the Salem side.

Colonel Mawhood asked Major Simcoe, "whether he thought, if he left a party in the house, the enemy would pass by it or not?" who replied, that he "thought they would be too cowardly to do it; but at any rate the attempt could do no harm, and, if he pleased, he would try." Colonel Mawhood directed Major Simcoe to do so, who accordingly profiting by the broken ground of the orchard which was behind it, and the clothing of his men, brought Captain Stephenson and his company into the house, undiscovered: the front windows were opened, and the back ones were shut, so that no thorough light could be seen; the women of the house were put in the cellar and ordered to be silent; the door was left open, and Lieutenant M'Kay stood behind it, with a bayonet, ready to seize the first person whose curiosity might prompt him to enter.

The Queen's Rangers were brought into the wood near to that part where it ended in clear ground, and two companies, under Captain Saunders, were advanced to the fences at the very edge of it, where they lay flat. Colonel Mawhood then gave orders for the detachment of the 17th, who were posted near the house, to call in their sentinels and retreat up the road in full view of the enemy.

This party had scarcely moved, when the enemy laid the bridge and passed it; a detachment of them went immediately across the marsh to the heights on the left, but the principal party, about two hundred, in two divisions, proceeded up the road; Captain Stephenson, as they approached the house, could hear them say, "let us go into the house," &c, but they were prevented, both by words and by action, by the officer who was at their head: he was on horseback, and spurring forward, quitted the road to go into the field, on the right, through a vacancy made by the rails being taken for fires. His party still proceeded up the road, and the first division passed the house: the officer, his

45

sight still fixed on the red clothes of the 17th, approached close up to the fence where Captain Saunders lay; he did not immediately observe the Rangers, and, it is probable, he might not, had he not heard one of the men stifling a laugh. Looking down he saw them, and galloped off; he was fired at, wounded, and taken.

The division that had passed the house attempted to return: Captain Stephenson sallied, drove them across the fields, Captain Saunders pursued them; the Huzzars were let loose and afterwards the battalion, Colonel Mawhood leading them; Major Simcoe directed the 17th back to the house, with the grenadiers, and Highlanders of the Rangers, ready to force the bridge, if ordered; the enemy, for a moment, quitted it, Colonel Mawhood thought it useless to pass it.

Some of the division, who passed the house, were taken prisoners, but the greater part were drowned in the Aloes creek. The officer, who was taken, proved to be a Frenchman. The Rangers had one Huzzar mortally wounded; and what was unfortunate, he was wounded by a man, whom in the eagerness of the pursuit he had passed, given quarters to, and not disarmed: the villain, or coward, was killed by another Huzzar. The corps returned to Salem.

The rebels still occupying the posts at Quintin and Hancock's bridge, and probably accumulating, Colonel Mawhood determined to attack them at the latter, where, from all reports, they were assembled to near four hundred men. He entrusted the enterprise to Major Simcoe, and went with him and a patrol opposite to the place: the Major ascended a tree and made a rough sketch of the buildings, which, by conversing with the guides, he improved into a tolerable plan of the place, and formed his mode of attack accordingly.

He embarked on the 20th, at night, on board the flat

boats; he was to be landed at an inlet, seven miles below Aloes creek, when the boats were immediately to be returned, and by a private road he was to reach Hancock's bridge, opposite to which, Major Mitchell was detached with the 27th regiment, to co-operate with him. Major Simcoe foresaw the difficulties, and dangers, but he kept them to himself: every thing depended upon surprise. The enemy were nearly double his numbers; and his retreat, by the *absolute orders* to send back the boats, was cut off; but he had just confidence in the silence, attention, and spirit of the corps.

By some strange error in the naval department, when the boats arrived off Aloes creek, the tide set so strong against them that, in the opinion of the officer of the navy, they could not reach the place of their destination till mid-day. Major Simcoe determined not to return, but to land on the marshes, at the mouth of the Aloes creek; there were good guides with him: they found out a landing place, and after a march of two miles through marshes, up to the knees in mud and water, labours rendered more fatiguing by the carriage of the first wooden planks they met with, to form bridges with them over the ditches, they at length arrived at a wood upon dry land. Here the corps was formed for the attack.

There was no public road which led to Hancock's bridge, but that which the Rangers were now in possession of; a bank, on which there was a footway, led from Hancock's to Quintin's bridge. Hancock's house was a large brick house; there were many store-houses round it, and some few cottages. Captain Saunders was detached to ambuscade the dyke that led to Quintin's bridge, about half a mile from the quarters, and to take up a small bridge which was upon it, as the enemy would, probably, fly that way, and if not pursued too closely, would be more easily defeated. Captain Dunlop was detached to the rear of Hancock's house; in which it was presumed the rebel officers quartered; directed to force it, occupy and barricade it, as it commanded the passage of the bridge.

Different detachments were allotted to the houses supposed to be the enemy's quarters, which having mastered, they were ordered to assemble at Hancock's; a party was appropriated to relay the bridge. On approaching the place, two sentries were discovered: two men of the light infantry followed them, and, as they turned about, bayoneted them; the companies rushed in, and each, with proper guides, forced the quarters allotted to it. No resistance being made, the light infantry, who were in reserve, reached Hancock's house by the road, and forced the front door, at the same time that Captain Dunlop, by a more difficult way, entered the back door; as it was very dark, these companies had nearly attacked each other.

The surprise was complete, and would have been so, had the whole of the enemy's force been present, but, fortunately for them, they had quitted it the evening before, leaving a detachment of twenty or thirty men, all of whom were killed. Some very unfortunate circumstances happened here. Among the killed was a friend of Government, then a prisoner with the rebels, old Hancock, the owner of the house, and his brother: Major Simcoe had made particular enquiry, and was informed that he did not live at home, since the rebels had occupied the bridge. The information was partly true; he was not there in the daytime, but unfortunately returned home at night: events like these are the real miseries of war.

The roads which led to the country were immediately ambuscaded; and Lieutenant Whitlock was detached to surprise a patrol of seven men who had been sent down the creek: this he effected completely. On their refusal to surrender, he fired on them, only one escaped. This firing gave the first notice of the success of the enterprise to the 27th regiment; with so much silence it had hitherto been conducted.

The bridge was now laid; and Major Simcoe communicated to Colonel Mitchell, that the enemy were at Quintin's bridge; that he had good guides to conduct them thither by a private road, and that the possession of Hancock's house secured a retreat Lieutenant-Colonel Mitchell said, that his regiment was much fatigued by the cold, and that he would return to Salem as soon as the troops joined.

The ambuscades were of course withdrawn, and the Queen's Rangers were forming to pass the bridge, when a rebel patrol passed where an ambuscade had been, and discovering the corps, galloped back. Lieutenant-Colonel Mitchell, finding his men in high spirits, had returned, purposing to march to Quintin's bridge: but being informed of the enemy's patrol, it was thought best to return. Colonel Mawhood, in public orders, "returned his best thanks to Major Simcoe and his corps, for their spirited and good conduct in the surprise of the rebel posts."

Chapter 6

Ambushcade

Two days after, the Queen's Rangers patrolled to Thompson's bridge; the enemy, who had been posted there, were alarmed at the approach of a cow the night before, fired at it, wounded it, and then fled; they also abandoned Quintin's bridge, and retired to a creek, sixteen miles from Aloes creek.

Major Simcoe, making a patrol with the Huzzars, took a circuit towards the rear of one of the parties sent out to protect the foragers: a party of the enemy had been watching them the whole day, and unluckily, the forage being completed, the detachment had just left its ground and was moving off; the enemy doing the like, met the patrol, were pursued, and escaped by the passage which the foragers had just left open. One only was taken, being pursued into a bog, which the Huzzars attempted in vain to cross, and were much mortified to see above a dozen of the enemy, who had passed round it in safety, within a few yards: they consisted of all the field officers and committee-men of the district. The prisoner was their adjutant

The enemy, who were assembled at Cohansey, might easily have been surprised; but Colonel Mawhood judged, that having completed his forage with such success, his business was to return, which he effected. The troops embarked without any accident, and sailed for Philadelphia. The horses were given back to the inhabitants, or paid for.

On the passage, the ships waiting for the tide, Major Simcoe had an opportunity of landing at Billing's port, where Major Vandyke's corps was stationed, and examining it, they arrived at Philadelphia, March the 31st.

The patrols of the Rangers were made systematically as ever, on their return; but as spring approached, the enemy's cavalry came nearer to the lines, and owed their escape, more than once, to the fleetness of their horses: one or two of them who were taken were decorated with eggs, women's shoes, &c. &c. that they had robbed the market people of, and, in that dress, were paraded through the street to prison.

Several loyalists were in arms, under the command of Mr. Thomas, their Captain; and, with Hovenden's, and James's troops of Provincials, made excursions into the country; and at Newton, many miles from Philadelphia, they brought off a large quantity of clothing; whenever they made an excursion, the Queen's Rangers pushed forward to bring them off.

One morning, about two o'clock, Major Simcoe, marching to support them in an attempt they were to make on Smithfield, met them about a mile from Philadelphia; they said, they had been repulsed: judging it necessary to support the advantages derived from the distance to which they made their excursions, he made enquiries into the matter, and found their accounts so various, that he determined to march to Smithfield, and accordingly took such of them with him as were not weary, for guides. His ideas were, that the party at Smithfield would probably be reinforced by another which was in its vicinity, and that he might possibly surprise them rejoicing at their success: at any rate, the recoil would add to the ascendancy necessary to be maintained in the country. The Queen's Rangers marched to Smithfield, but found no enemy there; and, it appeared, that they had also fled, having exchanged some shots with the refugees.

Mr. Washington drew his supplies of fat cattle from New England: a drove of this kind was met about thirty miles from Philadelphia, between the Delaware and Schuylkill, by a friend of Government, who passed himself upon the drivers for a rebel commissary, then billeted them at a neighbouring farm, and immediately galloped to Philadelphia, from whence a party of dragoons were sent for the cattle. The Queen's Rangers advanced forward to Chesnut Hill, and the brigade of guards were posted at Germantown; the whole drove was safely conducted to Philadelphia. Major Simcoe, as was his custom, with the Huzzars, patrolled in front, and took a minute survey of the ground, at Barren-hill church, which was near proving of consequence in the event.

A very great desertion happened from Washington's army this winter, which, had it not been difficult to effect, probably, would have been universal; the Queen's Rangers were benefited by it; Captain Armstrong's company of grenadiers, in size, youth, and appearance, was inferior to no one in the army. There were many reports, that Mr. Lacy, the rebel General of the Pennsylvania militia, was collecting them, professedly to impede the country people's intercourse with the markets.

Major Simcoe, besides employing his own intelligence, applied to Lieutenant-Colonel Balfour, who so successfully managed these matters, during the army's being at Philadelphia, for what he could furnish him with; and represented that it would be of the utmost consequence, to attack Lacy the moment he broke into the circle of country, which we had hitherto maintained possession of. In consequence of this conversation, he was sent for by Colonel Balfour, some time after, and informed, that Lacy's corps were to assemble at the Crooked Billett, twenty-five miles from Philadelphia, on the first of May.

Major Simcoe was anxious that they should be attacked on that night; and from the maps of the country arranged the plan, which was approved of. The main road led, past the Billett, to Philadelphia from York; at less than half a mile from it, on the Philadelphia side, there was another, that led to Washington's camp, by Horsham meeting. Major Simcoe proposed, that he should march with the Rangers, and, by a circuit, get to the road in the rear of the Billett; and that a detachment should march and ambuscade themselves in a wood, (the intelligencer said there was one adapted to the purpose,) on the road which led by the Horsham meeting-house to Washington's camp; this party was to remain in ambuscade till they heard the firing of the Queen's Rangers.

It was supposed, that if the surprise should not be complete, the ambuscade would render the success perfectly so, by supporting the Rangers if they were checked, and by intercepting the enemy if they attempted to retreat, which, probably, would be towards their army. Colonel Balfour proposed two hundred light infantry to go; to this Major Simcoe said, "that they would be commanded by older officers in the line, and yet of inferior local rank to himself, and that it was his wish, on that account, to avoid giving umbrage;" the result was, Lieutenant-Colonel Abercrombie was chosen, and marched with a large detachment of the light infantry, and with one of cavalry, and horses to mount part of his infantrymen, for greater expedition.

Major Simcoe's march was a difficult one: he thought it necessary to make many circuits to avoid places where he suspected the enemy had posts, or patrols. He was admirably guided; and, luckily, had information, about twilight, that prevented him from committing a serious error: the armed refugees, as Captain Thomas, their commander, informed him, were sent by Mr. Galloway, to convey in some of his furniture; they adventured out, hearing of the expedition by some means or other, and marched up the roads which the Rangers had so carefully avoided, but without meeting any interruption, or alarm. Luckily, they passed a house, which Major Simcoe called at, or he would, certainly, when he overtook them, have mistaken them for rebels: they were directed to keep themselves undiscovered; and the Rangers marched on so fast as possible.

Although daylight appeared, Major Simcoe was under no apprehensions of discovery, and certain of Colonel Abercrombie's having met with no accident, as the parties must have been within the hearing of each other's fire. He had now arrived at the point, where he quitted the road, in order to make his last circuit to reach the Billett, profiting by the covert that the irregularities of the ground would have afforded, and was informing the officers of his plan of attack, to be guided by circumstances, (Captain Kerr's division excepted, who was to force Lacy's quarters, and barricade them for a point to rally at, in case of misadventure,) when a few shot were heard. Major Simcoe immediately exclaimed, "the dragoons have discovered us;" so it was.

Colonel Abercrombie, although assisted by horses, could not arrive at his post at the appointed time, before daybreak; anxious to support Major Simcoe, he detached his cavalry, and mounted light infantry, to the place of ambuscade. The officer who commanded, patrolled to Lacy's outpost, and, being fired at by the rebel sentinels, did not retire; Lacy, of course, did, and collecting his force, began a retreat up the country. In this situation, the Rangers arrived nearly in his rear, upon his right flank; they stopped and turned some smaller parties who were escaping from the light infantry, and who were killed, but the main body retreated in a mass, without order, and by no efforts could the infantry reach them.

Unfortunately, the Huzzars of the Rangers were left at Philadelphia, their horses having been fatigued by a long course of duty, and a severe patrol the day before. Thirty dragoons, who were with the Rangers, were sent to intercept the baggage wagons, and stayed to guard them.

As the enemy were marching through a wood, Major Simcoe galloped up to the edge of it, and summoned them to surrender; they were in great consternation, but marched on; he then gave the words of command, "make ready, present, fire," hoping that the intervening fence and thickets between him and them might lead them to suppose he had troops with him, and that they might halt, when a few moments would have been decisive: at the word "fire" they crouched down, but still moved on, and soon got out of all reach.

A few men of the Rangers were wounded, as was the horse of Wright, Major Simcoe's orderly Huzzar; and Captain M'Gill's shoe-buckle probably saved the foot of that valuable officer: the enemy had fifty or sixty killed, and taken.

The troops returned to Philadelphia. The commander in chief ordered the baggage to be sold, for their benefit; it produced a dollar a man. The guides of the Queen's Rangers computed their march at fifty-eight miles; not a man was missing. This excursion, though it failed in the greater part, had its full effect, of intimidating the militia, as they never afterwards appeared, but in small parties, and like robbers.

CHAPTER 7

Leaving Pennsylvania

As the spring approached, the hopes of the army were pointed to an attack on Valley Forge: the surmise gave Major Simcoe particular pleasure; he had formerly been quartered in the house that was Washington's headquarters, and had made himself minutely master of the ground about it, and particularly, of those undulations which are so material in all attacks against batteries, and from all the plans and descriptions of Valley Forge, it appeared to him probable, that an attack would commence in this point.

These hopes vanished, when the news of Sir William Howe's recall reached Philadelphia, together with the orders for the army's abandoning that city. Mr. Washington's ignorance, however, exposed him to a check, from which his usual good fortune extricated him. He passed a corps, under the direction of the Marquis de La Fayette, over the Schuylkill; arrangements were made to cut it off; a column made a circuit for that purpose, under General Grant, the Queen's Rangers led it, and Major Simcoe was ordered to march at the rate of two miles an hour: this slow and tiresome pace was too quick to keep the column properly compacted, and he was frequently obliged to halt.

Nearly at daylight, a subaltern's party of dragoons were ordered to the front. Soon after a rebel patrol appeared, and while the young officer was deliberating what to do, got off; the column moved on, and arriving at three cross roads, the advance was directed to halt, there being some doubt which was the proper road. General Grant arrived, and *immediately* directed him to march on; the column was too late, the alarum guns were fired from Washington's camp, and Fayette had moved off from Barren-hill church, and passed the Schuylkill; the cavalry being detached in a fruitless pursuit of him, the Huzzars went with them, and Lieutenant Wickham compared a party of the rebels, whom he saw fording the Schuylkill, to the corks of a fishing seine.

As the time approached for the army's quitting Philadelphia, patrols were passed over the Delaware, from the Jersies; one of which, after a long chase, was taken by the Huzzars. The Quartermaster General being in great want of horses, Major Simcoe escorted the commissaries who were sent to procure them: he entered upon the office with great regret, as they were to be taken from people whom he had uniformly protected.

The enemy had some strong parties in the country. The whole corps made a long march, in four divisions, as has been before explained; he had also a three pounder, that had been lately attached to his corps. On his return he was ambuscaded, near the Bristol side of Pennypack bridge: the first division passed the bridge with the cannon, and immediately formed on the opposite banks, as Major Simcoe was apprehensive of some attack; its position secured the march of the successive divisions. It was afterwards known, that the enemy were in force, but were deterred from attacking by the position of the first division, and the order of march.

Sir Henry Clinton, when he took the command of the army, directed Lord Rawdon to raise a corps of Irish volunteers; and Captain Doyle, of the 55th regiment, was appointed Lieutenant-Colonel. Major Simcoe waited upon the commander in chief, and requested, that as he was Captain Doyle's senior in the army, he would be pleased to make him so in the Provincial line, adding, that if his Excellency, at any future time, should appoint a senior officer of the line, to a Provincial command, Major Simcoe, of course, could have no objection that he should have superior rank in the Provincials. Sir Henry Clinton was pleased to refer his request to Sir William Erskine, and General Paterson, the Quartermaster and Adjutant General, who, reporting that it was just, Sir Henry Clinton appointed him to the rank of Lieutenant-Colonel; and, to avoid similar inconveniences, antedated his commission to all Provincial Lieutenant-Colonels.

The procuring of the horses was the last service that the Queen's Rangers performed in Pennsylvania.

Embarking, and passing over to Cooper's ferry, on the 17th of June, 1778, Lieutenant-Colonel Simcoe observed, in public orders, "that he doubted not but that all ranks of the regiment were sensible that the undaunted spirit which had rendered them the terror of their enemies, was not more honourable to them than that abhorrence of plunder which distinguishes the truly brave from the cowardly ruffian, and which had left a favourable impression of the Queen's Rangers on the minds of such of the inhabitants of Pennsylvania as had been in their power; he assured himself, that, as they were to pass over to the Jersies, they would, in every respect, behave as became the character the corps had acquired, and which marks the disciplined soldier. He gave orders, that the Captains and officers, commanding companies, should march in the rear of their respective divisions, till such time as more active duties required their presence elsewhere, and should be answerable that no soldier quitted his rank on any pre-

A Grenadier of the Queen's Rangers

tence, but *particularly to drink:* this practice having been the death of many a valuable soldier, the permission of it was highly criminal"

The 18th, the Queen's Rangers, being part of General Leslie's division, marched to Haddonfield; on the 19th to Evesham; the Yagers being in front, there was a slight skirmish, in which the rebel party lost some men, and one of them being taken proved to be a British deserter, who was executed the next day. The army encamped at Mount Holly, the 20th and 21st; they marched to the Black Horse the 22nd; the Queen's Rangers formed the advance. By an error of the guides, at a cross road, they were pursuing the wrong one, a rebel officer called out to them, "You are wrong, you are wrong," but the corps passing by without heeding him, and afterwards taking the nearer way across the fields into the right road, in which he was, the advanced men got within a few yards of him, undiscovered; Lieutenant-Colonel Simcoe prevented them from firing, but called to him to keep at a greater distance, which he did.

The 23rd, the army marched to Crosswicks, the Queen's Rangers forming the advance of the left column. Hitherto there were no interruptions on this march but from a bridge, the boards of which had been taken up, but laid within a few yards, so that they were easily replaced. Approaching Crosswicks, a body of the enemy appeared; Lieutenant-Colonel Simcoe took the flanking party, under Lieutenant Wilson, and tried to cut them off before they could pass the creek at that place. He was too late for this purpose, but in time to prevent them from executing their design of cutting down the trees which stood close to the bridge, and throwing them across it; the enemy had taken up the planks, and were posted behind a wood, on the opposite bank. Captain Stephenson's company of light infantry, were directed, by the commander in chief in person, to the same post, on the left that Lieutenant Wilson had occupied.

Lieutenant-Colonel Simcoe, on his return, formed his corps behind the meeting-house, ready to pass the bridge. The dragoons arrived, and dismounted, lining the fences on the right, and Lieutenant M'Leod, of the artillery, bringing up his three pounders, and being fully exposed to the enemy, in case they had kept their position, it was determined to pass the bridge upon its rafters, which was affected without opposition. The enemy had fled from the wood, and a party on the right, which the Queen's Rangers made every effort to pursue, escaped; nor were the rest of the advanced troops more successful who followed the body which retreated on the left.

Captain Stephenson, exerting himself with his usual gallantry, became an object to a person, *said* to be a *Quaker;* who fired at him with a long fowling-piece, and dangerously wounded him; the escape of the commander in chief, distinguishable by his dress and activity to an enemy posted in security and intended to fire a single and well aimed shot, was very remarkable.

The Queen's Rangers, and some other troops, remained posted beyond the creek; the army did not pass the bridge: there were events here worth recording.

Lieutenant-Colonel Simcoe, in conversation with Captain Armstrong, happened to mention, that he was fully convinced of the truth of what an English military author had observed, that a number of firelocks were, in action, rendered useless, by being carried on the shoulders, from casual musket-balls, which could not be the case were the arms carried in the position of the advance; he added, that advanced arms, certainly, gave a compactness, and took off the appearance of wavering from a column more than any other mode of carrying them. Captain Armstrong had assented, and took occasion to exemplify it now, by advancing the arms of his grenadier company when under fire, and while he led over the rafters of the bridge.

The sluices had been shut, by which means the water was ponded; Lieutenant Murray plunged in, thinking it fordable, but finding it not so, he swam over, and got behind a tree before the corps passed the bridge, and was between both fires; luckily he escaped unhurt.

CHAPTER 8

A Skirmish and a Wound

Hitherto the march of the army pointed equally to Trenton, or Cranberry; it now, on the 24th of June, took the route to the latter, by marching to Allentown: the Queen's Rangers formed the advance of the column.

The bridge at Allentown, over a small rivulet, was taken up, and Colonel Simcoe fired two or three cannon shot, which drove a small party of the enemy from thence, and he passed over without the exchange of a musket, one of which might, unnecessarily, deprive him of a valuable officer, or soldier. Passing forward, a rebel patrol from the Cranberry road, came close to the front of the Rangers, mistaking them for their own people; they retired into a wood, which, as soon as the army halted, a party scoured, but to no purpose.

Lieutenant-Colonel Simcoe had a book, in which was inserted the names of every soldier in his corps, the counties in which they were born, and where they had ever lived, so that he seldom was at a loss for guides in his own corps; he had also many refugees with him, who served as guides. The commander in chief asked him, whether he had any guides? He answered, he had none who knew any of the roads to Brunswick; that the chief of his guides was born at Monmouth. Sir Henry

Clinton directed him to be sent to headquarters, as he might be useful in procuring intelligence, though not serviceable as a guide; this was done, and as soon as the army marched he came for two soldiers of the regiment, natives of Monmouth county.

This was the first idea which Lieutenant-Colonel Simcoe had of the army's being intended to march elsewhere than to South Amboy. An alteration in the disposition of the army took place; it marched in one column: the Yagers made the rear; the Queen's Rangers, light infantry, and dragoons, followed in succession. The army halted at the Rising Sun; the enemy's light troops appeared in greater force in the rear.

On the arrival at the camp, Lieutenant-Colonel Simcoe *immediately* passed a deep hollow that separated it from a high hill, with the Huzzars, in order to observe the ground in front, as was his constant custom. Two men came out of the wood to Lieutenant Wickham, who was patrolling, deceived by his green clothes; he gave into the deception, passed himself upon them for a rebel partisan, and introduced Lieutenant-Colonel Simcoe to them as Colonel Lee. One of the men was very glad to see him, and told him that he had a son in his corps, and gave him the best account of the movements of the rebel army, from which, Lieutenant-Colonel Simcoe said, he had been detached two days; the other proved to be a committee-man of New Jersey; they pointed out the encampment of the British army, and were completely deceived, till, having told all they knew, and on the party returning, the committee-man having asked, "I wonder what Clinton is about?"

"You shall ask him yourself," was the answer, "for we are British."

The army marched the next morning toward Monmouth, in the same order; and it now became evident, that

Sir Henry Clinton intended to embark from Sandy Hook. There was some skirmishing between the Yagers and the enemy; and one time, it having the appearance of being serious, the Rangers were divided into two divisions, to march on each flank of the Yagers, who, having no bayonets, might have suffered from an intrepid enemy; but the contrary was the case, as the alarm originated from a shout that Captain Ewald, who commanded the rear guard, set up on the enemy's approach, which with other preparations, sent them away upon the full run. Upon the arrival at Monmouth, the Queen's Rangers covered headquarters; the army halted the next day, and foraged.

On the morning of the 27th, the Queen's Rangers marched, at two o'clock, and occupied the post from which the second battalion of light infantry were drawn, to march with the second division, under General Kniphausen: a great extent of ground was to be guarded, and the whole corps lay upon their arms. In the morning, about seven o'clock, orders were brought to Lieutenant-Colonel Simcoe, "to take his Huzzars and try to cut off a reconnoitring party of the enemy, (supposed to be M. Fayette,) who was upon a bald hill, and not far from his left."

As the woods were thick in front, Lieutenant-Colonel Simcoe had no knowledge of the ground, no guide, no other direction, and but twenty Huzzars with him; he asked of Lord Cathcart, who brought him the order, whether he might not take some infantry with him, who, from the nature of the place, could advance nearly as expeditiously as his cavalry? His Lordship assenting, Lieutenant-Colonel Simcoe immediately marched with his cavalry, and the grenadier company, consisting of forty rank and file. He had not proceeded far, before he fell in with two rebel Videttes, who, galloping off, the cavalry were ordered to pursue them, as their best guides; they fled on the road down a small hill, at the bottom of which was a rivulet; on the opposite rising, the ground was open, with a high fence, the left of which reached the road, and along which, a considerable way to the right, a large corps was posted. This corps immediately fired, obliquely, upon the Huzzars, who, in their pursuit of the Videttes, went up the road, and gained their left, when Ellison, a very spirited Huzzar, leapt the fence, and others followed.

Lieutenant-Colonel Simcoe, in the meantime, brought up the grenadiers, and ordered the Huzzars to retreat; the enemy gave one universal fire, and, panic struck, fled. The Baron Stuben, who was with them, lost his hat in the confusion. Lieutenant-Colonel Simcoe rode along the fence, on the side opposite to which the enemy had been, posting the grenadiers there; the enemy fired several scattering shots, one of which wounded him in the arm. For some seconds, he thought it broken, and was unable to guide his horse, which, being also struck, ran away with him, luckily, to the rear; his arm soon recovering its tone, he got to the place where he had formed the Huzzars, and with fourteen of them, returned towards a house, to which the right of the enemy's line had reached.

Upon his left flank he saw two small parties of the enemy; he galloped towards them, and they fled: in this confusion, seeing two men, who, probably, had been the advance of these parties, rather behind the others, he sent Sergeant Prior, and a Huzzar, to take them, but with strict orders not to pursue too close to the wood. This the Sergeant executed; and, after firing their loaded muskets at the large body which had been dislodged and was now rallying, the prisoners were obliged to break them, and to walk between the Huzzars and the enemy.

The business was now to retreat, and to carry off whomsoever might be wounded in the first attack. The enemy opposite seemed to increase, and a party, evidently headed by some general officer, and his suit, advancing, to reconnoitre: it suggested to Lieutenant-Colonel Simcoe, to endeavour to pass, as on a similar design; and, for this purpose, he dispatched a Huzzar to the wood in his rear, to take off his cap, and make signals, as if he was receiving directions from some persons posted in it The party kept moving, slowly, close to the fence, and towards the road; when it got to some distance from the house, which has been mentioned. Lieutenant-Colonel Simcoe called out audibly, as if to a party posted in it, "not to fire till the main body came close," and moved on slowly parallel to the enemy, when he sent Ryan, an Huzzar, forward, to see if there were any wounded men, and whether the grenadiers remained where he had posted them, adding, "for we must carry them off or he with them;" to which the Huzzar replied, "*to be sure, your honour*"

On his return, and reporting there was nobody there, Lieutenant-Colonel Simcoe struck obliquely from the fence, secured by a falling of the ground from danger, over the brook to the wood, where he found Captain Armstrong had, with great judgment, withdrawn his grenadiers. From thence he returned to camp, and sending his prisoners to the General, went himself to the baggage, his wound giving him excruciating pain, the day being like to prove very hot, and there not appearing the least probability of any action.

Two Huzzars, and three of the infantry, were wounded in this skirmish; one of the Huzzars died at Monmouth after the action; the other, who was able to have marched, was left by the Hospital, and fell into the hands of the enemy. It is obvious that, of all descriptions of people, the Rangers were the last who should have been left as prisoners, since so many deserters from the enemy were in the corps: the soldiers had the utmost reliance upon their own officer's attention to this particular.

The enemy who were defeated, consisted of that corps of Jersey militia which in General Lee's trial, is said "to have given way," by the evidence of the field officer who brought up fresh troops and cannon to support it. They were those detachments, which Sir Henry Clinton's letter says, "the Queen's Rangers fell in with among the woods, and dispersed," and who, probably, as Washington's account says, "were the Jersey militia, amounting to about seven or eight hundred men, under the command of General Dickenson." They were destined to attack the baggage, but made no other attempt that day.

The American war shows no instance of a burger body of men discomfited by so small a number. The army saw not the combat; but every officer, every soldier, heard the heavy fire, and from that could form a judgment of the enemy's number. Lieutenant-Colonel Simcoe afterwards heard a person who was of this body call the grenadier's company, to use his own expression, "a power of Hessians."

Captain Ross took the command of the corps. He was detached, with the light infantry, under Colonel Abercrombie, to turn the enemy's left; went through the whole fatigue of that hot day, and though the corps had been under arms all the preceding night, it here gave a striking and singular proof of the vast advantages of the Philadelphia marches, by not having a man missing, or any who fell out of the ranks through fatigue. Captain Ross had an opportunity of more than once showing great military judgment and intrepidity, in checking different parties of the enemy; and the Highland company in particular, distinguished itself, under the command of Captain M'Kay, in covering a three pounder of the light infantry battalion, which was impeded by a swamp.

At night, when the army marched off, Captain Ross, with that silence which was remarked in Washington's account of the action, formed the rear guard. During the day, the baggage was not seriously attacked; but some very small parties ran across it, from one side of the road to the other: one of these Captain Needham, and Lieutenant Cooke of the 17th dragoons, (since Captain of the Queen's Rangers,) dispersed; the rumours of them, however, added personal solicitude to Lieutenant-Colonel Simcoe's public anxiety, and, for security, he got together the pioneers of his own and some other corps around his wagon. The uncertainty of what fate might attend his corps, and the army, gave him more uneasiness than he ever experienced; and, when the baggage halted, he passed an anxious night, till about the middle of it, when he had authentic information of the events.

CHAPTER 9

New York

The army encamped at Middleton, the 29th and 30th.
On the 1st of July, Lieutenant-Colonel Simcoe resumed his
command, and marched, to escort Sir William Erskine to
Sandy Hook.

The army remained in this vicinity till the 5th, when it
marched to Sandy Hook also: this peninsula had been made
an island by the storms of the preceding winter; a bridge of
boats was thrown across the channel, over which the army
passed, the Queen's Rangers excepted, who, forming the rear
guard, embarked in boats from the Jersey side, as soon as the
bridge was broken up. It is remarkable, and what few other
corps in the army could say, that in this march the Queen's
Rangers lost no men, by desertion. They landed at New York,
marched up to Morris's house, and encamped there.

Soon after, the troops returned from Philadelphia, it
appearing probable to Lieutenant-Colonel Simcoe, that
America would be quitted by the British forces, and the
war carried on in the West Indies; he applied to Colonel
Drummond, (then aid-de-camp,) to make the request from
him to Sir Henry Clinton, that he might be permitted,
with his corps, and other loyalists, to join the Indians and
troops under Colonel Butler, who had just been heard of
on the upper parts of the Delaware.

The Commander in Chief's answer to him was, "that he much applauded his spirit, but that he would find sufficient employment for him with his army." He had digested the detail of his route; his mode of subsistence, and operations: the idea he entertained, of what such a junction might have led to, was, and is still, unbounded.

Lieutenant-Colonel Simcoe was ill in New York, and did not join till the 14th, during this period, nothing material happened. On the 15th, the Queen's Rangers, and Emmerick's corps, encamped outside Kingsbridge; the three Provincial troops of Hovenden, James, and Sandford, also joined the Queen's Rangers: an Amuzette, and three artillery men, were now added to the three pounder attached to the regiment The post was of great extent, liable to insult, and required many sentinels: it was strengthened as much as possible; and, in all matters of labour, the soldiers worked with the greatest energy, under the inspection of their officers, and were easily made to comprehend, not only the general security, but the benefit which they, individually, received from their works, by its operating to lessen their duties; of course, they were taught that the work should not be slighted. Mr. Washington's army encamping at the White Plains, the Yagers, and Queen's Rangers, had full employment.

Lieutenant-Colonel Simcoe was ever averse to patrols, except, as in the case at Philadelphia, where they served to cover a well affected country, and were made systematically, and in force; or to ascertain some precise object; circumstanced as the armies now were, they appeared to him to be particularly dangerous, and totally useless. The inclinations of the Americans, though averse from tactical arrangement, had always been turned to patrolling, in their antiquated dialect, *scouting:* the Indians, their original enemies, and the nature of their country, had familiarized them to this species of warfare, and they were, in general, excellent marksmen.

There was nothing, either in the American generals or their troops, that could warrant a belief, that they would make a serious attempt upon Kingsbridge; added to the strong works within the island, the eminences in front of it were covered with a chain of redoubts within a distance from each other, barely more than necessary to secure the flanks of a battalion; and indeed, for the purpose of protecting a weak army, they had been originally constructed; half a mile in front of these redoubts, lay the light troops, to secure them from surprise, so that it was manifest any general move of Mr. Washington's army could not take place for so small an object, as that of beating up the huts of a light corps.

Washington's advance corps lay on the heights, near Tuckahoe, under the command of General Scott, to the amount of two thousand men, whose light troops occupied a line from Phillip's creek, on the north, to New Rochelle, on the East river. Small patrols frequently came to William's bridge, on the Bronx, and sometimes, General Scott came, in force, to Valentine's hill

The country between was irregular, intersected with woods, and so broken and covered with stone walls, as to be most liable to ambuscades: the inhabitants were, by no means, to be trusted, and, in general, so harassed by their country being the seat of war, that it was not reasonable to place any confidence in them. On the other hand, the Queen's Rangers had many of the natives of the country among them, and Lieutenant-Colonel Emmerick's corps was, in a great measure, composed of them.

Lieutenant-Colonel Simcoe made a few patrols, in force, merely to inform himself of the situation of the country; but he spared no pains to acquire an account of what posts the enemy occupied, at night; his determination being to attack them, whenever he saw a fit opportunity. Generals Clinton and Morgan, with a corps of fifteen hundred men, covered the forage of the country, on the side of the enemy. Colonel Wurmb, and Lieutenant-Colonel Simcoe, upon intelligence, had agreed to meet on Valentine's hill, one morning, in force, and, accordingly, Lieutenant-Colonel Simcoe, with his Huzzars, was upon the hill, waiting for him; the infantry, and Provincial cavalry, were left in the plain, under the command of Captain Ross; the light infantry and Highland companies being ambuscaded in an orchard, at the place where the roads fork to Hunt's bridge, and Valentine's hill. Colonel Wurmb, finding the enemy in force at Phillip's, did not choose to move to Valentine's hill, and sent the Yager cavalry to give the Rangers the necessary information.

At the same time the enemy appeared advancing to Valentine's hill As Lieutenant-Colonel Simcoe was quitting it, to return to his corps. Lieutenant M'Nab, of the Huzzars, who had been sent with a patrol beyond the Bronx, confirmed the intelligence which he had been furnished with the night before, that a strong body, with cannon, was approaching to Hunt's bridge, on the opposite side of the Bronx. This bridge was commanded by the heights on the side of Kingsbridge, which had been fortified by the rebels in 1776; their works were not demolished. In their rear was a wood; it had been designed to conceal the Rangers; and, while the Yagers and cavalry should have engaged with any corps who might patrol to Valentine's hill, it was thought probable, that the enemy on the opposite side of the Bronx would pass it to their assistance, when the corps in ambuscade was to rush from the wood, and, occupying the fleches, do severe and cool execution upon them, as they were on the bridge, and occupied in the deep hollow.

An advanced party of the enemy, notwithstanding the circumstances which made the troops quit Valentine's hill, had already passed the Bronx. The Yager cavalry were ordered to proceed towards Kingsbridge, slowly, and in full sight of the enemy, who were on Hunt's Hill There were still hopes, by forming the ambuscade, to do some service; when, to Lieutenant-Colonel Simcoe's great surprise, the enemy's cannon were fired at the infantry, whom he expected to have been hidden from their sight, by the intervention of the woods: but, it appeared, that while Captain Ross was with the advanced companies, some officers imprudently had got upon a fence, out of curiosity, and discovered themselves to the enemy.

Lieutenant-Colonel Simcoe immediately withdrew his men out of the reach of any chance shot, and made use of the low ground (the crossing of which would have led him into the ambuscade) to march his infantry under its cover, out of their sight, or the reach of their cannon. He sent orders to Captain Ross to withdraw, and again ambuscaded the cavalry, in a position to take advantage of the enemy, if any party of them should pursue him, or from Valentine's hill should endeavour to incommode his retreat.

Observing the movement of the Yager cavalry, the enemy marched a party to watch their motions, on the opposite bank, while their main body formed the line. Captain Ross thought proper to wait for the party which had passed the Bronx. He permitted them to come close to him, when his fire threw them into confusion. He then retreated, making a small circuit to avoid some riflemen who had occupied the wood; the corps returned to their camp.

The grand guard was constantly advanced in the daytime to a height, from whence it had a view of the passage over the Bronx, at William's bridge; at night it was withdrawn. Lieutenant-Colonel Simcoe being on duty at New-York for a day, Captain Ross, in visiting the piquet at night, found the sentinels so ill placed, that he ordered Sergeant

Kelly and two Huzzars to patrol forwards for its security; they passed a few hundred yards only from the post, when they were surrounded by a party who lay between two stone walls, and taken; nor was Captain Ross to be blamed for ordering the patrol, but the Captain of cavalry, who had omitted a principal sentinel. This patrol made, in contradiction to Lieutenant-Colonel Simcoe's principles, was the only one that had been taken under his command: the Sergeant having been in the rebel service, forced thereto by all want of work, was thrown into prison and threatened with death; Lieutenant-Colonel Simcoe offered a Sergeant whom he had lately taken, in exchange for him; and threatening to leave to the mercy of his soldiers the first six rebels who should fall into his hands, in case of Kelly's execution, soon obtained his release.

Chapter 10

Indians!

July the 18th Captain Lord Cathcart was appointed Colonel, and on the 1st of August Captain Tarleton, Lieutenant-Colonel of the Legion: Captain Hovenden and James's troops were incorporated in that corps. Captain Ross was appointed to the rank of Major of the Queen's Rangers. Lord Cathcart joined the light troops at Kingsbridge, and took the command of them.

Lieutenant-Colonel Simcoe having information that three distinct patrols of thirty men each, set out early in the morning from General Scott's camp at the same time, by different roads, proposed to his Lordship to ambuscade them, on a supposition that they had orders to assist each other in case of necessity; to which his Lordship assenting, the infantry of the Queen's Rangers marched and occupied a wood two miles in front of Kingsbridge, and Lord Cathcart, with the cavalry of the Rangers, Legion, and Emmericks, lay half a mile in the rear, from whence he sent out a patrol, which passing by a road on the right of the Rangers, advanced a quarter of a mile in its front, and returned.

On its return, Lord Cathcart began firing to attract the enemy's notice, a party of whom crossed the country, and came near to the Queen's Rangers, but passed no further,

and, after firing into the wood, to the right of the ambuscade, marched off; this patrol had approached, as was
expected, on hearing the firing, and would inevitably have
been taken, but, as it afterwards appeared, a girl, from a gar-
ret window, had seen some of the soldiers on their march
to the wood, and gave the enemy intelligence.

Lt. Colonel Simcoe was much affected at Lord Cathcart's having the rank of Colonel of Provincials, and made,
in consequence of it, application to the Commander in
Chief. Sir Henry Clinton, though he waved for the present
the giving Lt. Colonel Simcoe rank of Lord Cathcart, offered to him that of Colonel, which he respectfully (but as
the event has proved most unfortunately) declined: every
motive that he had to solicit this rank, by Lord Cathcart's
being employed on other duties, was done away, and Lt.
Colonel Simcoe remained at Kingsbridge, in command of
his corps, Lt Col. Emmerick's, and the cavalry of the Legion. In Lt. Col. Tarleton, he had a colleague, full of enterprise and spirit, and anxious for every opportunity of
distinguishing himself.

These officers, when making observations on the country in front, had a very singular and narrow escape, as they
were patrolling with a few Huzzars.

The Stockbridge Indians about sixty in number, excellent marksmen, had just joined Mr. Washington's
army. Lt Col. Simcoe was describing a private road to Lt
Col. Tarleton: Wright, his orderly dragoon, alighted and
took down a fence of Devou's farmyard, for them to pass
through; around this farm the Indians were ambuscaded.
Wright had scarce mounted his horse, when these officers, for some trivial reason, altered their intentions, and,
spurring their horses, soon rode out of sight, and out of
reach of the Indians. In a few days after, they had certain
information of the ambuscade, which they so fortunate-

ly had escaped: in all probability, they owed their lives to the Indians' expectations of surrounding and taking them prisoners.

Good information was soon obtained, by Lt. Col. Simcoe, of General Scott's situation, and character; and he desired Sir William Erskine would lay before the Commander in Chief his request, that he would permit the York Volunteers to join him, for a week; that, during that time, he might attack Scott's camp He particularly named the York Volunteers, as he wished to unite the Provincials in one enterprise; unfortunately, that regiment could not be spared, as it was ordered for embarkation. Scott soon altered his position; and the source of intelligence, relative to him, was destroyed.

The rebels had, in the daytime, a guard of cavalry, near Marmaroneck, which was withdrawn at night: it was intended to cover the country, and protect some sick horses, turned into the salt marshes in the neighbourhood. Lt. Col. Simcoe determined to attempt its surprisal. General Scott's camp was not above three miles from it; and, in case of alarm, he had a shorter march to intercept the party, at Eastchester bridge, than it had to return there.

The troops, consisting of the Queen's Rangers, and the cavalry of the Legion, marched at night; at Chester bridge, Captain Saunders, an officer of great address and determination, was left in ambuscade in a wood, with a detachment of the Rangers, and in the *rear* of the post that the enemy would, probably, occupy, if they should attempt to cut off the party in its retreat His directions were, to remain undiscovered; to let all patrols pass; and, in case the enemy should post themselves, to wait until the party, upon its return, should be engaged in forcing the passage, and then to sally upon their rear. The troops continued their march, passing the creek, higher up, with the greatest silence; they went through fields, obliterating every trace of their passage when they crossed roads, to avoid discovery from disaffected people, or the enemy's numerous patrols.

When they arrived at their appointed station, Lt Col Tarleton, with the cavalry, ambuscaded the road, on which the enemy's guard was to approach; Lt. Col. Simcoe occupied the centre, with the infantry, in a wood, and Major Ross was posted on the right, to intercept whomsoever Lt. Col. Tarleton should let pass. Two or three commissaries, and others, who were on a fishing party, were taken.

At six o'clock, as he was previously ordered, Lt Col. Tarleton left his post, when the party of the enemy instantly appeared in his rear: they owed their safety to mere accident. The information that both the old and new piquet of the enemy generally arrived at this post at five o'clock, was true; a horse, belonging to a Sergeant, breaking loose, the officer chose to wait till it was caught, and this delayed them for a full hour. Three dragoons, who had previously advanced to a house within the ambuscade, were now taken, and about thirty or forty lame or sick horses.

The troops, followed at a distance by the rebel dragoons, returned home without any accident. Scott, upon the alarm, ordered off his baggage; and Washington sent cannon, and troops, to his assistance, and put his army under arms.

Captain Saunders permitted two patrols to pass, having effectually concealed his party. The prisoners said, that, two mornings before, General Gates had been there fishing.

Lt Col. Simcoe, returning from headquarters, the 20th of August, heard a firing, in front, and being informed that Lt. Col. Emmerick had patrolled, he immediately marched to his assistance. He soon met him retreating; and Lt Col. Emmerick being of opinion the rebels were in such force, that it would be advisable to return, he did so.

Lt. Col. Simcoe understood that Nimham, an Indian

chief, and some of his tribe, were with the enemy; and by his spies, who were excellent, he was informed that they were highly elated at the retreat of Emmerick's corps, and applied it to the whole of the light troops at Kingsbridge. Lt. Col. Simcoe took measures to increase their belief; and, ordering a day's provision to be cooked, marched the next morning, the 31st of August, a small distance in front of the post, and determined to wait there the whole day, in hopes of betraying the enemy into an ambuscade: the country was most favourable to it.

His idea was, as the enemy moved upon the road which is delineated in the plan as intersecting the country, to advance from his flanks; this movement would be perfectly concealed by the fall of the ground upon his right, and by the woods upon the left; and he meant to gain the heights in the rear of the enemy, attacking whomsoever should be within by his cavalry and such infantry as might be necessary. In pursuance of these intentions, Lt Col. Emmerick, with his corps, was detached from the Queen's Rangers, and Legion; as, Lt Col. Simcoe thought, fully instructed in the plan; however, he, most unfortunately, mistook the nearer house for one at a greater distance, the names being the same, and there he posted himself, and soon after sent from thence a patrol forward, upon the road, before Lt Col. Simcoe could have time to stop it. This patrol had no bad effect, not meeting with any enemy: had a single man of it deserted, or been taken, the whole attempt had, probably, been abortive.

Lt Col. Simcoe, who was half way up a tree, on the top of which was a drummer boy, saw a flanking party of the enemy approach. The troops had scarcely fallen into their ranks, when a smart firing was heard from the Indians, who had lined the fences of the road, and were exchanging shot with Lt. Col. Emmerick, whom they had discovered. The

Queen's Rangers moved rapidly to gain the heights, and Lt. Col. Tarleton immediately advanced with the Huzzars, and the Legion cavalry. Not being able to pass the fences in his front, he made a circuit to return further upon their right; which being reported to Lt. Col. Simcoe, he broke from the column of the Rangers, with the grenadier company, and, directing Major Ross to conduct the corps to the heights, advanced to the road, and arrived, without being perceived, within ten yards of the Indians.

They had been intent upon the attack of Emmerick's corps, and the Legion; they now gave a yell, and fired upon the grenadier company, wounding four of them, and Lt Col. Simcoe. They were driven from the fences; and Lt. Col. Tarleton, with the cavalry, got among them, and pursued them rapidly down Courtland's-ridge. That active officer had a narrow escape; in striking at one of the fugitives, he lost his balance and fell from his horse; luckily, the Indian had no bayonet, and his musket had been discharged. Lt Col. Simcoe joined the battalion, and seized the heights. A Captain of the rebel light infantry, and a few of his men, were taken; but a body of them, under Major Stewart, who afterwards was distinguished at Stony Point, left the Indians, and fled.

Though this ambuscade, in its greater part, failed, it was of consequence. Near forty of the Indians were killed, or desperately wounded; among others, Nimham, a chieftain, who had been in England, and his son; and it was reported to have stopped a larger number of them, who were excellent marksmen, from joining General Washington's army. The Indian doctor was taken; and he said, that when Nimham saw the grenadiers close in his rear, he called out to his people to fly, "that he himself was old, and would die there;" he wounded Lt. Col. Simcoe, and was killed by Wright, his orderly Huzzar.

The Indians fought most gallantly; they pulled more than one of the cavalry from their horses; French, an active youth, bugle-horn to the Huzzars, struck at an Indian, but missed his blow; the man dragged him from his horse, and was searching for his knife to stab him, when, loosening French's hand, he luckily drew out a pocket-pistol, and shot the Indian through the head, in which situation he was found. One man of the Legion cavalry was killed, and one of them, and two of the Huzzars, wounded.

Colonel Gist, who commanded a light corps of the rebels, was posted near Babcock's house, from whence he made frequent patrols. Lt Colonel Simcoe had determined to attack him; when, a deserter coming in, at night, who gave an accurate account of his position, the following morning was fixed upon for the attempt General Kniphausen, who commanded at Kingsbridge, approved of the enterprise, and ordered a detachment of the Yagers to co-operate in it. Lt Col. Emmerick undertook to lead the march, having, in his corps, people who were well acquainted with the country.

The following disposition was made. Emmerick's infantry, followed by the Queen's Rangers, were to march through the meadows on the side of Valentine's hill, opposite Courtland's-ridge, and pass between the rebel sentries to Babcock's house, when they would be in the rear of Gist's encampment, which they were immediately to attack. Lieut. Col. Tarleton, with the whole of the cavalry, was to proceed to cover the right, and arrive at Valentine's hill by daylight; a detachment of Yagers, under Captain Wreden, were to march on Courtland's ridge, and to halt opposite to Gist's encampment; and a larger detachment of Yagers, under Major Pruschank, were, at the same time, to be ready to force Phillip's bridge, then to proceed to the bridge opposite Babcock's house, and to cut off the enemy's retreat by that road. The signal for these divisions' moving on was to be the noise of storming Gist's encampment.

Lt. Col. Emmerick conducted the march in so able a manner, and the whole corps followed with so much silence, that the enemy's sentinels were passed without alarm, and this division gained the heights in the rear, and could see the whole chain of sentinels walking below them. Major Ross was detached to possess himself of Post's house, to preserve a communication with Lt. Col. Tarleton, on Valentine's hill; the remainder of the Rangers inclined to the right, towards Gist's camp, and Lt. Col. Emmerick was directed to secure the saw-mill road.

Firing soon began; and it was apparent from Lt. Col. Emmerick's quarter, whom the enemy had discovered. Lt. Col. Simcoe immediately moved rapidly into the road, and directly up the steeps to the enemy's camp, as a nearer way than through the thickets; he attained it, and, to his great surprise, found that Major Pruschank had not forced Phillip's bridge, as had been intended, but had crossed and joined Captain Wreden on Courtland's Ridge, and that Colonel Gist had escaped through the passage which had been so unaccountably left open.

Lt Col. Tarleton fell in with a patrol of cavalry, and dispersed it; and the Queen's Rangers, as soon as they got possession of Gist's camp, having ambuscaded themselves, took a patrol which came forward on hearing the firing. The troops set fire to Gist's huts, and returned to their camp.

Soon after, Mr. Washington quitted the White-plains; and Lt. Col. Simcoe was not a little gratified at the country people, among other reasons, attributing this measure to the continual checks which his light troops had received. The next day, he patrolled so near as to be certain of the enemy having decamped. Soon after, patrolling again to that spot, Lt. Col. Tarleton, who was in front, sent to inform Lt. Col. Simcoe that he understood there was a piquet of the enemy two miles off to the right of the White-plains, and desired that he would send a party to the Plains to watch that quarter, while he galloped on to the enemy's post.

Lt. Col. Simcoe went himself to the White-plains, and observed and sketched the inaccessible ground which Mr. Washington had occupied, in 1776, and which hitherto had not been visited by any British officer. Lieut. Col. Tarleton, soon after, returned; he had put the enemy's piquet to flight, and taken some prisoners.

CHAPTER 11

Capture of Colonel Thomas

Colonel Campbell advanced, the latter end of September, with the 71st regiment and the light troops, to Milesquare, where, soon after, Major-General Grant, with a larger force, occupied the ground, from the Bronx, at Hunt's bridge, to the North river. The Provincial troops, consisting of the Queen's Rangers, Delancey's, Emmerick's, and Legion cavalry, under Lieut. Col. Simcoe, were on the right, beyond the Bronx, and formed a flying camp between that and Chester creek: as this corps was liable to be struck at, it seldom encamped two days and nights in the same place, and constantly occupied a strong position.

Their patrols, crossing the country, together with the Yagers, who were on the left, effectually covered the camp. An, ambuscade was laid by Colonel Lee, for the Yager patrols, which, in part, was successful. General Grant, wishing to retaliate upon the enemy, an attempt was made to surprise a post at Hammond's house. The Provincial troops were to make a circuit to gain its rear, and the Yagers were to approach to the front. After a very fatiguing and long march, the party gained their position, but the enemy had gone off.

On the return to camp, Lieutenant Colonel Simcoe met General Grant, and requested, that, as the corps under his command was severely fatigued and incapable of exertion, he might pass the Bronx, and be within the guards of the line. The General assented: nor was it useless, for the next day, when they returned to their former position, Major Ross made a patrol, and brought *certain intelligence* that a large body of the enemy's infantry, pressing horses, had approached the post, at night, within two miles, intending to attack it.

Earl Cornwallis, being foraging near the English neighbourhood, in the Jerseys, it was thought easy whilst his lordship pushed a body of militia, who were watching his motions in front, to intercept their retreat by passing a corps over the North river; for this purpose, Colonel Campbell, with the 71st and Queen's Rangers, were ordered to embark from Phillip's house; they arrived there, and waited for the boats from New York, which did not come, or land them till three hours after the appointed time.

However, the enemy had changed their position, and Colonel Campbell joined General Grey, who had just surprised Baylor's dragoons; his troops being fresh he offered his services to penetrate further into the country, and to collect what cattle he could; which being done, the detachment re-crossed the river, and returned on the evening to their several encampments.

It requires great skill, and still greater attention, to adapt the movements of any embarkation in boats to the tides and shoals of rivers: this was the second expedition mentioned in this journal, which might have failed, from the want of such knowledge, or attention in its execution.

General Grant, being to embark for the West Indies, was so well satisfied with the Queen's Rangers, that he told Lt. Col. Simcoe, if he could get Sir Henry Clinton's permission, he would readily take him, and his corps, among the number of chosen troops destined for that service. This kind and generous offer, could not but be highly agreeable to him and to the officers of the Queen's Rangers, and nothing could have made them decline it, but a conviction that it would not be just in them to the many very valuable native Americans who were among their non-commissioned officers, and soldiers.

Lieut. Col. Simcoe, therefore, respectfully declined this very advantageous offer, and the certainty of British rank which must have resulted from it. Major Ross went upon the expedition as Brigade-Major, and Lt. Col. Simcoe was deprived of the assistance of his valuable friend, as his country was, too soon, of the services of this gallant officer, he being unfortunately killed at St Christopher's. Captain Armstrong was appointed Major in his room. Lieut. Col. Simcoe, Captain in the 40th, which regiment went with General Grant, was permitted to remain in the Rangers, by a very honourable distinction which the Commander in Chief was pleased to make, in public orders. The army, soon after, returned to York Island; and the Rangers fell back nearer to the redoubts.

Captain Beckwith, (now Major), aid-de-camp to General Kniphausen, procured intelligence of the strength, and of the views of the enemy's advanced corps; and he informed Lieut. Col. Simcoe, that Colonel Armand lay in a situation easily to be surprised. In a few days, some deserters came in. Upon their arrival, Captain Beckwith examined them, and sent them on to headquarters at New York. Lieut. Col. Simcoe, went immediately to New York, to get the deserters, as guides; unfortunately, they had enlisted in the Legion, and been sent to Long-island, where that corps, having left Kingsbridge, was quartered. Their information was, that one sentry was posted by each house, that Armand had neither videttes nor piquets, and that his horses were unsaddled during the night, and in different stables.

Before the troops went into winter quarters, it was necessary, that sufficient boards should be procured to hut those who were to remain in the vicinity of Kingsbridge, and the light troops were of the parties who collected them. Lt. Col. Simcoe proposed to General Tyron, who commanded the British, to take down Ward's house, and the buildings in its vicinity; and that, while a covering party should haLt. there, he would attempt to surprise Colonel Thomas, a very active partisan of the enemy, and a post of dragoons, nearly twenty miles beyond it. General Tryon acquiesced in the proposal, and directed it to be put in execution, but seemed very doubtful, whether so wary a person as Thomas could be circumvented.

Lt. Col. Simcoe marched all night, with Emmerick's and the Queen's Rangers, and surrounded Thomas's house by daybreak. He never lay at home before that night, and had done so in consequence of the British troops, in general, being gone into winter quarters, and one of his own spies being deceived, and made to believe that the Queen's Rangers were to march to Long Island. One shot was fired from the window, which, unfortunately, killed a man, by the side of Lt. Col. Simcoe; the house was immediately forced, and, no resistance being made, the officers shut the doors of the different rooms, to prevent the irritated soldiers from revenging their unfortunate comrade. The man, who fired was the only person killed; but Thomas, after Lt. Col. Simcoe had personally protected him and ensured his safety, jumped out of the window, and, springing over some fences would have certainly escaped, notwithstanding most of Emmerick's riflemen fired at him, had not an Huzzar leapt after him and cut at him with his sword, (which he crouched from and luckily escaped,) when he surrendered.

The cavalry proceeded on to the enemy's piquet, at a

mile distance. They had been alarmed by the firing, and were formed; they fired their carbines (by which Captain Ogden, of Emmerick's was wounded) and fled: they were pursued, but to no purpose. The troops returned to General Tyron, who was, in person, at Ward's house, and who was much pleased at this mischievous partisan's being taken. This march was above fifty miles.

CHAPTER 12

The 1st American Regiment

The season had been, for some time, dreadfully inclement, and was severely felt. by the troops encamped on the exposed heights of Kingsbridge. It was, therefore, with great pleasure, that Lieut. Col. Simcoe received orders to march for winter quarters to Oyster bay, in Long Island, where he arrived on the 19th of November.

As it was understood that this village was to be the winter cantonment of the corps, no time was lost in fortifying it; the very next day, the whole corps was employed in cutting *fascines*. There was a centrical hill, which totally commanded the village, and seemed well adapted for a place of arms; the outer circuit of this hill, in the most accessible places, was to be fortified by sunken fleches, joined by abatis, and would have contained the whole corps; the summit was covered by a square redoubt, and was capable of holding seventy men; platforms were erected, in each angle, for the field pieces, and the guard-house, in the centre, cased and filled with sand, was rendered musket proof, and looped so as to command the platforms, and surface of the parapet; the ordinary guard, twenty men, were sufficient for its defence. Some of the militia assisted, in working, one day, when Sir William Erskine came to Oyster bay, inten-

tionally to remove the corps to Jericho, a quarter the
Legion was to quit in order to accompany him to the
east end of the island.

Lt. Col. Simcoe represented to him, that in case of the
enemy's passing the sound, both Oyster Bay and Jericho
were at too great a distance from any post to expect suc-
cour, but that the latter was equally liable to surprise as
Oyster bay, that its being farther from the coast was no
advantage, as the enemy, acquainted with the country, and
in league with the disaffected inhabitants of it, could have
full time to penetrate, undiscovered, through the woods,
and, that the vicinity of Oyster bay to the sea coast would
enable him to have a more watchful eye over, the landing places, and to acquire a knowledge of the principles
of the inhabitants in these important situations; and that
provisions from New York might be received by water.
Sir William Erskine was pleased to agree with Lt. Col,
Simcoe; and expressed himself highly satisfied with the
means that had been taken to ensure the post; and, on his
representation, the corps was permitted to remain in its
present cantonments.

There was a small garrison at Lloyd's neck, within
twelve miles of Oyster bay: a feint, in case of attack, would
serve to have kept this post within its redoubts. The nearest cantonment was at Jamaica, where the British grenadiers lay; this was almost thirty miles from Oyster bay. The
New-England shore was not more than twelve, and in
many places but seven or eight miles over; and there were
many favourable landing places within a mile or two of
Oyster bay. The enemy could raise any number of men for
such an expedition; General Parsons lay with some regular
troops in the vicinity, and there were whale-boats sufficient to carry two-thousand men, who, in three hours,
might attack the cantonment.

The situation was an anxious one, and required all the vigilance and system of discipline to prevent an active enemy from taking advantage of it Every separate quarter was loop-holed, and surrounded with abatis in such a manner that it could not be forced. A house was moved, bodily, to the rear, near to the beach, where the Highland and Grenadier companies were quartered. A general plan of defence was calculated for the whole; and proper orders were given, in case of attack. Patrols were frequently made; the friendly inhabitants were on the watch, and some depredations having been committed, convalescent soldiers, of good characters, were sent to lodge in the houses of those of the vicinity who chose it; and signals were appointed to be made by the country people, in case any plunderers were out, on which, sentinels were to be placed on each barrack, and the rolls immediately called; by these, and other precautions, marauding was effectually prevented.

Since the conclusion of the war, Lieut. Col. Simcoe has had the satisfaction of hearing, that his precautions were not in vain, for that, more than once, an attack on Oyster bay was meditated, and laid aside.

There being little probability of the Queen's Rangers recruiting, notwithstanding the exertions of the parties on that service, while much greater bounties were given, by regiments now raising, than Government allowed the Provincials, it was, in public orders, recommended to the consideration of the officers, "whether a strict soldier-like, and honourable economy, which their present situation would admit of, might not enable them, by adding to the bounties allowed by Government, to recruit their companies, and give them opportunities of acting in a wider sphere at the commencement of the next campaign, which, from every appearance, was like to be most active?"

The officers subscribed liberally to the recruiting fund.

The Commander in Chief intending to augment the Huzzars of the Queen's Rangers, to a troop of fifty, or more, Lt. Col. Simcoe applied, through Sir William Erskine, that Lieut. Wickham should be captain; Lieut. M'Nab lieutenant; Quartermaster Spencer, of the 16th dragoons, cornet; and Sergeant Spurry, of the same regiment, quartermaster. That regiment had been drafted, and Lt. Col. Simcoe, with his utmost solicitations, could not procure the quartermaster, or a single dragoon from the corps.

The regular and methodical mode of dressing, and feeding the horses, was the point of service that the troop wished to be instructed in, by the regular dragoons. The situation at Oyster Bay was extremely well calculated to secure the health of the soldiery; the water was excellent; there was plenty of vegetables, and oysters to join with their saLt. provisions, and bathing did not a little contribute, with the attention of the officers to cleanliness, to render them in high order for the field, nor were they without sufficient exercise.

The garrison in New York being in great want of forage, Oyster Bay became a central and safe deposit for it, and frequent expeditions, towards the eastern and interior parts of the island, were made to enforce the orders of the Commander in Chief in this respect; excursions were also frequently made to execute other orders, relative to the intercourse with the inhabitants of the rebel coast, and to escort messengers, &c. between Sir William Erskine, who commanded on the east end of the island, and Jamaica.

Lt. Whitlock, having a perfect knowledge of the country about Norwalk, proposed to burn the whale-boats, which were harboured there, and had infested the sound, and taken several of the wood and provision vessels. He was immediately dispatched to the Commander in Chiefs to lay his proposals before him. Sir Henry Clinton, at this period, did not think it advisable to put Lieut. Whitlock's plan in execution. The officers of the Queen's Rangers always understood, that whatever plans they might offer for the good of the King's service, would be patronised, and fairly represented to the Commander in Chief, by the Lieutenant-Colonel, that they might reap the fruit of their own exertions.

The corps had constantly been exercised in the firing motions, and the charging with bayonets, upon their respective parades; as the season opened, they were assembled together. They were, particularly, trained to attack a supposed enemy, posted behind railing, the common position of the rebels. They were instructed not to fire, but to charge their bayonets with their muskets loaded, and, upon their arrival at the fence, each soldier to take his aim at their opponents, who were then supposed to have been, driven from it. They were taught that, in the position of running, their bodies afforded a less and more uncertain mark to their antagonists, whose minds also must be perturbed by the rapidity of their approach with undischarged arms.

The light infantry, and Huzzars, were put under the direction of Captain Saunders, who taught them to gallop through woods, and acting together, the light infantry learnt to run, by holding the horses' manes; the cavalry were, also, instructed, as the infantry lay flat upon the ground, to gallop through their files.

The grand divisions were exercised in the manual, and firing motions, by their respective commanders, but they were forbidden to teach them to march in slow time, they were "to pay great attention to the instruction of their men in charging with their bayonets, in which case, the charge was never to be less than *three hundred yards,* gradually increasing in celerity from its first outset, taking great care that the grand division has its ranks perfectly close, and the pace adapted to the shortest men. The soldier is, particularly, to be taught, to keep his head well up, and erect: it is graceful, on all occasions, but absolutely necessary if an enemy dare stand the charge; when the British soldier, who fixes with his eye the attention of his opponent, and, at the same instant, pushes with his bayonet without looking down on its point, is certain of conquest"

When the weather permitted, the corps was frequently exercised together, particularly in occupying ground, on the supposition of the enemy's landing to attack the post; they were shown how to make, and navigate rafts, constructed on the simplest principles, and with the slightest materials.

On the 18th of April, a party of refugees went from Oyster Bay, being furnished with arms, agreeable to an order from headquarters, to take the Generals Parsons and Silliman from the opposite shore. They did not risk the attack on General Parsons, but they brought Brigadier Silliman to Oyster Bay: he was sent, the next day, to New York.

Lt. Col. Simcoe had been directed towards the centre of the island, to enquire into a supposed intercourse held with Connecticut; he had the Huzzars, and some infantry, with him. The weather was inclement, and the troops occupied two or three different houses: such precautions were taken as the quarters would admit of.

At night, the advance sentinel, on the Lieutenant-Colonel's quarters, fired The man was questioned; he persisted, that he challenged three or four men, with arms: though he was a steady soldier, it appeared so improbable, that any enemy could be in Long Island, that he was not credited. It was afterwards known, that a party of twenty men had been concealed there, in hopes to take some officer, for near three weeks, and that could they have surprised Lt. Col. Simcoe's quarters, it was meant to have attacked them.

On the 2nd of May, the Commander in Chief was pleased to signify, in general orders, to the Provincial troops, "that his Majesty, anxious to reward their faithful services, and spirited conduct, upon several occasions, has been pleased to confer upon them the following marks of his Royal favour." The articles were then enumerated, and were all material to that service: the principal were: "That the officers of Provincial corps shall rank as juniors of the rank to which they belong, and if disabled in service, should be entitled to the same gratuity as officers of the established army; and, to distinguish the zeal of such regiments as shall be completed, his Majesty will, upon the recommendation of the Commander in Chief, make the *rank of those officers permanent in America,* and will allow them half-pay, upon the reduction of their regiments, in the same manner as the officers of the British reduced regiments are paid."

In consequence of this order, the Queen's Rangers were recommended by the Commander in Chief, and styled, and numbered, as the *first American regiment:* the doubt whether they came under the letter of the description, as they were not at present actually complete, was graciously explained, by his Majesty, in their favour, as, they had formerly been so; the New York Volunteers, and the Volunteers of Ireland, were, at the same time, placed upon this establishment.

Chapter 13

Casualties

The Queen's Rangers, consisting of three hundred and sixty, rank and file, in great health and activity, left their cantonments on the 18th of May, and, by a given route, arrived at Kingsbridge, and encamped there on the 27th, and formed the advance of the right column of the army, which marched from thence, on the 29th, to a position extending from Phillip's house to East Chester heights; Sir William Erskine commanding the cavalry, and light troops, he encamped, with a division of the line, and the light troops, on the 1st of May, at Dobb's ferry.

Lt. Col. Simcoe marched, on the 3rd of June, to Croton bridge, where the enemy had been collecting the cattle of the country, which he seized upon; at the same time, he covered the retreat of Lt. Col. Tarleton, who had passed that bridge and beat up the quarters of a party, four miles farther: he took some prisoners, and returned to Dobb's ferry.

On the 6th, Sir William Erskine fell back towards Valentine's hill; the Queen's Rangers encamping at Odle's hill: soon after they formed part of the escort which accompanied the Commander in Chief to the White-plains.

On the 24th of June, the Queen's Rangers, and Legion, marched by different routes to Croton bridge; the Queen's Rangers arriving first, and being discovered, the Huzzars attacked and routed a small patrol of the enemy, taking a few prisoners. Lieutenant Whitlock, who was on a piquet while the troops halted to refresh themselves, ambuscaded a patrol, and took a Captain, and some privates.

The Queen's Rangers, and Legion, marched to Northcastle, and lay there that night: the enemy having several parties in the neighbourhood. Before day, Captain Moncrief, of the Rangers, was detached to take post, without discovering himself, in a wood, which commanded a dangerous pass through which the troops were to march; they fell back, without molestation, on Colonel Wurmb, who had advanced to the White-plains to support them, and returned, the next day, with him to the army.

The army marched, on the 8th of July, in two columns, to Marmaroneck; the Queen's Rangers were, in front of that, on the right. On the 9th, the Commander in Chief marched with the army to Byram's bridge: on leaving this camp, to return to Marmaroneck, the next day, the Queen's Rangers formed the rear guard. Upon this march, three soldiers, straggling at a small distance from their huts, were taken by some militia.

Lt. Col. Simcoe expressed, in orders, "that he is most sensibly affected at the loss of the three men, who straggled from their post during the last march. He feels himself but ill repaid for the confidence he has placed in the regiment, and his inclination to ease their duty, by never posting an unnecessary sentinel; at the same time, he trusts, that, as this has been the *first instance* of the kind during the time he has had the honor of commanding the Queen's Rangers, it will be the last; and that the soldiers will reflect what they must suffer by a long imprisonment, from a mean and despicable enemy, who never has, or can gain any advantage over them, but what arises from their own disobedience of orders."

Captain Saunders, patrolling towards Byram bridge, pursued a party of rebels. Their leader, Colonel Thomas, escaped, by quitting his horse and running into a swamp: he had his parole when made prisoner, the year before; but he was guilty of some malpractices on Long Island, and made his escape, pretending to justify his breaking of his parole by saying, that he understood it was meant to imprison him.

An ambuscade, for a party of the enemy's militia, and dragoons, was projected, with every appearance of success; and General Vaughan, having approved of it, had directed Lt. Col. Simcoe, and Major Delancey, to put it into execution, the next morning; but, at night, the firing at Verplank's-point was heard, and the news of the capture of Stony-point was brought to the camp. The Commander in Chief embarking for Verplank's-point, on the 19th of July, Colonel Birch was detached from General Vaughan's army, with the 17th dragoons, Queen's Rangers, and Legion, to make a display of force, and to occupy the heights on Croton river, above Pine's bridge. The troops made great fires, and every demonstration of their being in force. The heights they occupied were visible from Verplank's and Stony-point.

Two of the Rangers, who knew the country, passed the Croton river, and, returning, brought information that a brigade of the enemy's militia were to encamp, in the evening, on a particular spot, within three or four miles; that provisions were prepared for them, and that there was not the smallest suspicion of the King's troops being in the neighbourhood; it appeared evident that it would be easy to surprise and destroy this corps, but Colonel Birch's orders, to his great regret, were positive not to pass the Croton.

On the 20th, the troops marched back to Dobb's ferry, where the army had arrived, with whom they returned, on the 23rd, to the old camp, in front of Valentine's hill: the Queen's Rangers closing the rear of the left column. Major-General Matthews commanded the troops in the new camp; and on the 30th, he directed his light troops to make, respectively, strong patrols, and at a given time, and to a prescribed point. Lt. Col. Tarleton on the right; Emmerick, and Simcoe, in the centre; and the Yagers on the left.

Lt. Col. Emmerick fell in with a strong party of the enemy's cavalry, who charged his dragoons, which retreated, and drew them into an ambuscade of the infantry, upon whose firing, the enemy fled. Colonel Wurmb, and Lt. Col. Simcoe heard the firing, and pushed to cut off the retreat of the enemy, which was so very precipitate, that, after a long pursuit, only two or three of their rear fell into the hands of the Yagers.

The troops fell back to Kingsbridge: the Queen's Rangers, Emmerick's, and the Legion, occupying the same position they had done the year before.

On the 5th of August, Lt. Col. Simcoe, returning, at midnight, from New York, had not alighted from his horse, when a refugee came in, from Westchester, and informed him, that a rebel party of dragoons had surprised several of their quarters, had taken many prisoners, and that he had escaped in the confusion.

Lieut. Col. Simcoe called "to arms," and sent to the Legion, and Lt. Col. Emmerick, to join him; he marched immediately, with the cavalry of the three corps: Major Cochrane commanded that of the Legion, Lt. Col. Tarleton being in New York. The infantry was directed to follow, with all expedition; and information was sent to Colonel Wurmb. The enemy were pursued so expeditiously, that most of the loyalists, whom they had taken, escaped; and, at New Rochelle, Lt. Col. Simcoe, with the advanced guard, overtook Colonel White, who commanded the enemy, with his rear guard; they fired their pistols at the Huzzars, who did not return a shot

The cavalry being arrived, Colonel White was so pressed, that he left his infantry, and passed a bridge: the enemy's infantry, unable to attain it, threw themselves over a stone wall, close to the left of the road. This bridge was a mile from Marmaroneck; where, it was understood, the enemy were in force. It was obvious, that there would be little probability of cutting off White's fatigued cavalry, unless the fire of the infantry could be passed; Lt. Col. Simcoe attempted to rush past it, hoping that the enemy's confusion, and their position close to the road, would, as the event justified, hurry them to give their fire *obliquely;* unluckily, it was fatal on the most essential point; four Huzzars, and five horses, being either killed or disabled in the front, which was checked; and, at the same time, from some unknown cause, the rear moved about, and the confusion reached to the centre.

Lieut. Col. Simcoe, in this disorder, ordered Captain Deimar, who commanded an independent troop of Huzzars, which followed the Queen's Rangers, to pass the wall in pursuit of the enemy's infantry, who had fled from it; he did so; and Captain James, with his troop, and others of the Legion followed him, two or three of whom without orders, and, unsupported, passed the bridge, and were killed there. Lt. Col. Simcoe tried to get information of any *collateral* road, by which, without passing the bridge, he could pursue the enemy, who naturally supposing that the check might have stopped his party, would be induced to retreat at a slower rate than if they were *directly* pursued; but he could procure no guide, and, in the mean time, a refugee, who had escaped, brought certain intelligence that the enemy were unsupported by any infantry but those with whom the skirmish had happened.

One of the enemy was killed by their own fire, close to the fence; two, or three, by Captain Deimar, in the pursuit, others were drowned in passing the creek; and, by the enemy's gazette it appeared, "that driven into a bad position, they were compelled to fight at disadvantage, and lost twelve men."

The cavalry, on Captain Deimar's return, immediately continued the pursuit to Byram bridge, beyond which it was not prudent or useful to follow. Some more of the loyalists were rescued, but none of the enemy overtaken. On the return, the cavalry were divided, by troops, and scoured the woods back to Marmaroneck, but without effect; there they met with the British and Hessian light troops, with whom they returned to camp.

On the 8th of August, the light troops fell back to the redoubts: A grand guard being in advance, which reported to Lt. Col. Simcoe, as senior officer of the Provincials, the Queen's Rangers were, for the first time since they left winter quarters, permitted to take off their coats, at night, until further orders. In case of sudden alarm, they were ordered to form on their company's parade, undressed, with silence and regularity; the bayonets were never to be unfixed.

The Commander in Chief was pleased to place Captain Sandford's troop of Buck's county dragoons under the command of Lieut. Col. Simcoe, till further orders; Captain Deimar's Huzzars were also added to his command; and this whole corps marched for Oyster Bay on the 13th of August: the cavalry, and cannon, by the route of Hell-gates, and the infantry by Frog's neck, where they embarked, passed over on the 15th, and joining the cavalry, arrived at Oyster Bay on the 17th.

In this interval, the officers, commanding grand divisions, were ordered to make their men perfect in the whole of the manual exercise. Sergeant M'Pherson, a corporal, and twelve men, were selected, and placed under the command of Lieutenant Shaw: they were armed with swords and rifles; and, being daily exercised in firing at objects, soon became most admirable and useful marksmen.

There was every reason to believe that the enemy meant to attack some of the posts on Long Island; that at Lloyd's neck had been the object of frequent expeditions; and Lt. Col. Simcoe's orders were to assist it, in case of necessity. On some musketry being fired in that quarter, at midnight, he galloped there with the cavalry, and cannon; the infantry followed. The alarm proved to be a false one; but Colonel Ludlow, who commanded that post, was of opinion, that this appearance of attention might prevent the attack on it, which he had certain information, was seriously intended against Long Island, a part only of the general operations meditated against New York on the expected arrival of D'Estaing, with his fleet, from the West Indies.

CHAPTER 14

Burning Boats

On the 9th of October, it was hinted to Lieut. Col. Simcoe, to hold his corps in readiness for embarkation.

On the 19th, it marched for that purpose; the cavalry to
Jericho, where they were to remain under the command
of Lieut. Col. Tarleton, and the infantry to Jamaica, which
proceeded to Yellow-hook, and embarked on the 24th. Earl
Cornwallis commanded this expedition, consisting of the
7th, 23rd, 22nd, 33rd, 57th regiments, Rangers, and Volunteers of Ireland commanded by Lord Rawdon. It was supposed to be intended for Jamaica, at that time presumed to
be threatened with an invasion from M. D'Estaing.

On intelligence being received, that his designs were
pointed elsewhere, the troops were re-landed; and were
ordered to continue in readiness to embark at the shortest notice. The Queen's Rangers marched to Richmond,
on Staten Island: they relieved a regiment which had been
very sickly while there. Lieut. Col. Simcoe immediately ordered their huts to be destroyed, and encamped his corps;
Signals, in case of alarm, were established on the island by
General Patterson, who commanded there.

There was a general rumour of an intended attack
on New York. Lt. Col. Simcoe had information that fifty flat-boats, upon carriages, capable of holding seventy

men each, were on the road from the Delaware to Washington's army, and that they had been assembled to Van Vacter's bridge, upon the Rariton. He proposed to the Commander in Chief to burn them. Sir Henry Clinton approved of his plan, as did Earl Cornwallis, and directed it to be put into execution.

Colonel Lee, with his cavalry, had been at Monmouth: Sir Henry Clinton, upon Lieut. Col. Simcoe's application to him for intelligence of this corps, told him, that by the best information he had, Lee was gone from that part of the country. There were no other troops in the vicinity: the Jersey militia only, and those, tumultuously assembled at the moment of the execution of the enterprise, could, possibly, impede it

The coasts of Jersey had been the common receptacle of the disaffected from Staten, Long, and York islands, on the British troops taking possession of them; of course, they were most virulent in their principles, and, by the custom they had of attacking, from their coverts, the British foraging parties, in 1776, and insulting their very out-posts, they had acquired a great degree of self-confidence, and activity.

Lieut. Col. Simcoe's plan was, to burn the boats with as much expedition as possible; to return, with silence, to the heights beyond the town of Brunswick, before day; there to show himself, to entice all who might follow him into an ambuscade; and if he found that his remaining in the Jersies could effect any valuable purpose, the Commander in Chief proposed to reinforce him.

To execute this purpose, he was to draw his cavalry from Jericho in Long Island, by easy marches, to Staten Island. Stuart, an active and gallant man, a native of New-Jersey, commanded some cavalry on that island: these were to be added to him; and he requested ten guides. Three hundred infantry of the Queen's Rangers, with their artillery, were also to accompany him. Two days were lost by a misunderstanding of the General's order: the Huzzars, of the Queen's Rangers only, being sent from Jericho, without Captain Sandford's troop, which was not merely necessary in regard to numbers, but particularly wished for, as it was known that Captain Sandford, when quartermaster of the guards, had frequently been on foraging parties in the country he was to pass through.

On the 25th of October, by eight o'clock at night, the detachment, which has been detailed, marched to Billop's-point, where they were to embark. That the enterprise might be effectually concealed, Lt. Col. Simcoe described a man, as a rebel spy, to be on the island, and endeavouring to escape to New-Jersey; a great reward was offered for taking him, and the militia of the island were watching all the places where it was possible for any man to go from, in order to apprehend him.

The batteaux, and boats, which were appointed to be at Billop's-point, so as to pass the whole over by *twelve o'clock* at night, did not arrive till *three o'clock* in the morning. No time was lost; the infantry of the Queen's Rangers were landed: they ambuscaded every avenue to the town; the cavalry followed as fast as possible.

As soon as it was formed, Lt. Colonel Simcoe called together the officers; he told them of his plan, "that he meant to burn the boats at Van Vacter's bridge, and crossing the Rariton, at Hillsborough, to return by the road to Brunswick, and, making a circuit to avoid that place as soon as he came near it, to discover himself when beyond it, on the heights where the Grenadier Redoubt stood while the British troops were cantoned there, and where the Queen's Rangers afterwards had been encamped; and to entice the militia, if possible, to follow him into an ambuscade which the infantry would lay for them at South-river bridge."

Major Armstrong was instructed to re-embark, as soon as the cavalry marched, and to land on the opposite side of the Rariton, at South-Amboy: he was then, with the utmost despatch and silence, to proceed to South-river bridge, six miles from South-Amboy, where he was to ambuscade himself, without passing the bridge or taking it up.

A smaller creek falls into this river on the South-Amboy side: into the peninsula formed by these streams, Lieut. Col. Simcoe hoped to allure the Jersey militia.

In case of accident, Major Armstrong was desired to give credit to any messenger who should give him the parole, of "Clinton and Montrose."

It was daybreak before the cavalry left Amboy. The procuring of guides had been by Sir Henry Clinton entrusted to Brigadier Skinner: he either did not or could not obtain them, for but one was found who knew perfectly the cross-road he meant to take, to avoid the main road from Somerset court-house, or Hillsborough, to Brunswick. Captain Sandford formed the advance guard, the Huzzars followed, and Stuart's men were in the rear; making in the whole about eighty.

A Justice Crow was soon overtaken; Lt. Col. Simcoe accosted him roughly, called him "Tory," nor seemed to believe his excuses, when in the American idiom for courtship, he said "he had only been sparking," but sent him to the rear guard, who, being Americans, easily comprehended their instructions, and kept up the justice's belief that the party was a detachment from Washington's army.

Many plantations were now passed by, the inhabitants of which were up, and whom the party accosted with friendly salutations.

At Quible-town, Lt. Col. Simcoe had just quitted the advance guard to speak to Lieut. Stuart, when, from a public house on the turn of the road, some people came out with knapsacks on their shoulders, bearing the appearance of a rebel guard. Captain Sandford did not see them till he had passed by, when, checking his horse to give notice, the Huzzars were reduced to a momentary halt opposite the house; perceiving the supposed guard, they threw themselves off their horses, sword in hand, and entered the house. Lt. Col. Simcoe instantly made them remount: but they were afraid to discover some thousand pounds of paper-money which had been taken from a passenger, the master of a privateer, nor could he stay to search for it.

He told the man, "that he would be answerable to give him his money that night at Brunswick, where he should quarter;" exclaimed aloud to his party, "that these were not the Tories they were in search of although they had knapsacks," and told the country people who were assembling around, "that a party of Tories had made their escape from Sullivan's army, and were trying to get into Staten Island, as Iliff (who had been defeated, near this very spot, taken, and executed) had formerly done, and that he was sent to intercept them:"

The sight of Justice Crow would, probably, have aided in deceiving the inhabitants, but, unfortunately, a man personally knew Lt. Col. Simcoe, and an express was sent to Governor Levingstone, then at Brunswick, as soon as the party marched. It was now conducted by a country lad whom they fell in with, and to whom Captain Sandford, being dressed in red, and without his cloak, had been introduced as a French officer: he gave information, that the greater part of the boats had been sent on to Washington's camp, but that eighteen were at Van Vacter's bridge, and that their horses were at a farm about a mile from it. He led the party to an old camp of Washington's above Bound brook. Lt. Col. Simcoe's instructions were to burn these huts, if possible, in order to give as wide an alarm to the Jersies as he could. He found it impracticable to do so, they not being joined in ranges, nor built. of very combustible materials.

He proceeded without delay to Bound brook, from whence he intended to carry off Col. Moyland, but he was not at Mr. Vanhorn's. Two officers who had been ill were there; their paroles were taken; and they were ordered to mark "sick quarters" over the room door they inhabited, which was done; and Mr. Van-horn was informed, that the party was the advanced guard of the left column of the army, which was commanded by General Birch, who meant to quarter that night at his house; and that Sir H. Clinton was in full march for Morris-town, with the army. The party proceeded to Van Vacter's bridge.

Lieut. Col. Simcoe found eighteen new flat-boats, upon carriages; they were full of water. He was determined effectually to destroy them. Combustibles had been applied for, and he received, in consequence, a few port-fires; every Huzzar had a hand-grenade, and several hatchets were brought with the party. The timbers of the boats were cut through; they were filled with straw and railing, and some grenades being fastened in them, they were set on fire. Forty minutes were employed in this business.

The country began to assemble in their rear; and as Lt. Col. Simcoe went to the Dutch-meeting, where the harness, and some stores, were reported to be, a rifle-shot was fired at him from the opposite bank of the river. This house, with a magazine of forage, was now consumed, the commissary, and his people, being made prisoners.

The party proceeded to Somerset court-house, or Hillsborough. Lt. Col. Simcoe told the prisoners not to be alarmed, that he would give them their paroles before he left the Jersies; but he could not help heavily lamenting to the officers with him, the sinister events which prevented

110

him from being at Van Vacter's bridge some hours sooner, as it would have been very feasible to have drawn off the flat-boats to the South river, instead of destroying them. He proceeded to Somerset court-house.

Three Loyalists, who were prisoners there, were liberated; one of them was a dreadful spectacle, he appeared to have been almost starved, and was chained to the floor; the soldiers wished, and it was permitted to burn the court-house: it was unconnected with any other building, and, by its flames, showed on which side of the Rariton he was, and would, most probably, operate to assemble the neighborhood of Brunswick at its bridge, to prevent him from returning by that road.

The party proceeded towards Brunswick. Alarm guns were now heard, and some shots were fired at the rear, particularly by one person, who, as it afterwards appeared, being out a shooting, and hearing of the incursion, had sent word to Governor Levingstone, who was at Brunswick, that he would follow the party at a distance, and every now and then give a shot, that he might know which way they directed their march. Passing by some houses, Lt. Col. Simcoe told the women to inform four or five people who were pursuing the rear "that if they fired another shot, he would burn every house which he passed."

A man or two were now slightly wounded.

As the party approached Brunswick, Lieut. Col. Simcoe began to be anxious for the cross road, diverging from it into the Prince-town road, which he meant to pursue, and which having once arrived at, he himself knew the bye ways to the heights he wished to attaint where having frequently done duty, he was minutely acquainted with every advantage and circumstance of the ground. His guide was perfectly confident that he was not yet arrived at it; and Lt. Col. Simcoe was in earnest conversation with him, and making the necessary enquiries, when a shot, at some little distance, discovered there was a party in the front.

He immediately galloped thither; and he sent back Wright, his orderly Sergeant, to acquaint Captain Sandford "that the shot had not been fired at the party," when, on the right at some distance, he saw the rail fence (which was very high on both sides of the narrow road between two woods) somewhat broken down, and a man or two near it, when putting his horse on the canter, he joined the advance men of the Huzzars, determining to pass through this opening, so as to avoid every ambuscade that might be laid for him, or attack, upon more equal terms, Colonel Lee, (whom he understood to be in the neighborhood, and apprehended might be opposed to him,) or any other party; when he saw some men concealed behind logs and bushes, between him and the opening he meant to pass through, and he heard the words, "now, now," and found himself, when he recovered his senses, prisoner with the enemy, his horse being killed with five bullets, and himself stunned by the violence of his fall.

His imprisonment, the circumstances which attended it, and the indelible impressions which it has made on his memory, cannot, even at this distance, be repeated without the strongest emotions: as they merely relate to personal history, they, with his correspondence with Sir H, Clinton, Governor Levingstone, Col. Lee, Gen. Washington, &c. &c. are referred to in the appendix.

Lt. Col. Simcoe had no opportunity of communicating his determination to any of his officers, they being all with their respective divisions ready for what might follow upon the signal shot of the enemy, and his resolution being one of those where thought must go hand in hand with execution, it is no wonder, therefore, that the party, who did not perceive the opening he was aiming at, followed with the accelerated pace which the front, being upon the canter, too generally brings upon the rear; they passed the ambuscade in great confusion. Three horses were wounded, and the men made prisoners, two of them being also wounded.

The enemy who fired were not five yards off: they consisted of thirty men, commanded by Mariner, a refugee from New York, and well known for his enterprises with whale-boats. They were posted on the very spot which Lt. Col. Simcoe had always aimed at avoiding. His guide misled him: nor was the reason of his error the least uncommon of the sinister events which attended this incursion.

When the British troops quitted the camp at Hillsborough, and marched to Brunswick, among other houses which were unwarrantably burnt was the one which the guard relied upon, as marking out the private road the party was to take: he knew not of its being burnt, and that every vestige had been destroyed, so that he led them unintentionally into the ambuscade; which when the party had passed by on the full gallop, they found themselves on the high grounds beyond the barracks at Brunswick. Here they rallied; there was little doubt but Lt. Col. Simcoe was killed: the surgeon, (Mr. Kellock,) with a white handkerchief, held out as a flag of truce, at the manifest risk of his life, returned to enquire for him.

The militia assembling, Captain Sandford drew up, and charged them, of course, they fled: a Captain Vorhees, of the Jersey Continental troops, was overtaken, and the Huzzar, at whom he had fired, killed him. A few prisoners were taken. Captain Sandford proceeded to the South river, the guides having recovered from the consternation. Two militia-men only were met with upon the road thither: they fired, and killed Molloy, a brave Huzzar, the advance man of the party, and were themselves instantly put to death.

At South river the cavalry joined Major Armstrong; he

had perfectly succeeded in arriving at his post undiscovered, and, ambuscading himself, had taken several prisoners. He marched back to South-Amboy, and re-embarked without opposition, exchanging some of the bad horses of the corps for better ones which he had taken with the prisoners.

The alarm through the country was general; Wayne was detached from Washington's camp in the highlands, with the light troops, and marched fourteen miles that night, and thirty the next day; Colonel Lee, who was in Monmouth county, as it was said, fell back towards the Delaware. The Queen's Rangers returned to Richmond that evening. The cavalry had marched upwards of eighty miles, without halting or refreshment, and the infantry thirty.

In the distribution of quarters for the remaining winter, Richmond was allotted to the Queen's Rangers. This post was in the centre of Staten Island, and consisted of three bad redoubts, so constructed, at various times and in such a manner, as to be of little mutual assistance. The spaces between these redoubts had been occupied by the huts of the troops, wretchedly made of mud; these Lieut. Col. Simcoe had thrown down, and his purpose was to build ranges of log houses, which might join the redoubts, and being loop-holed, might become a very defensible curtain. Major Armstrong followed the plan, and set the regiment about its execution, in parties adapted to the different purposes of felling the timber, sawing it, and making shingles for the roofings. In the beginning of December, the regiment was ordered to embark; which order was, soon after, countermanded.

CHAPTER 15

Winter

On the last day of December, Lt. Col. Simcoe returned to Staten Island, from his imprisonment He was mortified to find the expedition, under the Commander in Chief, had failed; especially as, upon his landing at Staten Island, he received a letter from Major Andre, adjutant-general, saying; "If this meets you a free man, prepare your regiment for embarkation, and hasten to New York yourself."

He joined his corps at Richmond; Major Armstrong had been indefatigable in getting the regiment hutted in a manner which rendered their post both comfortable and defensible: and they soon found the advantages of their very extraordinary labours.

The day which Lt. Col. Simcoe passed the sound was the last on which it became navigable for a considerable time, the frost setting in with most unusual inclemency, and, by the 10th of January, the communication with New York was totally shut up by floating ice; and General Stirling was reduced to the necessity of restraining the troops to half allowance of provisions, but with every precaution to impress the inhabitants, and soldiers, with the belief that this restriction was precautionary against the possibility of the communication being closed for several weeks; and care was taken to investigate what resources of fresh provisions might be obtained from the island.

The sound, which divides Staten Island from the Jersies, being totally frozen over and capable of bearing cannon, information was received that several of the rebel Generals had been openly measuring the thickness of the ice, and it was universally rumoured that an attack was soon to take place upon Staten Island. General Stirling commanded there, and he was with the main body at the watering place, the heights of which were occupied with several redoubts; Colonel Lord Rawdon, with the volunteers of Ireland, was quartered near a redoubt at the point of the narrows; and Lt. Col. Simcoe with the Queen's Rangers, at Richmond: the whole force on the island being under one thousand eight hundred effective men.

On the 15th of January, early in the morning, the rebel detachment of near three thousand men, under the command of the person styled Lord Stirling, crossed the ice and entered Staten Island; Lord Stirling marched immediately towards the landing place, and by his position cut off General Stirling's communication with the Volunteers of Ireland and the Queen's Rangers. Lt. Col. Simcoe occupied the high grounds near Richmond with small parties of cavalry, and the infantry were sedulously employed in what might strengthen that post. There were three pieces of cannon (a nine and two six-pounders) mounted on platforms, without embrasures, in the redoubts. These were pointed at the eminences, where it was expected the enemy would first appear, and where the stones were collected in heaps, so that a round shot, if it struck among them, might have the effect of grape. If batteries, or any cannon, should be opened against Richmond, it was obvious these guns must be dismounted: they were, therefore, not intended to be exposed to such accidents, but the redoubt on the right was meant, on the first appearance of assault, to be abandoned, and its area filled with abatis which were provided, and its gate left open and exposed to the fire of the cannon of the other redoubts placed at their respective gates, of the two regimental field pieces, and of the musketry from the doors, windows, and loop-holes of the barracks.

The officers' barracks, which were within the triangular area formed by those of the soldiers and the redoubts, were intended to be taken down, and the logs of which they were composed were to be heaped within a hut, and to form a traverse on a part exposed to the enemy. The rear of the works were secured by their position on the edge of the hill from any possibility of attack, and some of the huts, which ran below the surface of it, were in perfect safety from any shot whatsoever, and nearly so from shells, against the splinters of which their logs were very respectable traverses. There was a gun-boat, which was frozen up in the creek, at the foot of Richmond Hill: this gun was elevated so as to fire a single round of grape shot; some swivels also were brought into the redoubts. Spike nails, which there were a quantity for the barrack purposes, were driven through boards, ready to be concealed under the snow in places which were most accessible. All the cattle in the neighbourhood were brought into the precincts of the garrison, as were the sledges, harness and horses, and the most cheerful and determined appearance of resolution ran through the whole corps.

About midday, many deserters came in from the rebel army; by them a perfect knowledge of the enemy's force was gained: and one of them affirmed that he overheard some of their principal officers say, "That it was not worth-while to attack Richmond where they were sure of obstinate resistance, and which must fall of itself whenever the main body was taken."

Lt. Col. Simcoe was anxious to communicate with Lord Rawdon, and to obtain any intelligence, or orders, his lordship might have for him: he sent his adjutant, Lt. Ormond, with directions to get some of the militia, to convey a letter for that purpose, by the sea shore. Some scattering parties of the enemy had been that way, on which account Lieut. Ormond could get no one to venture, he therefore went himself, and putting on coloured clothes that he might not be distinguished, in case of any small parties lying in ambuscade, he got safely to the flagstaff, and returned without discovery.

The rebels making no attempt in the day time upon the redoubts, where General Stirling was, led Lt. Col. Simcoe to conclude that they waited for cannon or more forces, and meant to storm them at night or the next morning; for, though no person could hold more cheaply than he thought himself authorised to do, those men on whom the enemy had conferred the office and title of Generals, it appeared totally unreasonable that having so well chosen the moment of invading the island, they had no determined point to carry, or had neglected the proper means to ensure its success.

On these ideas, he desired Col. Billop, (who commanded the militia of Staten Island,) to get them to assemble to garrison Richmond; but neither entreaties, the full explanation of the advantage such a conduct would be of, nor the personal example of Col. Billop, had any effect: not a man could be prevailed upon to enter the garrison. They assembled to various public houses, and to hear the news, busy in providing for the temporary security of their cattle and effects; and these were not disaffected persons, but men who were obnoxious to the rebel governors, many of them refugees from the Jersies, some who had every reason to expect death, if the enemy succeeded, and all the total destruction of their property.

Lieut. Col. Simcoe was therefore obliged to lay aside

his intentions, which were to march with his cavalry, carrying muskets, with as many infantry as he could justify the taking from Richmond, with his field pieces in sledges, together with the swivels fixed upon blocks, and to get near the enemy undiscovered, and to make as great an alarm and as much impression as possible upon their rear, whensoever they attempted to storm the British redoubts.

All the roads between Richmond and the headquarters, led through narrow passes, and below the chain of hills: these, where they had been beaten only, were passable, the ground being covered with several feet of snow, so that no patrols were made during the night, which would have been useless and dangerous; and the cavalry were assembled within the redoubts: the night was remarkably cold. A person from the Jersies brought the report of the country, that Washington was expected the next day, at Elizabethtown, and that straw, &c. was sent to Staten Island. He went back again, commissioned by Lt. Col. Simcoe, to observe what stores were in Elizabethtown, and particularly to remark what air-holes were in the ice on the sound between the mouth of Richmond Creek and Elizabethtown, as it was intended, if nothing material intervened before the next night, to send Capt. Stephenson with a detachment to burn Elizabethtown, and to give an alarm in the Jersies.

The intelligence which this zealous and trustworthy loyalist brought was very probable: the making a. winter campaign in America had always appeared to Lt. Col. Simcoe a matter of great facility, and by frequently ruminating upon it, he was alive to the advantages which would attend Mr. Washington in its prosecution. He would without hesitation have abandoned the post of Richmond, and joined Lord Rawdon, or Gen. Stirling, taking on himself all consequences, had it not appeared to him that the possession of Richmond would insure to Mr. Washington a safe retreat, even should the ice become impassable, and would probably inculcate on him the propriety of his seriously attempting to keep Staten Island at this very critical period, when the Commander in Chief was absent with the greatest part of the army, and the troops in New York, under Gen. Kniphausen, were probably not in a capacity to quit it and take the field: particularly as in that case, the nominal militia whose numbers were so well displayed, as sufficient to garrison it, must for the greater part have melted away in their attendance on the army, to whose various departments they in general belonged.

Mr. Washington might without difficulty have assembled from the smaller creeks, and even from the Delaware, and Hudson's river, a multitude of boats, which, while the snow was upon the ground, might be conveyed overland to the Staten Island Sound; and with these, added to those which attended his army, he might transport his troops or form bridges, securing all approaches to them from the water, by batteries constructed on the Jersey shore, while by other attacks and preparations, he certainly could have thrown great difficulties in the way of Gen. Kniphausen, and the British army in the three islands. Lt. Col. Simcoe, reasoning on the possibility of these events, waited to be guided by circumstances.

If Gen. Stirling could hold out, and was neither overwhelmed by numbers, or reduced by famine, which was most to be dreaded, it was obvious Richmond would be safe: if matters happened otherwise, he was perfectly certain, from Lord Rawdon's character, that he should receive some directions from him, who would never remain in an untenable post, with the certainty of being made prisoner; and at all events Lieut. Col. Simcoe determined, in case Gen. Stirling should be defeated, and that he should receive no orders, he would attempt to escape; for since the rebels had shown a total defect in every private and public principle of honour, when they violated the convention with Gen. Burgoyne's army, he and the officers of the Queen's Rangers had determined in no situation to surrender, where by escaping, if it should be but a mile into the country, the corps could disband itself individually, and separately attempt to rejoin the British armies; proper inducements being held out to the soldiers, and great aid being reasonably to be expected from the loyal inhabitants, scattered throughout every colony, and in very great numbers.

This, which had been his common conversation and steady resolution, in case of any unfortunate events, was now determined on by Lieut. Col. Simcoe. His ideas were to forerun all intelligence, and to attempt to surprise Col. Lee, at Burlington, and then to escape to the back countries. For this purpose, he had sledges which could carry a hundred men, and he had no doubt of soon increasing them in the Jersies, to a number sufficient to convey the whole corps; the attempt was less dangerous in itself, and less injurious, if it failed, to the community, than the certainty of being destroyed by heavy artillery, of ultimately surrendering, of mouldering in prison, and becoming lost to all future service to their king and country. There was no corps between General Washington's army, and that of Lincoln hastening into Charles-town, but Col. Lee's.

When once in possession of his horses, there was little doubt in the mind of Lt. Col. Simcoe, and the officers to whom he communicated his ideas, but that he should effect his retreat into the back parts of Pennsylvania, join his friends there, probably release the Convention army, and not impossibly join the commander in chief, in Carolina.

Full of these ideas, it was with great surprise and pleasure, that Lt. Col. Simcoe understood the enemy were retreating from the island. He immediately pursued them with the flank companies and Huzzars; and was overtaken by an order from General Stirling to effect the same purpose; but the enemy had passed to the Jersey shore before he could come up with them. While the troops in the enemy's front, on their arrival at the heights opposite to the British redoubts, halted for the rear to close up, they were permitted to make fires, which increased the power of the frost, and rendered them totally unable to proceed, and the severity of the night affecting the whole of them, many lost their limbs, and several their lives.

There were vast mounds of snow drifted before the redoubts, which Lord Stirling gave as his reason for not attempting them; and General Kniphausen, on the first signal of Staten Island being attacked, embarked troops to support it The enemy in the dark of the evening saw these vessels, (which, whether the passage could be effected or not, were wisely directed to be kept plying off and on,) but they did not wait to see if they could reach the island, which in fact the drifting ice prevented, but immediately determining to retreat, they effected it the next morning, losing many men by desertion, and many British soldiers, who had enlisted with them to free themselves from imprisonment, embraced the opportunity of being in a country they were acquainted with, to return to their old companions. The Queen's Rangers obtained a great many recruits; and it is very remarkable that neither that corps, or the Volunteers of Ireland had a single man who deserted from them, while there were such opportunities and apparent reasons to do it.

Lt. Col. Simcoe on his return from Elizabethtown Point, where the enemy passed, had information that a party of plunderers had crossed from the Jersies to the other end of the island; he detached the Huzzars in pursuit of them, but they fled, on the Staten Island militia collecting together.

The frost still continuing, there were many reports and a general expectation that the enemy would again adventure upon the island, with superior force, with sufficient provision to attempt some greater purpose; and patrols were constantly made on all the roads, by which they could possibly approach, by order of Gen. Stirling. The Queen's Rangers had formerly experienced how ready Gen. Stirling was to represent their services; and they, now in common with the other troops, had a further proof of his good inclinations, it being inserted in the general orders of the 21st of January, "Brigadier Gen. Stirling is happy to inform the troops on this island, of his Excellency Gen. Kniphausen's fullest approbation of their behaviour, and the good countenance they showed when the rebels were upon this island, which the brigadier had reported to the Commander in Chief; and his Excellency desires his thanks may be given to them."

On the 25th Lieut. Col. Simcoe gave out the following order: "That he expects the order relative to officers and soldiers sleeping in their clothes be strictly complied with, such recruits excepted, whom the officers commanding companies may judge as yet unequal to the duties of the regiment; if any half-bred soldier disobeys this order, the first officer, or non-commissioned officer, who meets with him, will deliver him to the officer on guard to be put on some internal duty. The Lt. Col. has particular satisfaction in seeing the General's approbation of that good countenance which enabled him, on the late inroad of the enemy, to rest perfectly at ease, without augmenting the duty of the regiment; he knows its universal spirit, and certain from the fidelity of those on guard, that the garrison cannot be snatched away by surprise, is confident that Richmond redoubts will be too dear for the whole rebel army to purchase."

CHAPTER 16

Over the Ice

Soon after the rebel army returned to their former winter quarters, a very important enterprise suggested itself to Lt. Col. Simcoe.

He understood by deserters and other intelligence, that Mr. Washington was quartered at a considerable distance from his army, or any corps of it, and nearer to New York: by the maps of the country, and all the information he could collect, he thought that it would not be difficult. to carry him off. He communicated his ideas to a gentleman, who had been persecuted by the rebels, and whose family had been the object of their cruel resentment, for his early and uniform loyalty, and by his assistance, a very minute and perfect map of the country was drawn. Some few particulars were necessary to be ascertained, which a trusty person was sent out to inquire into, but without any idea being given to him that might lead him to guess at the enterprise, which was only made known to Capt Shaw, of the Queen's Rangers, until the 31st of January, when, preparatory to the necessary application to Generals Tryon and Kniphausen, Lt. Col. Simcoe communicated his ideas to Gen. Stirling, which, as appears by his letter in the appendix, met with his full approbation.

Lieut. Col. Simcoe's plan was to march by very secret ways, made the more so by the inclement season, and to arrive near Gen. Washington's quarters by daybreak, to tie up his horses in a swamp, and to storm the quarters, and attack his guard on foot: for this purpose, his party were to carry muskets as well as swords, and he meant it to consist of eighty men, indiscriminately taken from the cavalry or infantry, with an officer, besides those of the staff, to every six men, and he was to select those he should command. The party were to halt. at two cottages in a wood, if they should arrive before the appointed time.

Lt. Col. Simcoe waited for his conclusive information with great impatience, and in his conversations with Capt. Shaw always expressed his sanguine hopes, almost his certainty of success; his only apprehension being in case Mr. Washington should personally resist, by what means he could bring him off, and preserve his life; when, to his great surprise, his Huzzars were ordered to march with a convoy over the ice to New York. It should seem, the same negligence in Gen. Washington's quartering in front of his army, had attracted the notice of Capt. Beckwith, Gen. Kniphausen's aid-de-camp, and he had formed a plan to carry off that general; for which purpose, cavalry were collected at New York, and among others, Captain Beckwith obtained the Huzzars of the Queen's Rangers, of whom he had a good opinion, as he often accompanied Lt. Col. Simcoe in the patrols he had made from Kingsbridge.

Brigadier-Gen. Stirling communicated to Lt. Col. Simcoe the purpose for which his cavalry was withdrawn, as it was intended that a general movement from Staten Island should favour the enterprise. Since it did not take place on so large a scale as was at first designed, Lt. Col. Simcoe received orders "to send a party to surprise the enemy's post at Woodbridge or Rahway, and to give a general alarm." This party was to cross the ice at one o'clock in the morning, and not to return till nine or ten.

Accordingly, Lt. Col. Simcoe passed the ice with two hundred infantry, at one o'clock; Major Armstrong with some infantry, the cavalry, and cannon occupying the heights, at the Old Blazing-star, to cover their return. The snow prevented all possibility of marching, but on the beaten road: there were no posts in Woodbridge. But, as he was anxious to fulfil the spirit of his orders, and to give every assistance in his power to his friend, Capt Beckwith's enterprise, he determined to proceed until he beat up some of the enemy's quarters, or fell in with their patrols. On the arrival at the cross roads, from Amboy to Elizabethtown, the troops were challenged, the whole body halted, and with such profound silence, added to their being in the middle of the road, and at night when the beaten path in it appeared among the snow like a dark streak, that the enemy were deceived and thought themselves mistaken, as was learnt from their conversation, which was plainly overheard. But another patrol on horseback, falling in on the flank of the march, discovered the party; the enemy's sentinels fired, and in succession the bugle-horns, drums, and bagpipe of the Queen's Rangers sounded; an universal alarm being given and propagated, the party returned towards Woodbridge. A soldier was unfortunate enough to be killed by the chance shot of the sentinels.

The enemy assembled in the rear, and appeared at eight o'clock, when the party passed Woodbridge creek. The snow was so deep that it was scarce possible to quit the road, which was of advantage to the Rangers; for the companies, alternately advancing in front of the march, occupied such orchards or trees, as were at a small distance from the road, and checked the enemy who pressed upon

the rear. Upon his approach to the Sound, Lt. Col. Simcoe could hear them determine to occupy the houses at the Ferry, and to fire on the Rangers as they passed back; this they could have done with considerable effect, and without being exposed. Sergeant Wright was dispatched to gallop over the ice to Major Armstrong, and to desire him to point his cannon at the Ferry house; and Capt Shank was detached to cross it, previous to the return of the troops, and to conceal himself behind the ridges of the ice, which the tide had heaped up, and cover the retreat of the party, which would pass the Sound in security, between the angle formed by the fire of this detachment, directly opposite, and of Major Armstrong's cannon, at a greater and more oblique distance.

These arrangements being made, and the enemy approaching, the Rangers suddenly turned about and charged them upon a steady run, the rebels immediately fled, and they were pursued till they passed over a small hill, when the Rangers were ordered to go to the right about, and without altering their pace get upon the ice. They were halfway over before the rebels perceived them, which as soon as they did, they occupied the houses, and some of them followed upon the ice. Capt Shank, firing upon them from his ambuscade, drove them instantly back while the cannon shot struck the houses at the same time, and, as it was reported, killed some of them.

The party returned to Richmond without further molestation. The Queen's Rangers lost only the man already mentioned; a few were wounded, but they bore no proportion to the numbers whose clothes were struck by the enemy's bullets, fired at a distance, through intervening thickets, or more probably by those who had not recollection sufficient to ram down their charges. The enemy's loss was supposed to be more considerable, as many of them were seen to fall, and the whole of the affair being between single men, the Rangers were infinitely better marksmen than the Jersey militia.

Capt. Beckwith had found it impracticable to carry his attempt into execution, from an uncommon fall of rain, which encrusting the top of the snow, cut the fetlocks of his horses, and rendered it absolutely impossible for him to succeed. The Huzzars soon after returned to Staten Island.

The ice floating on the 22nd of February, the Sound became impassable; the soldiers were permitted to undress themselves at night, and in case of alarm they were directed to accoutre in their shirts, and to form at their posts.

CHAPTER 17

Cavalry Action

Lt. Col. Simcoe on his arrival at Staten Island from imprisonment, had applied to the Commander in Chief to request that he might join the army to the southward; he had also written in the strongest terms to Earl Cornwallis, soliciting his lordship to support his application. In case his wishes should not take place, he was anxious to be of what service he thought the present situation of the Queen's Rangers would admit.

For this purpose he made application through the proper channel to Gen. Kniphausen, for discretionary permission to beat up the enemy's posts in the Jersies, and to have boats sufficient to transport three hundred infantry and sixty cavalry, to be manned by the Rangers, and to be left totally to his own disposal. He proposed by these means to countenance desertion, then prevalent in Washington's army, and to keep the whole coast in continual alarm: he had the most minute maps of the country and the best guides: and the Loyalists, without doubt, would have universally joined him.

The first enterprise he meant to attempt was, to surprise Col. Lee, at Burlington: he intended to land at night with his cavalry in an unfrequented part of the coast, and march in three separate bodies, each of thirty rank and file, carrying firelocks, and in the minutest particular, each party to be so like to the other, that if they should be discovered by any accident, they might not be easily discriminated, particularly as the separate routs were to be nearly parallel, through bye paths, and seldom at more than two miles distance. Before daybreak they were to meet at an appointed swamp, where they were to remain concealed till the next night, when they were to continue their march, dismount when they arrived close to Burlington, and with fixed bayonets rush into the town, and attempt to conquer Lee's corps. In the meantime the infantry were to land on the second evening, and, with as much secrecy as possibly, march twenty-five miles into the country to secure the retreat.

From time to time, during this enterprise, Lt. Col. Simcoe would have had the best intelligence, without the Loyalists who managed it being entrusted with the secret of his destination; they would have arrived at specified spots from different places, in expectation of meeting those who carried on a contraband traffic with Philadelphia.

Lee's corps were excellently mounted and disciplined; he himself was active and enterprising, and had that weight in the Jersies, which capacity and power, with a very free use of it, could give to the possessor; the importance it would have been of to the intended system of operations, to have seized upon Col. Lee and demolished his corps, is best illustrated by remarking that, although Burlington is near seventy miles from Staten Island, he was understood to have his piquets eight or ten miles in his front for his security.

Lt. Col. Simcoe's proposals were approved of by Generals Kniphausen, Stirling, and Tryon. Some of the boats were sent to him, and the remainder, with the preparations detailed in the appendix, were in forwardness, when, on the 23rd of March 1780, the infantry of the corps received orders to embark for Charleston, which it did on the 4th of April.

Capt. Wickham was left with the Huzzars in the town of Richmond, and the duty of the redoubts was taken by a party of two subaltern officers and sixty rank and file, from the 82nd regiment, under his directions. This detachment was in a few days after relieved by the 22nd regiment.

The Hessian regiment of Ditforth, Queen's Rangers, Volunteers of Ireland, and Prince of Wales's volunteers, under the command of Col. Westerhagen, sailed on the 7th. The Queen's Rangers anchored in Stone inlet on the 18th, and passing the Ashley river, arrived at the camp before Charles Town on the 21st: they immediately marched to the quarter-house, four miles from Charles Town and covered the troops employed on the siege, by extending between the Ashley and Cooper rivers.

The infantry consisted of four hundred rank and file: there was not a sick man among them, for great attention had been paid to whatever might preserve them in health; and Mr. Kellock and Macauley, the surgeons, were very capable and attentive in their duties. The soldiers were new clothed and accoutred, and the regiment had substituted light caps, neat and commodious, in the room of the miserable contract hats, which had been sent from England. To the personal congratulations of his friends, on his release from imprisonment Lt. Col. Simcoe had great pleasure, as he expressed himself in orders, "in hearing the uniformity and appearance of the regiment universally approved: he trusts that soldier will vie with soldier and officer with officer in maintaining in their respective stations the very favourable impression which their superior officers entertain of them, that their discipline and appearance on the parade reflects credit on their soldier-like behaviour in the field."

On the arrival of this reinforcement, Sir Henry Clinton augmented the detachments which he had thrown over the

Cooper river, to cut off the intercourse between Charles Town and the countiy: and Earl Cornwallis took their command. The siege was pushed with vigour.

Lt. Col. Simcoe was very apprehensive that Gen. Lincoln, under the pretext of a sally, would embark in boats, and passing up the Ashley river land beyond his post; when, a few hours' march in a country intersected by rivers and swamps, would enable him to baffle all pursuit. He therefore obtained two six pounders to be added to his field pieces, and placed to command the river; and he endeavoured to procure a fire-raft, to be moored on the opposite bank, which, being set on fire, would throw a light across sufficient to direct the cannon on any boats which might attempt to pass. He had brought with him a Sergeant and nine Huzzars, with their accoutrements, these and his riflemen he soon mounted, and patrolled in his front between Dorchester and Goose creek; but particularly to examine the points which he thought most practicable for Gen. Lincoln to land on.

He found a sloop on the shore at Goose creek, which on the 9th of May Lt. Murray, a gentleman who had been bred in the navy, was indefatigable in getting off and bringing down to the post, to assist in blocking up the passage: however, Mr. Lincoln either did not intend to escape, or thought of it too late; for all possibility of effecting such a design was effectually precluded by Earl Cornwallis's sending down from Wando inlet a water force, which, by Capt Elphingstone's arrangement, effectually blocked up the river: and the place surrendered on the 12th of May.

Lt. Col. Simcoe going to headquarters to congratulate the Commander in Chief, Sir H. Clinton was pleased to show him where he had intended to storm the town, had the enemy's obstinacy obliged him to that measure. The point from whence this attack was to have been made, had been privately reconnoitred by that gallant officer Capt. Hanger; and that Charles Town was not stormed must ever be imputed to that humanity which is so bright a feature in the character of the British general.

The Queen's Rangers marched to Dorchester and its environs, immediately after the capitulation. The air or the water at the quarter-house, had rendered the men sickly. They advanced to Fourhole-bridge, where they remained a day or two at Caton's, (an unfortunate loyalist, whom the rebels some time after assassinated,) from whence, by express order, they returned to Charles Town, as it was supposed, to embark on an expedition to Georgetown. They covered the headquarters on the 30th, and embarked on the 31st for New York.

Capt Wickham of the Huzzars had by no means been idle while at Richmond: the post was such as might have been a temptation to an enterprising enemy; but Gen. Kniphausen, by frequent and well-concerted expeditions, had kept the rebels fully employed in their own cantonments, the Jersies.

On one of these attempts, the Huzzars of the Rangers were eminently distinguished, as was detailed to Lt. Col. Simcoe by Capt Wickham, and by him read to the Commander in Chief, who was highly satisfied with it The report mentions that:

> On the 15th of April, the cavalry on Staten Island, consisting of Cornet Tucker and twenty of the 17th regiment, light dragoons, Capt Wickham with his troop of forty-five men, and Capt Deimar with his Huzzars, forty men, crossed at Cole's ferry, and marched to the English neighbourhood, where they joined Major Du Buy, with three hundred of the regiment, De Bose and fifty of Col. Robinson's corps. At New-bridge Sergeant M'Laughlin, with six of the

Rangers in advance, fell in with and either killed or took the whole of a small rebel outpost The detachment then continued their march, leaving fifty infantry for the security of the bridge. At a convenient distance from Hopper Town, Major Du Buy gave his last orders for his surprise of Col. Bailey, with three hundred rebels, posted at that place: the major was particularly attentive to a minute description of their situation. Cornet Spencer with twelve ranger Huzzars, and Cornet Tucker with the like number of the 17th regiment to support him, made the advance guard; then followed Capt Deimar with his troop: the infantry and the remainder of the cavalry closed the rear. Hopper Town is a straggling village, more than a mile long; the farthest house was Col. Bailey's quarters; the nearest, a court-house which contained an officer's piquet of twenty men, and which, if properly disposed, covered a bridge over which the troops must pass. The advance was ordered to force the bridge, and to push forward at full speed, through the town, to headquarters: this they effected after receiving an ineffectual fire from the piquet and from some of the windows: the rest of the cavalry dispersed, to pick up the fugitives and to take possession of the rebel's quarters, now abandoned. Cornet Spencer, on his arrival at his post with six men only, the rest not being able to keep up, found about five and twenty men drawn up on the road, opposite him, and divided only by a hollow way and small brook, with Hopper's house on their right, and a strong fence and swamp on their left. The officer commanding them, whom he afterwards found to be Bailey, talked to his men and asked his officers, " Shall we fire now or take possession of the house;" the latter was agreed on. The house was of

136

stone, with three windows below and two above: at the moment of their going in, Cornet Spencer with his party augmented to ten of his own, and by two of the 17th regiment, passed the ravine, and taking possession of the angles of the house, ordered some of his men to dismount and to attempt to force one of the windows. Some servants from a small out-house, commenced a fire: Corporal Burt with three men was sent to them, who broke the door open and took nine prisoners. Cornet Spencer made several offers to parley with those who defended headquarters, but to no purpose; they kept up a continual fire: finding it impossible to break the door open, which was attempted, and a man wounded through it, or to force any of the windows, he ordered fire to be brought from the out-house, with which he set one angle of the roof, which was of wood, in flames: he again offered them quarter if they would surrender; they still refused, though the flames were greatly increased. By this time some of the speediest of the cavalry had come to his assistance: the firing ceased. Captains Diimar and Wickham, &c, who had collected a great number of prisoners, and left some few men to guard them, until the infantry should come up, now joined the advance. Col. Bailey, as he opened the door to surrender, was unfortunately shot by one of Captain Deimar's Huzzars, and died three days after. Of the advance guard two men and three horses were killed, and two men and two horses wounded: and one man and one horse of the 17th regiment were also killed. In this house Col. Bailey, two captains, three subalterns, and twenty-one soldiers were taken. In the whole, twelve officers, with one hundred and eighty-two men were made prisoners. The party returned by the same route they had advanced, with little opposition and no loss. The plan of this expedition was well laid, and as well executed: Major Du Buy seemed to be master of the country through which he had to pass, and was well seconded by Capt. Deimar. Major Du Buy was pleased to honour the Huzzars of the Rangers with his particular thanks and approbation. The house was well defended, and the death of the gallant Colonel Bailey was very much regretted by his opponents.

CHAPTER 18

Retreat

On the 21st of June the regiment landed at Staten Island, and marched to Richmond redoubts.

At midnight Lt. Col. Simcoe received orders to proceed instantly to the Jersies, where General Kniphausen having thrown a bridge of boats over the Sound, near Elizabethtown Point, was encamped: the Huzzars of the Rangers here joined the corps. Lieut. M'Nab had found an opportunity of distinguishing himself by the intrepidity and boldness with which he advanced into Elizabethtown, amidst the fire of the enemy who possessed it, in order to entice them to follow him into an ambuscade, which Capt. Archdale, of the 17th dragoons (who had the temporary command of the Provincial cavalry) had very skilfully laid for them; but which they were too cautious to fall into.

That evening the Queen's Rangers and Yagers, under the command of Col. Wurmb, attacked the enemy's advance post, for the purpose of taking some prisoners, who might give intelligence; in which they succeeded, with the loss of a Yager, and an Huzzar of the Rangers, who were killed.

On the 23rd of June, Maj. Gen. Mathews with a division of the troops, marched before day towards Springfield: the Rangers made the advance guard. The enemy's smaller parties fell back upon a larger one, which was well posted on an eminence, covered on the right by a thicket, and on the left by an orchard: the road ran in a deep hollow between them. While the battalions of Gen. Skinner's brigade, who flanked the march, were exchanging shot with these troops, Lt. Col. Simcoe closed the companies of the Rangers, and directed them to rush down the hollow road in column without firing, and then by wheeling to the right, to ascend to the orchard and divide the enemy's parties: this was done, and Capt Stevenson who led with the riflemen and light infantry company, obtained the ground on their flank without loss, making several prisoners: the enemy fled, and the Rangers pursued closely on the right, where the ridge continued, and which commanded the road, virtually, becoming a flanking party to the line of march.

In the meantime, the enemy who had been posted on the left retreated up the road, which led through a plain, unpursued: the line for some time leaving it to follow the Queen's Rangers, who having dispersed the party they pursued, now made the utmost exertions to cut off the retreat of the other division: the circuit they had to take rendered this design ineffectual.

The enemy retired over the bridge near Springfield, where they had some troops and cannon; they fired a few shot, by which two of the Rangers were killed as they slept, Maj.-General Mathew, halting till the arrival of Gen. Kniphausen, with the main body of the army; he then made a circuit with his division to pass the river higher up, on the right The troops halted for a considerable time on a height, below which ran a little brook, and cannonaded small parties, of the enemy scattered up and down in the fields and woods, which shelved at a considerable distance from the Newark hills. A very heavy fire being heard from Gen. Kniphausen's column, the troops proceeded unopposed over the brook: the enemy appeared beyond a second bridge, and possessing the heights, seemed to be drawn up in small bodies by echelon, so as to concentre their fire upon the road.

Lt. Col. Simcoe advanced towards the bridge in column, when rapidly forming the line, and extending it to the left, he passed the deep gully covered by the thickets, and by the riflemen whom Lt. Shaw had well disposed of, and outreached the enemy's left: they immediately fell back, with too much precipitation to be overtaken by the Rangers who were forming for that purpose, and with too much order to be adventured upon by a few men, whom Lt. Col. Simcoe had collected and brought secretly through the thickets upon their flank. The Rangers met with no loss; the gallant Lt. Shaw was slightly wounded.

The column then marched to Springfield, which Gen. Kniphausen, on hearing the cannonade from Gen. Mathews, had forced; on their arrival there, most of the army re-crossed the river, and the Rangers received orders to follow in the rear over the bridge, where it was intended to halt for two or three hours to refresh the troops, who, it was now evident, were to return to Elizabethtown Point.

Lt. Col. Simcoe thought proper to accompany the officer, who brought this order, to Gen. Kniphausen, and to represent to him that the Rangers, who lay in an orchard full of deep hollows, which secured them from the enemy's shot, were in a much more favourable position to cover the army than if they crossed the river; and it being obvious, that while this position was maintained, the enemy could not be certain whether the British army meant to return towards Staten Island or advance, they would not hazard the passing their light troops over the river on the flanks of the army in readiness to molest them in their present position and future march.

Gen. Kniphaosen directed Lt. Col. Simcoe to maintain his post, and some Yagers were sent to cover his left, and a battalion of Gen. Skinner's his right flank. In the meantime Gen. Greene, with the gross of his army, occupied a strong position upon the hills, near a mile and a half in front of the advanced corps: his troops and his cannon in general were in ambuscade. He detached two or three field pieces to the right flank of the British, which cannonaded them for some time, but with little effect; and his militia and light troops in great numbers came as close to the front as the intervening thickets could shelter them, and kept up a constant though irregular fire from every side. Most of these shot passed over the heads of the Rangers, while some, which were fired at a greater distance, dropped with little effect in the hollows which concealed them.

On their right ran a rivulet, forming small and swampy islets, covered with thickets; as under favour of this ground the enemy were gradually approaching, Lt. Col. Simcoe waded to one of them with Captain Kerr, whom with his company he left in ambuscade, with orders, if the enemy advanced, to give them one well directed fire, and immediately to re-cross to the regiment Captain Kerr executed his orders judiciously, many of the enemy were seen to fall: the thicket he quitted was not again attempted by them, but it became the centre to which the principal part of their fire was directed.

The troops having halted two or three hours, began their march to Elizabethtown: the advance corps covered the retreat, and re-passed the bridge without molestation. It was a considerable time before the enemy perceived their movement, nor did they become troublesome till the Yagers, who made the rear guard, had nearly ascended the heights where the army was to divide into two columns; the one on the right was closed by the Yagers, that on the left by the

Rangers. The columns marched on, and it appearing that the Yagers might be pressed, the Rangers returned to their assistance, and the enemy retired. The troops proceeded towards Elizabethtown with little interruption.

The riflemen of the Queen's Rangers, now commanded by Sergeant M'Pherson, were eminently distinguished on this retreat. The enemy's militia, who followed the army, were kept by them at such a distance, that very few shot reached the battalion; and they concealed themselves so admirably that none of them were wounded, whilst they scarcely returned a shot in vain.

There being at one time an appearance that the enemy meant to occupy a tongue of wood, which ran between the columns, Lt. Col. Simcoe requested of Colonel Howard, who commanded the guards, to post some divisions of them in echelon behind the various fences, so as to protect his flank, masque the wood, and in some measure to extend and to approach nearer to the right column; the Colonel assented: but as the enemy were not in sufficient numbers to advance, the army returned to their former encampment The Rangers had two men killed, Lieut. Shaw and nine privates slightly wounded: the huzzar, Wright, had his horse wounded; but a great many soldiers had marks of the enemy's bullets in their clothes and knapsacks: the Jersey militia suffered considerably, and among others Fitz Randolph, one of their best officers, was killed.

At night the troops passed over the bridge to Staten Island; the retreat being covered by two redoubts, occupied by troops of the line, who embarked, on the bridge being broken up, without molestation.

The Rangers embarked the next morning, and sailing up the North river, landed on the 25th, and proceeded to Odle's Hill, their position in front of the line.

It now appeared, that the commander in chief had hurried from Charles Town, and withdrawn Gen, Kniphausen from the Jersies, on the intimation of a French armament being destined for Rhode Island, and with the hopes of attacking it to advantage, on its arrival: he had encamped the army near Kingsbridge, for the purpose of embarking them with the greater facility.

Lt. Col. Simcoe was obliged to go to New York to recover his health; and the regiment was in general very sickly. The refugees, who had taken post on the banks of the North river, in the rebel country, were attacked by Gen. Wayne, whom they gallantly repulsed: amidst the fire, Cockrane, the brave huzzar, who had been left at Monmouth, quitted the rebels with whom he had enlisted, and risking every hazard, got in to the post, and rejoined his comrades.

Chapter 19

Long Island

On the 19th of July Lieut. Col. Simcoe joined his corps, and proceeded with it to Long Island, crossing the sound at Flushing. He marched to Huntingdon, where an hundred of the militia cavalry, of the island, joined him: this corps was destined to secure the communication over-land between the fleet, which lay off the eastern end of the island, and New York.

Lieut. Col. Simcoe proceeded on his route without delay; at the same time, through the adjutant general, Major Andre, he communicated his wishes, and his hopes to the Commander in Chief, that in case of any attack on Rhode Island, he would employ the Rangers in it; to which Major Andre replied: "The General assures you, that the Rangers shall be pitted against a French regiment the first time he can procure a meeting."

The Queen's Rangers remained about the Points, on the east end of the island, till the 9th of August, when they fell back to Coram, from whence they returned eastward on the 15th, being joined by the King's American regiment, which Lt. Col. Simcoe was ordered to detach to Riverhead, and he himself met the Commander in Chief, who was now on his journey by the Admiral's invitation to hold a conference with him. Sir H. Clinton sent him to the Admiral Arbuthnot, whose fleet at that time was anchored in Gardiner's Bay, but which sailed from thence before the Commander in Chief could arrive.

The Queen's Rangers returned to Oyster Bay on the 23rd of August This march, of near three hundred miles, had been made very fatiguing by the uncommonly hot weather, which rendered the Pine barren, through which the roads principally lay, as close and sultry in the night as in the day time. The troops had been obliged to subsist on the country. A militia dragoon who was sent express to the Adjutant General to inform him what difficulty there was in procuring provisions for the troops, and the hardship which consequently fell upon the inhabitants, was waylaid, taken and robbed, by a party from the rebel shore, at Smith Town. As this had been formerly the case, and it was obvious that no party could remain secreted unknown to the inhabitants, Lieut. Col. Simcoe obtained leave of the Commander in Chief, to raise a contribution from the inhabitants of eighty pounds currency, one half to reimburse the militia man, for what was taken from him, and the other to recompense him for the chagrin he must necessarily have been under in not being able to execute his orders. This, probably, was the only contribution levied by the King's troops during the war.

On the 26th of August, the Commander in Chief augmented the Rangers with two troops of dragoons, appointed Lt. Col. Simcoe to be Lieutenant Colonel of cavalry; and the infantry Captains, Saunders and Shank, officers of distinguished merit, to the additional troops. The corps remained at Oyster Bay and its vicinity, until the 22nd of September, when it marched to Jamaica.

Sir H. Clinton had been pleased to entrust Lt. Col. Simcoe with knowledge of the important negotiation, which terminated so unfortunately in the death of Major Andre;

and at the same time, he informed him on what service he should eventually employ him if it took effect, and directed him to obtain as minute a knowledge as he could of the country, where future operations were likely to be carried on. The preparations for the execution of this great design were effectually concealed, by an expedition being in forwardness to proceed to the southward, under General Leslie. The Queen's Rangers were generally supposed to be destined for this service.

Lt. Col. Simcoe, had this been the intention, must have commanded the cavalry; and he had in a former conversation with Gen. Leslie, represented, that although no men could possibly be more useful or more brave than the Huzzars of the Rangers, yet as he never had leisure properly to instruct them in the regular system of cavalry, or, indeed, had any occasion to employ them on any but desultory services, and, on the other hand, as the enemy had every means of establishing a well-mounted and solid body of cavalry, he requested, that the General would ask from the Commander in Chief, a detachment of forty of the Seventeenth of dragoons, to whom he would add a similar number from his dragoons now forming, and the stoutest of the huzzars, and that this squadron should be carefully preserved from all the smaller services of light troops, and kept as a constant reserve to support the huzzars, and to be opposed to the enemy's cavalry. Gen. Leslie was pleased to approve of Lt. Col. Simcoe's representations.

The Commander in Chief's design proving abortive, the Queen's Rangers crossed from Long to Staten Island, and marched to Richmond redoubts on the 8th of October.

Some circumstances relative to Major Andre's unfortunate attempt, will be more fully detailed in the appendix. The Commander in Chief thinking it proper, in the general orders, to publish the high idea which he entertained of him both as a gentleman and an officer, and the sense he entertained of the loss his King and country had met with in his death, Lt. Col. Simcoe, who considered his execution as a barbarous and ungenerous act of power in the American general, and who had certain and satisfactory intelligence that the French party in general, and M. Fayette in particular, who sat upon his trial, urged Mr. Washington to the unnecessary deed, took the opportunity in his orders to the Queen's Rangers, the officers and soldiers of which personally knew and esteemed Major Andre, to inform them, that "He had given directions that the regiment should immediately be provided with black and white feathers as mourning, for the late Major Andre, an officer whose superior integrity and uncommon ability did honour to his country, and to human nature. The Queen's Rangers will never sully their glory in the field by any undue severity: they will, as they have ever done, consider those to be under their protection who shall be in their power, and will strike with reluctance at their unhappy fellow subjects, who, by a system of the basest artifices, have been seduced from their allegiance, and disciplined to revolt: but it is the Lt. Colonel's most ardent hope, that on the close of some decisive victory, it will be the regiment's fortune to secure the murderers of Major Andre, for the vengeance due to an injured nation, and an insulted army."

Capt Saunders with his Lieut. Wilson, and Cornet Merit embarked for Virginia, with Gen. Leslie: he was a native of Princess Anne County, possessed property there, and had distinguished himself in the Earl of Dunmore's active enterprises in that colony: he carried with him several dragoons, and expected to complete his troop in that province. At this time Lt. Col. Simcoe, who had frequently in conversation with the Commander in Chief, expatiated on the advantages he thought might accrue to his Majesty's service, by a post being seized and maintained at Billing's Port, on the Delaware river, recapitulated some of his ideas, by the letter which is in the appendix.

From the earliest period of the war, Lt. Col. Simcoe had felt it his duty to cultivate the good opinion of the loyalists: he had been fortunate in obtaining it by his conduct to the inhabitants of Pennsylvania, and upon the abandoning of that province had still maintained it.

The Buck's County volunteers, commanded by Capt Thomas, had, as much as suited with their independent spirit, acted with the Queen's Rangers, embarked on expeditions with them, and had considered themselves as under Lt. Col. Simcoe's protection. A considerable body of the loyalists, seated near the waters of the Chesapeake, had associated themselves for the purpose of restoring the royal government, and this they began at a period when, from the British troops having evacuated Pennsylvania, they saw, that it was from their own exertions only, that they could expect emancipation from the fetters of usurpation. A correspondence was carried on with the leaders of these loyalists by Major Andre, and to which Lieut. Col. Simcoe was privy. Soon after his death, their agent, who was in New York, gave to Lt. Col. Simcoe a paper from them, the purport of which was, to desire that he would forward to Lord George Germain their requisition, which accompanied it: "that he, Lt. Col. Simcoe, might be detached with a thousand men to a certain place, with arms, and that they to the amount of some thousands would instantly join and declare for government: it concluded with the strongest encomiums on the character of the officer whom they wished to command them, and of the confidence with which they would take up arms under his direction."

Lieut. Col. Simcoe answered the agent, that although nothing on earth could be more grateful to him than the terms of this letter, yet, as a subordinate officer, he would upon no account forward any plan, or offer, to Great Britain, without the knowledge of the Commander in Chief; and that although, as he gathered from their language, Sir Henry Clinton might appear to the loyalists to be slow in his progress to give them effectual support, yet that he was confident, this opinion would be found to be the result. of their anxiety and zeal, rather than any knowledge which they could possibly have of the means within his power, or of his intentions in their application.

In a short time, the paper was sent back, and returned in such a form as made it not improper for Lt. Col. Simcoe to show it to the Commander in Chief; and then, with his approbation, he returned the following answer to the associates:"The gentleman, to whom our situation has been by your directions entrusted, is most sensible of the honour conferred upon him; to say, that he is ready to risk his life in our service, is only to say, that he is ready to do his duty as a citizen and as a British officer. He hopes, that Providence will permit him to establish the good opinion our friends entertain of him by more than words: he bids me assure you that he has authority to say, that you are and have been a great and constant object of the concern and attention of the Commander in Chief, whose system you cannot but see is to unravel the thread of rebellion from the southward; and that in his progress your most valued assistance will be depended upon; but that he is anxious not to expose you, nor must you expose yourselves in aid of any kind of desultory expeditions, neither meant nor calculated to take possession of or to keep your country: such may be made to distress the enemy; but you are most strictly enjoined, not to consider them as intended for any other object, until by his public proclamation, or such private intelligence as you can depend upon, it shall be signified to you, that you are to take up arms, and actively maintain that hallowed cause, for which you have suffered so much, and which you have so nobly, and so conscientiously supported."

It was generally supposed about the latter end of October that the enemy meditated some attempt on Staten Island. M. de Fayette was in the neighbourhood of Elizabethtown, in force and with boats on travelling carriages. Lt. Col. Simcoe by public conversation, the means of spies, and by marching to Billop's point in the dusk of the evening, so as to be discovered from the opposite shore, and then returning by ways which the enemy could not see, had endeavoured to attract their notice, and to possess them with a belief, that an inroad into the Jersies was in contemplation.

As M. Fayette arrived in the vicinity the very day subsequent to this feint, it was reasonable to believe that his march was in consequence, and that the boats with him were destined to facilitate his passage across the small creeks with which the Jersies are intersected, in case of the British troops making any incursions into that country.

Every proper precaution was taken by the troops in Richmond to prevent a surprise: on the 12th of November, official information was sent by the Adjutant General to Lt. Col. Simcoe, that his post was the object of Fayette's design, and that it probably would be attacked on that or the ensuing night. He immediately declared in orders, "The Lt. Colonel has received information that M. Fayette, a Frenchman, at the head of some of his Majesty's deluded subejects, has threatened to plant French colours on Richmond redoubts. The Lt. Colonel believes the report to be a gasconade; but as the evident ruin of the enemy's affairs may prompt them to some desperate attempt, the Queen's Rangers will lay in their clothes this night, and have their bayonets in perfect good order."

The Highlanders immediately assembled and marched to the redoubt, which, in the distribution of posts, was allotted to them to defend, and displaying their national banner, with which they used to commemorate their saint's day, fixed it on the ramparts, saying, "No Frenchman, or rebel, should ever pull that down."

The Rangers were prepared if an attack should be made on the watering place, which appeared to be most probable, to march out and attack any division which might be placed, as had been in Lord Stirling's attempt, to mask the troops in Richmond: two field pieces, six pounders, and Capt. Althause's company of riflemen had reinforced them. Lt. Col. Simcoe made himself acquainted with the landing places, and the intervening grounds, in the minutest particular, and he had the Commander in Chief's directions to abandon his post, "If the enemy should land in such force as to make, in his opinion, the remaining there attended with risk."

The defects of Richmond were not sufficiently obvious for such inexperienced men as the rebel generals, to seize upon and profit by at once: how far they might attract the instantaneous notice of the scientific French officers, supposed to be acting with them, it was not easy to foresee. Had the enemy been in a situation to have attacked the place by regular approaches, Lt. Col. Simcoe would have done his best endeavours to have maintained it; but had any General, at the head of a very superior force on the moment of his appearance, placed twenty or thirty field pieces, on two separate eminences which enfiladed the redoubts, and formed a column to penetrate under cover of the cross fire, he had resolved to abandon what he considered in case of such a disposition to be untenable.

A false alarm, which was given by an armed vessel stationed in Newark Bay, occasioned a considerable movement in the army; and troops from New York embarked to reinforce Staten Island. The post at Richmond was supposed to be the object of an attack. On the first gun being fired, patrols had been made on all sides by the cavalry, and the infantry slept undisturbed. Lieut. Col. Simcoe apprehending the alarm to be false, the Rangers were very alert on guard, and proud of their regimental character, of not giving false alarms, or being surprised; and the sentinel, as Lt. Col. Simcoe remarked in orders upon the only omission, which ever came under his cognizance, "Felt. a manly pleasure in reflecting, that the lives and honour of the regiment was entrusted to his care, and that under his protection his comrades slept in security."

CHAPTER 20

The Virginia Expedition

On the 11th of December, the Queen's Rangers embarked on an expedition to Virginia, under the command of Gen. Arnold: Capt Althause's company of York Volunteers embarked with them, as did Capt Thomas of the Bucks County Volunteers. The Commander in Chief had directed Lt. Col. Simcoe to raise another troop of dragoons, the command of which was given to Lt. Cooke of the 17th of dragoons, who remained in New York to recruit it.

The troops under Gen. Arnold being embarked, he issued an order on the 20th of December against depredations in the country where the expedition was bound to, and in the most forcible terms and strongest manner, called upon the officers to second his intentions and the Commander in Chiefs orders in this respect. The expedition sailed from Sandy Hook on the 21st of December, and arrived in the Chesapeake, but in a dispersed manner, on the 30th: several ships were missing. General Arnold without waiting for them, was enabled, by the fortunate capture which the advance frigate, under Capt. Evans, had made of some small American vessels, to push up the James river, and this was done with incomparable activity and despatch: the whole detachment showing an energy and alacrity that could not be surpassed.

The enemy had a battery at Hood's point, and there was as yet no certainty whether or not it was defended by an enclosed work. The vessels anchored near it late in the evening of the 3rd of January; one of them, in which was Capt. Murray of the Queen's Rangers, not perceiving the signal for anchoring, was fired at. Upon the first shot the skipper and his people left the deck; when Capt. Murray seized the helm, and the soldiers assisting him, he passed by the fort without any damage from its fire, and anchored above it.

Gen. Arnold ordered Lt. Col. Simcoe to land with one hundred and thirty of the Queen's Rangers and the light infantry, and grenadiers of the 80th regiment. The landing was effected silently and apparently with secrecy about a mile from the battery, and a circuit was made to surprise its garrison: in the meantime the fleet was fired upon, but ineffectually on account of its distance.

On the detachment's approach through bye paths, to Hood's, the flank companies of the 80th were ordered to file from the rear and to proceed rapidly to the battery, while the Rangers were ready to support them, or to receive any enemy who might possibly be on their march from the adjacent country. Major Gordon on his approach found the battery totally abandoned; the concerted signal was made, and the fleet anchored near it. General Arnold came on shore; and it appeared that a patrol had discovered the boats as they rowed to the landing. Capt Murray had heard them as they approached the shore, and with his accustomed zeal had got into his boat ready to assist if called for: the battery was dismounted and the troops re-embarked in the morning, Gen. Arnold pushing the expedition up the river with the utmost celerity.

On the arrival at Westover, the troops were immediately disembarked. At first, from the reports of the country of the force that was assembling to defend Richmond, Gen. Arnold hesitated whether he should proceed thither or not, his positive injunctions being not to undertake any enterprise that had much risk in it; but Lt. Colonels Dundas and Simcoe, concurring that one day's march might be made with perfect security, and that by this means more perfect information might be obtained, the troops were immediately put in motion and proceeded towards Richmond, where the enemy was understood to have very considerable magazines: it was above thirty miles from Westover; several transports had not arrived, and Gen. Arnold's force did not amount to eight hundred men.

On the second day's march, whilst a bridge was replacing over a creek, the advanced guard only having passed over, some of the enemy's militia, who had destroyed it the evening before, and were to assemble with others to defend it, were deceived by the dress of the Rangers, and came to Lt. Col. Simcoe, who immediately reprimanded them for not coming sooner, held conversation with them, and then sent them prisoners to General Arnold.

Within seven miles of Richmond a patrol of the enemy appeared, who, on being discovered, fled at full speed: the Queen's Rangers, whose horses were in a miserable condition from the voyage, could not pursue them.

Soon after Lt. Col. Simcoe halted, having received the clearest information that a road, made passable by wood carts, led through the thickets to the rear of the heights on which the town of Richmond was placed, where they terminated in a plain, although they were almost inaccessible by the common road. On giving this information to Gen. Arnold, he said it was not worthwhile to quit the road, as the enemy would not fight. On approaching the town, Gen. Arnold ordered the troops to march as open and to make as great an appearance, as possible; and the ground was so favourable that a more skilful enemy than those who were now reconnoitring, would have imagined the numbers to have been double.

The enemy at Richmond appeared drawn up on the heights to the number of two or three hundred men: the road passed through a wood at the bottom of these heights, and then ran between them and the river into the lower town. Lt. Col. Simcoe was ordered to dislodge them: he mounted the hill in small bodies, stretching away to the right, so as to threaten the enemy with a design to outflank them; and as they filed off, in appearance to secure their flank, he directly ascended with his cavalry, where it was so steep that they were obliged to dismount and lead their horses. Luckily the enemy made no resistance, nor did they fire; but on the cavalry's arrival on the summit, retreated to the woods in great confusion.

There was a party of horsemen in the lower town, watching the motion of Lt. Col. Dundas, who, the heights being gained, was now entering it. Lt. Col. Simcoe pushed on with the cavalry unnoticed by the enemy in the lower town, till such time as he began to descend almost in their rear, when an impassable creek stopped him, and gave the enemy time to escape to the top of another hill beyond the town. Having crossed over lower down, he ascended the hill, using such conversation and words towards them as might prevent their inclination to retreat. However, when the Rangers were arrived within twenty yards of the summit, the enemy greatly superior in numbers, but made up of militia, spectators, some with and some without arms, galloped off. They were immediately pursued, but without the least regularity.

Capt. Shank and Lt. Spencer, who had met with good horses in the country, far distanced the rest of the cavalry. Lt. Col. Simcoe left an officer to mark the position he meant his infantry to take on their arrival, and collecting all the men he could overtake, followed Capt. Shank, anxious lest his ardour should prove fatal. He had pursued the enemy four or five miles, six or seven of whom he had taken with several horses; a very well timed capture.

On Lt. Col. Simcoe's return, he met with orders from Gen. Arnold to march to the foundry at Westham, six miles from Richmond, and to destroy it; the flank companies of the 80th, under Major Gordon, were sent as a reinforcement. With these and his corps he proceeded to the foundry. The trunnions of many pieces of iron cannon were struck off, a quantity of small arms and a great variety of military stores were destroyed. Upon consultation with the artillery officer, it was thought better to destroy the magazine than to blow it up. This fatiguing business was effected by carrying the powder down the cliffs, and pouring it into the water; the warehouses and mills were then set on fire, and many explosions happened in different parts of the buildings, which might have been hazardous had it been relied on, that all the powder was regularly deposited in one magazine; and the foundry, which was a very complete one, was totally destroyed.

It was night before the troops returned to Richmond; the provisions which had been made for them were now to be cooked. Fatigued with the march, the men in general went to sleep, some of them got into private houses and there obtained rum.

In the morning Gen. Arnold determined to return; but Lt. Col. Simcoe requested that he would halt half the day. The enemy were drawn up on the opposite side of the river so that no enterprise could be expected from them; and the whole of the Rangers having been extremely fatigued the day before, without any men having been left to cook for them, were in a great measure in want of sustenance. Gen.

Arnold was sensible of the reasonableness of the request, but he thought it most advisable to return; and he gave as his reason, that if Gen. Tryon and Sir William Erskine had marched two hours sooner from Danbury, on their expedition there, they would have met with no opposition; and if they had delayed it much longer, they would have found it absolutely impossible to have regained their shipping.

The roads were rendered by the rain slippery and difficult, and in most places were narrow and overhung by bushes, so that the troops were frequently obliged to march by files, which made it impossible for the officers, who were on foot, to see far before them, and to take their customary precautions. When it became dark, if any man through an intention of deserting quitted his ranks, or in the frequent haltings, overpowered by fatigue, fell asleep, (which those who have suffered it, well know brings on a total disregard of all consequences, even of life itself,) he escaped notice and was irrecoverably lost. Nine men of the Rangers either deserted or were taken by the country people on this march. The troops arrived at a very late hour at the ground on which they were to encamp, and where they passed a wet and tempestuous night.

Gen. Arnold returned the next day to Westover, preceded by Lt. Col. Simcoe with the huzzars, to communicate the earliest intelligence to the fleet. While the troops were halting at Westover to refresh themselves, no intelligence could be received: the militia of the lower counties gathering together and blocking up the country; parties of them appeared in force on the heights divided from Westover by a creek, and covered the peninsula which it formed with the James river.

Gen. Arnold directed a patrol to be made on the night of the eighth of January towards Long Bridge, in order to procure intelligence. Lt. Col. Simcoe marched with forty cavalry, for the most part badly mounted, on such horses as had been picked up in the country; but the patrol had not proceeded above two miles before Sergeant Kelly, who was in advance was challenged. He parlied with the videttes, till he got nearer to them, when rushing at them, one he got hold of, the other flung himself off his horse and escaped into the bushes; a negro was also taken whom these videttes had intercepted on his way to the British army. From these people information was obtained that the enemy was assembled at Charles City Court house, and that the corps which had appeared in the day time opposite Westover, nearly to the amount of four hundred men, lay about two miles in advance of their main-body, and on the road to Westover.

The party were immediately ordered to the right about, and to march towards them; Lt. Holland, who was similar in size to the vidette who had been taken, was placed in advance: the negro had promised to guide the party so as to avoid the high road, and to conduct them by an unfrequented pathway, which led close to the creek, between the body, which was supposed to be in advance, and that which was at Charles City Court house. Lt. Col. Simcoe's intention was to beat up the main body of the enemy, who trusting to those in front might reasonably be supposed to be off their guard. In case of repulse he meant to retreat by the private way on which he advanced, and should he be successful it was optional to attack the advance party or not, on his return.

The patrol passed through a wood, where it halted to collect, and had scarcely got into the road when the advance was challenged; Lt. Holland answered, "A friend," gave the countersign procured from the prisoner, "It is I, me, Charles," the name of the person he personated. He passed one vidette whom Sergeant Kelly seized, and himself caught hold of the other, who in a struggle proved too strong for him, got free, presented and snapped his carbine at his breast; luckily it did not go off, but the man galloped away, and at some distance fired, the signal of alarm.

The advance division immediately rushed on, and soon arrived at the Court house; a confused and scattered firing began on all sides. Lt. Col. Simcoe sent the bugle horns, French and Barney, through an enclosure to the right, with orders to answer his challenging, and sound when he ordered; he then called loudly for the light infantry, and hollowed "sound the advance;". The bugles were sounded as had been directed, and the enemy fled on all sides, scarcely firing another shot

The night was very dark, and the party totally unacquainted with the ground. Part of the dragoon were dismounted and mixed with the huzzars; some of the enemy were taken, others wounded, and a few were drowned in a mill-dam.

In saving three armed militia men from the fury of the soldiers, Lt. Col. Simcoe ran a great risk, as their pieces were loaded, pointed to his breast, and in their timidity they might have discharged them. From the prisoners he learnt that the whole of their force was here assembled, and that there was no party in advance: the soldiers were mounted as soon as possible, nor could they be permitted to search the houses where many were concealed, lest the enemy should gain intelligence of their numbers, and attack them; and this might easily be done as the darkness of the night prevented the. Rangers from seeing around them, while they were plainly to be distinguished by the fires which the enemy had left.

It appeared that the militia were commanded by Gen. Nelson, and consisted of seven or eight hundred men. They were completely frightened and dispersed, many of them not stopping till they reached Williamsburgh. Sergeant Adams of the huzzars was mortally wounded; this gallant soldier, sensible of his situation, said "My beloved Colonel, I do not mind dying, but for God's sake do not leave me in the hands of the rebels." Trumpeter French and two huzzars were wounded; about a dozen excellent horses were seasonably captured. The enemy did not appear during the time the troops stayed at Westover, nor attempted to harass their rear as had been threatened: the remainder of the forces arrived the next day.

In the embarkation from New York, the horse vessels were very bad, infamously provided, and totally unfit for service, in consequence, above forty horses had been thrown overboard; the very Skippers were fearful of sailing, and it required every exertion of the Quarter-Masters to oblige them to weigh anchor, and, at sea, the utmost industry and labour could barely prevent them from foundering.

Sergeant Adams died at Westover the 9th; the corps attended his funeral; he was buried in the colours which had been displayed and taken from Hood's battery.

CHAPTER 21

M'Gill's Account

On the 10th of January Gen. Arnold embarked and dropped down to Flour de Hundred. At night he ordered Lt. Col. Simcoe to land. The General had information that a party of militia, with cannon, were assembled at Bland's mills, and he intended to surprise them.

On the approach to the shore, people were plainly heard talking, who galloped off on the imaginary gun-boats being loudly ordered to point their cannon towards the shore. On the Queen's Rangers landing, Lt. Col. Simcoe placed Capt. Ewald in ambuscade; that gallant and able officer, with the remainder of his Yagers, had joined at Westover. Gen. Arnold had scarcely landed, and Col. Dundas, with the 80th regiment, was not yet on shore, when a patrol of the enemy fell into the ambuscade of the Yagers, and exchanged shot with them. The night was very dark. Gen. Arnold directed Lt. Col. Simcoe immediately to march towards Bland's, with Col. Robinson's regiment and his own infantry; but the cavalry did not land.

The detachment had not proceeded above two miles, when Robinson's corps in front received a heavy fire. There was no room for disposition, for the road ran through a wood which was remarkably thick, at the forks of which, as the clearest ground, the enemy had placed themselves.

Upon the firing, the troops were immediately ordered to charge; they rushed forward and the enemy fled. Near twenty of Col. Robinson's regiment were killed and wounded; among the latter was Capt Hatch who commanded the advance guard.

Lt. Col. Simcoe seeing no probability of accomplishing the business he had been ordered upon, halted till Gen. Arnold's arrival, who had followed with the main body. The troops returned to Hood's battery, which having totally dismantled, they carried off the heavy artillery and quitted it; the next day re-embarking and falling down the river.

The troops landed on the 14th at Harding's ferry, and marched to Smithfield.

The next morning Gen. Arnold sent Major Gordon with a detachment over the Pagan creek, and ordered Lt. Col. Simcoe to cross at M'Kie's mills with the cavalry, to cooperate with him in dispersing a body of militia, who were supposed to be assembled in that neighbourhood. Lt. Col. Simcoe desired Gen. Arnold to permit him to take Capt Ewald with the Yagers as far as M'Kie's mills, in case the enemy should have seized that pass. The General assented.

When the party arrived there, the enemy were in possession of the pass; and in some force. The demonstration of the cavalry and the advancing of the Yagers, after a few shot, obliged them to retire; the bridge being taken up, prevented an immediate pursuit. The Yagers returned and the cavalry proceeded to fulfil their orders. They joined Major Gordon, who had met with no enemy.

Parties of militia being understood to be at the points on each side of the creek, stationed there to fire on the boats, Lt. Col. Simcoe proceeded with some cavalry to disperse them. The advanced man, Molloy, soon perceived two sentinels, when watching till their backs were turned, he slowly followed them, and, as they turned round, sprung his horse between them crying out, "lay down your arms, I have you both," which they readily did. Proceeding to the house, the party was immediately surrounded and taken, it consisted of an officer and twelve men. A similar party was on the other side. The officer who had been taken was sent over in a boat, to inform them that if they surrendered and delivered up their arms, they should have their paroles; if not, they must abide by the consequences, as a party would be sent to surround and cut them in pieces. The militia immediately accepted the offers, the officer commanding returning with him who had carried the alternative; they were very happy to have any reason that might be pleaded to their oppressors, not to be forced to take up arms.

However, this did not answer the views of the rebel legislatures, and Governor Jefferson soon after published a proclamation, declaring the paroles of all the Virginia militia, in a similar predicament, null and void.

Lt. Col. Simcoe and Major Gordon passed the night opposite to Smithfield, and the next day the army continued its march; its route was by Sleepy-hole ferry, across which the boats had arrived to carry them. The Queen's Rangers proceeded to Portsmouth. Gen. Arnold being apprehensive that the enemy might burn the houses there, two or three small patrols were taken or dispersed during the march, and Lt. Col. Simcoe entered the town early in the morning of the 19th of January. A party of the enemy had just crossed over to Princess Ann; the advance ship of the squadron came up soon after, and Gen. Arnold with the army arrived in the course of the day.

On the 25th, Colonel Dundas, with a part of the 80th and a detachment of the Queen's Rangers, crossed Elizabeth river, and went into Princess Ann. This party returned at night and on its arrival at the ferry an account came from

Gen. Arnold, that some of the artillery, who had been foraging on the road to the Great bridge, had been attacked, their wagons taken and the officer killed. The General ordered a detachment to be passed over from Norfolk, to endeavour to retake the wagons. The troops had just arrived from a fatiguing march; the night was closing in, and it began to rain tremendously. Lt. Col. Simcoe ferried over, as ordered, to Herbert's point, with fourteen Yagers and Rangers; they were joined by the conductor of the artillery who had escaped, and from his account it appeared that the officer was not dead, and that the enemy were but few in number.

After the party had advanced a mile, an artillery man, who had escaped and lay hid in the bushes, came out, and informed him that the Lt. Rynd lay not far off. Lt. Col. Simcoe found him dreadfully mangled and mortally wounded; he sent for an ox cart from a neighbouring farm, on which the unfortunate young gentleman was placed. The rain continued in a violent manner, which precluded all pursuit of the enemy; it now grew more tempestuous, and ended in a perfect hurricane, accompanied with incessant lightning.

This small party slowly moved back toward Herberts ferry, it was with difficulty that the drivers and attendants on the cart could find their way; the soldiers marched on with their bayonets fixed, linked in ranks together, covering the road. The creaking of the wagon and the groans of the youth added to the horror of the night. The road was no longer to be traced when it quitted the woods, and it was a great satisfaction that a flash of lightning, which glared among the ruins of Norfolk, disclosed Herbert's house. Here a boat was procured which conveyed the unhappy youth to the hospital ship, where he died the next day. Lt. Col. Simcoe barricaded the house in which he passed the night.

Gen. Arnold employed the garrison in fortifying the post at Portsmouth, the primary object of his expedition; the same line to the front was occupied, which Gen. Leslie had begun. On the 29th Lt. Col. Simcoe was sent to fortify the post at Great bridge. Much lumber that was found there was floated down to Portsmouth; and the troops, with unremitted attention, applied themselves to raise a star work, which commanded the bridge and the causeway; it was intended to abaty the ditch, and then to fill it with water, which, the smaller bridges being taken up, would have effectually prevented a surprise.

The rebels continually fired at night on the sentinels, and perfect information was gained of a party being intended for that purpose: the extent of the post prevented any ambuscade from being laid with certainty, and the fatigue the men underwent in the day, demanded as much quiet as possible during the night. A figure was dressed up with a blanket coat, and posted in the road, by which the enemy would probably advance, and fires resembling those of a piquet, were placed at the customary distance. At midnight the rebels arrived, and fired twenty or thirty shot at the effigy. As they ran across the road they exposed themselves to the shots of two sentinels, they then went off.

The next day an officer happening to come in with a flag of truce, he was shown the figure and was made sensible of the inhumanity of firing at a sentinel, when nothing farther was intended. This ridicule probably had good effects, as during the stay of the Queen's Rangers at Great bridge, no sentinel was fired at.

The works being in a state of defence, and capable of receiving a garrison, the Rangers were relieved on the 5th of February, by Major Gordon with a detachment. Col. Dundas arrived that day and marched out with the Rangers, and part of the 80th. The cavalry soon fell in with a patrol, which Captain Shank pursued over Edmond's bridge, dispersing them and making an officer prisoner. The Rangers returned the next day to Portsmouth, and were constantly employed on the works till the 10th, when Gen. Arnold thought proper to detach them to Kemp's landing.

The disaffected inhabitants of Princess Ann, for the most part, had left it; but it was much infested by a party under the command of a New Englander, of the name of Weeks. To drive him from the county was the object of Lt. Col. Simcoe's march, and for this purpose, he detached Capt Ewald with the Yagers, and a party of the Queen's Rangers to the Great bridge, and with the remainder of the corps marched to Kemp's. He advanced on the 16th up the country, by the main road towards the north-west landing, while Capt Ewald, by almost impassable ways and bye paths proceeded to the same point: he fortunately surprised and totally dispersed Weeks's party.

The next day, Lt. Col. Simcoe proceeded with a detachment of cavalry to the northwest landing: Weeks was again fallen in with, and with great difficulty escaped from the pursuit of the huzzars into a swamp. The whole corps returned the next day to Kemp's; and from thence, on the 18th, to Portsmouth.

The north-west landing was the only passage from North Carolina, excepting the Great bridge, and this excursion was luckily timed. Gen. Arnold, on the 13th of February, receiving information of the arrival of three French ships of the line, had sent Lt. Col. Simcoe orders to march from Kemp's, where he then was, to the Great bridge, intimating that he should send up boats to bring off the cannon, and that the post should be withdrawn if necessary.

Lt. Col. Simcoe wrote to Gen. Arnold, informing him, that he certainly should march at the time prescribed by his orders, if not countermanded, giving at the same time such

168

reasons as to him appeared most forcible, why the Great bridge should not be hastily abandoned, but that rather Weeks and his party should be driven from the county into North Carolina. The General was pleased to approve of his reasons, and on the 16th he marched against Weeks as has been related. Gen. Arnold, in case Capt. Symonds thought it expedient, offered the army to assist in any attacks on the French fleet.

Captain Alberson, the gallant master of the *Empress of Russia*, Lt. Col. Simcoe's transport, was anxious, and offered his services, to lay him and the Queen's Rangers on board any of the French ships. The army was employed in strengthening their works. On the 19th the French ships left the bay.

Gen. Arnold had issued a proclamation, for the inhabitants of Princess Ann to assemble at Kemp's on the 21st. On that day the Queen's Rangers escorted him thither; and Captain M'Kay, of that corps, was left at this post. He fortified and barricaded his quarters in the best manner possible, and having some dragoons with him kept the country clear of small parties.

It being reported that Lord Cornwallis was near Petersburg, Lieut. Col. Dundas embarked with five hundred men, on the 23rd, and such provisions as were thought necessary, to make a diversion in his Lordship's favour; but more certain advices of his operations being received, he returned.

Gen. Arnold ordered Lt. Col. Dundas to march at night with the 80th regiment and the cavalry, to endeavour to surprise a body of the enemy, within eight or nine miles of Portsmouth, upon the Suffolk road, while Lt. Col. Simcoe, with the infantry of the Rangers, embarked in boats and proceeded by water to gain their rear undiscovered. The plan was well laid, nor did it fail through any fault in the execution. When Lieut. Col. Simcoe landed and marched on, he found a party sent by Lt. Col. Dundas to meet him; the enemy had flown. Since the war it has appeared, that a woman, probably a double spy, left Portsmouth half an hour before Colonel Dundas marched, and gave the enemy information.

The militia assembling at Hampton, Lt. Col. Dundas passed over from Portsmouth to dislodge them. What part the Rangers bore in this expedition, cannot be better detailed than in the modest recital of Quarter-Master M'Gill, who went with Lt. Col. Dundas, and whose bravery and conduct were honoured with the highest commendations, by that most respectable officer:

Col. Dundas with part of his regiment, a few Yagers, Lt. Holland, myself and twelve huzzars, of the Queen's Rangers, went on an expedition towards Hampton. We embarked on the night of the 6th of March, and landed early next morning at Newport-news, from thence marched to a village about three miles from Hampton, where we destroyed some stores, and burned four large canoes without opposition; but on our return to the boats, we saw about two hundred militia drawn up on a plain, and a wet ditch in front. As I was advanced with the huzzars, and first saw them, I informed the Colonel, and at the same time asked his permission to advance against them, without thinking of Lt. Holland, whom in truth I did not see at the time. He granted my request, and ordered the mounted men of the 80th to join me, who had, as well as the Rangers, been mounted in the morning upon the march: with these, and some officers of the 80th, who had also got horses, we made up twenty-six horsemen. The rebels were about three hundred yards from the road; and I had to wheel to the left, full in their view, which discovered our numbers, and, I believe, encouraged them a good deal, as they did not fire until we were within thirty yards of them. This checked us, and gave them time to give us a second salute, but not with the same effect; for, with the first, they killed Capt Stewart, of the 80th, wounded Lieut. Salisbury, of the navy, who commanded the boats, and came for pleasure. Col. Dundas, myself, and Sergeant Galloway, were unhorsed, and some of the infantry, who were an hundred yards in our rear, were wounded. Poor Galloway lamented the loss of the heel of his boot, which was shot away, more than the wound he received. My horse had three balls through him, and he received a fourth before all was over. It was much against us, that we were obliged to advance on the centre of the rebels, a thick wood bounding both their flanks, otherwise I thought to have made them give an oblique fire as the least destructive. However, we happily broke them before they could attempt a third fire, and the infantry coming among them did good service. The rebels had sixty killed, wounded and taken; among the latter was their commander, Col. Curl, and a few of their officers. I cannot ascertain our loss more than I have mentioned; they let us embark quietly, and we landed at Portsmouth the same evening.

General Arnold having information that some of the enemy's Continental forces were at Williamsburg, sent Lt. Allen, of the Queen's Rangers, in a boat to land at night, and gain information. This intelligent officer executed his commission much to the General's satisfaction; and Lt. Col. Dundas embarked with part of the 80th regiment and the Queen's Rangers, to endeavour to surprise them: he fell down the Elizabeth river in the evening; but at its mouth, the night became so very dark and tempestuous, as to render the attempt totally impracticable.

It was with difficulty that the troops reached Newport-news, a point on the enemy's shore, where they landed and passed the night unmolested; and the next day returned to Portsmouth. Fortunately, by the skill of the naval conductor, and Lt. Col. Dundas's indefatigable attention, not a single boat foundered.

CHAPTER 22

The Great Bridge

There being indications that a serious attack upon Portsmouth was in agitation, Gen. Arnold was very active in putting it into a respectable state of defence. Lt. Col. Simcoe had given his opinion, by letter to the Commander in Chief, "that Portsmouth, considered as a post was very weak; from its extent, and from its left being so entirely flanked, that its whole front was taken in reverse; I conceive it to be tenable against any force in this country. It did not appear to be a proper situation for a small garrison; but looked upon as an entrenched camp, it might be made a respectable one; nor was it, and its dependencies, ill suited for combined defence, and the preserving a small naval and military force from the operations of a superior armament.

To explain this opinion, it is necessary to observe, that directly opposite to Portsmouth a branch of the Elizabeth river, which it stands upon, ran eastward, dividing Herbert's point from Norfolk: this eastern branch was not to be forded within eight miles. The occupying a good redoubt at Norfolk, another at Herbert's point, and reestablishing an old work at Mill point below Portsmouth, would reduce any force which, in the present appearance of affairs, was likely to be brought against Gen. Arnold's army, to a direct assault on some part, as it was evident, the regular siege of the whole, or any single work, would take up more time than any French squadron could venture to employ before it.

Gen. Arnold had constructed a great many boats, excellently adapted for the transportation of soldiers, and capable of carrying eighty men besides the rowers. By these means, he had it in his power to reinforce any of the points within ten minutes. Lt. Col. Simcoe had previously sounded all the creeks, at low water, with Capt. Richard Graves, of the royal navy; and that officer, upon leaving Portsmouth to go to Hampton road, sent him on the 14th of March his opinion on the subject of forming a regular system of defence, applicable to the stationing of the ships under Captain Symonds (the largest of which was the *Charon* of 44 guns), from Mill point to the brewery, at Norfolk. "Three ships can be placed in an oblique line, mooring across the channel one third of a cable each way, besides two ships lying in the intervals at the same distance, either in front or rear, which, in my opinion, with vessels sunk and proper dispositions made of fire vessels, may effectually stop the passage."

Lt. Col. Simcoe had converted the bodies of his wagons into small pontoons, capable of holding six men, as boats, and well adapted to form bridges over the small creeks in the country, through which, if it had become necessary to quit Portsmouth, the retreat might have been made, by the north-west landing to North Carolina. These were the opinions which he had always held when any conversation took place upon the subject; and the system of defence is the same which appears on his arrival, to have been thought of by Gen. Phillips. Much would have depended on the science of the enemy's General. The ground of Portsmouth was not only enfiladed on the left flank, but the enemy had on the right, favourable positions to place their batteries wherever they advanced to the assault; and, if the points on the river could not be secured, the fleet must inevitably fall into their hands, without contributing to the defence of the place. The garrison was in great spirits, full of confidence in the daring courage of Gen. Arnold; and the enemy had everything to fear from a sally.

About this time a singular event took place: the passage from the Great bridge upon Elizabeth river had hitherto been secure; but a party of the enemy from its banks fired upon a gun-boat, that was returning with the baggage of the detachment which had been relieved; and having wounded some of the people in it, took the boat. Capt. Stevenson, who had commanded at the Great bridge, lost his baggage; and among his papers was found a fictitious letter, which he had written by way of amusement, and of passing his time, to Gen. Gregory, who commanded the North Carolina militia at the West landing, detailing a plan which that officer was to follow to surrender his troops to Lt. Col. Simcoe; the whole plausibly written and bearing with it every appearance of being concerted. The manner of its falling into the enemy's hands strengthened these appearances.

At first it served for laughter to the officers of the Rangers; but when it was understood that Gen. Gregory was put in arrest, Capt. Stevenson's humanity was alarmed, and the letters, which are in the appendix, passed between Lt. Col. Simcoe and Col. Parker, who had taken the boat. They prevented all further bad consequences.

The 6th of March, Gen. Arnold ordered Lt. Col. Simcoe to send two or three small parties every night, from the piquet, as far, or a little beyond the crossroads, four miles in front of Portsmouth. They were to consist of four or five men. The woods, to the right and left of the road, being intersected with paths on which the enemy generally patrolled, rendered their destruction almost inevitable. Two of them, one of the Yagers and another of the Rangers, being taken, they were discontinued.

The enemy assembling in force, the troops were constantly under arms at four o'clock in the morning, at their alarm post, if the weather was favourable; if otherwise, at their respective barracks.

There being various reports of the enemy making a road through the dismal swamp to the left of Great bridge, and small parties infesting the country, Lieut. Col. Simcoe marched the 10th of March to the Great bridge. Capt. M'Kay, who commanded at Kemp's, had received information, that Weeks was to pass over on the night of the 11th, and that he would be at a house between the Great bridge and Kemp's. He proposed to Lieut. Col. Simcoe to surprise him, and Gen. Arnold approved of it, as it was necessary to check every inroad into Princess Ann.

Capt M'Kay marched at a concerted hour from Kemp's, and Lieut. Col. Simcoe from the Great bridge, in order to support him. The former met the enemy before he arrived at the place where he expected to find them; and he instantly detached Lt. Dunlop to their rear, who attacked, and effectually surprised them: eight or ten were killed or taken. In the pocket of the Lieutenant, who was killed, was found a letter saying, to his Captain, that with four or five men, he could every night seize one or two of the refractory men belonging to his company." These violences were necessary to force the militia, of the lower counties of Virginia, to arms.

The Queen's Rangers returned the next day to Portsmouth, as did Capt. M'Kay to Kemp's; which post, he maintained with singular vigilance and propriety.

Lt. Col. Simcoe thought it proper, in public orders, to desire, "That his best thanks might be accepted by Lt. St.

John Dunlop, and the party under his command, for their obedience to their orders, and gallantry in the surprise of a rebel party, the night of the 11th instant. The Lt. Colonel is satisfied, that if the information Capt. M'Kay received had been true, the rebel *banditti* he marched against would have been annihilated in consequence of his proper disposition, and the steadiness of the officers and soldiers under his command. It is with great pleasure the Lieutenant-Colonel hears of the orderly and soldier-like behaviour of the whole party stationed at Kemp's: he hopes the regiment will equally pride themselves in protecting, as in the present case, the unarmed inhabitants of the country, as in scourging the armed *banditti* who oppress it."

The Great bridge was situated at the head of Elizabeth river, close to the great dismal swamp, from whence it rises. It was the great road, while Norfolk was in affluence, between that town and North Carolina. Small parties only could pass through the swamps, the season being uncommonly dry; but the surprisal of that which had attempted it, rendered it not very advisable. The post was easily to be maintained until such time as an enemy should venture to throw bridges over the Elizabeth river, between the Great bridge and Portsmouth; and then, it was to be weighed whether a hundred men, the usual garrison of the Great bridge would not find more employment for an enemy, and be more than adequate to any services the same number could be of, in Portsmouth. Like other field works it could not hold out a moment against mortars: it was calculated to keep the Carolina militia out of Princess Ann, and every hour that this could be done was of great importance: the hopes of plunder and the certainty of their escaping, would have deluged the country with this *banditti*.

About this time, Capt M'Crea, of the Queen's Rangers, having the command of this post, with that gallantry which had so eminently distinguished him at Kingsbridge, on the first formation of the Rangers, sallied upon a party of the enemy, who had frequently fired upon his sentinels, surprised them, put them to the rout and pinned a label upon one of the men who had been killed, threatening to lay in ashes any house, near his front, that they should harbour in. This vigorous sally had its use. The enemy, as their custom was when they were corrected, complained of cruelty, and Gen. Muhlenberg wrote to Gen. Arnold on that subject. Lt. Col. Simcoe had also some correspondence, on this subject, with Col. Parker, a gentleman of more liberality than was commonly found in those who commanded parties of the militia.

Capt M'Crea had taken two prisoners, they were offered to be exchanged for Ellison, the gallant huzzar who had signalised himself at the battle of Monmouth, and another soldier, who, their horses being killed, had been taken in a skirmish, a few days before, towards the north-west landing; but so little did the enemy value their militia, that it was refused on the ungenerous plea of their having been wounded. It is not improbable but the unfortunate men might have been loyalists, averse from the service of the rebels and forced into it. Ellison was soon after exchanged; he had been ill-treated while prisoner, but nothing hurt him equally with the being robbed of the silver half moon which he wore on his huzzar cap, with the word "Monmouth" engraven on it, as a mark of his bravery in that action.

On the 18th of March, Gen. Arnold gave orders for every person to work on the lines, and the town people, who should refuse, to quit it. M. de La Fayette appeared in the front of the works, and the Yager piquet, posted near the head of Scott's creek, was attacked in force. A deep ravine passable at this post, and above it, separated them from the enemy. Capt Ewald was with his piquet, and by demonstrations and the countenance of his people, more than once checked the enemy, who showed every inclination to pass over the gully, and totally prevented them from reconnoitring the right of Portsmouth; Capt Ewald was wounded.

Gen. Arnold in his letter to Sir Henry Clinton says, "That he did not think it prudent to leave his works and sally, as Lieut. Col. Simcoe was in Princess Ann with near four hundred men." It is not improbable that the enemy had intelligence of the Queen's Rangers being detached to secure forage, &c, as on Lieut. Col. Simcoe's return, the small bridges were destroyed between Kemp's and Portsmouth; which, though they were but trifling impediments, must have been done by a lurking party, or the disaffected of the country, in consequence of some concerted order.

Lt. Col. Simcoe, to whom the Yagers had been attached, felt this a proper op-portunity to represent Captain Ewald's conduct and gallantry to Gen. Kniphausen.

On information of a squadron with French colours being at anchor, on the 19th, in Lynnhaven bay, Lt. Col. Simcoe was sent there with a patrol, to observe them. He had the pleasure to find that it was Admiral Arbuthnot's fleet, and to see a rebel cruiser, deceived by their colours, taken by them. The action which the Admiral had with the French fleet, saved the armament in Virginia from a serious attack.

Gen. Arnold had received information, from the officer at the Great bridge, that General Gregory, on the 18th, had approached within two miles of him, with six pieces of cannon and twelve hundred men. General Arnold sent him orders, "To defend it to the last extremity;" and then directed Lt. Col. Simcoe, after he had informed himself what fleet was below, to take such measures as he thought necessary respecting the Great bridge; the situation of which has been heretofore stated.

Gen. Phillips arrived on the 27th of March, and was soon followed by the forces under his command. The light infantry went into cantonments at Kemp's, and the Queen's Rangers at New Town, under instructions to hold themselves liable to move on the shortest notice, and in case of Lieut. Col. Abercrombie's requisition, Lt. Col. Simcoe was to place himself under his orders.

There being every appearance of the army taking the field, Lt. Col. Simcoe made application to Gen. Phillips, for the same number of artillerymen to his cannon as had been attached to them on similar occasions. The General chose only to allow him some men for a short time, to instruct soldiers of the Queen's Rangers; this Lt. Col. Simcoe declined. His corps was weak in numbers, and he considered the number of men, who must have attended his guns, more useful with their muskets; while the corps acted separately, cannon always furnished a reason for an enemy to avoid action.

In some situations, even such contemptible guns as three-pounders might be of great use in particular, in defence of a house or any position which might enable a corps, in case of necessity, to rally; but the Queen's Rangers were now not likely to be detached, and if they were and it became necessary, the Commander of the army would send them cannon. The three-pounder and amuzette were therefore sent to the artillery park on the 20th of April. The Commander in Chief was pleased to add Capt Deimar's troop of huzzars, then at New York, to the, Queen's Rangers, and they were placed under the command of Capt. Cooke.

Gen. Phillips gave out the following orders for exercising the troops, preparatory to their taking the field: "It is the Major General's wish, that the troops under his command may practice forming from two to three and to four deep; and that they should be accustomed to charge in all those orders. In the latter orders, of the three and four deep, the files will, in course, be closer, so as to render a charge of the greatest force. The Major General also recommends to regiments the practice of dividing the battalions, by wings or otherwise, so that one line may support the other when an attack is supposed; and, when a retreat is supposed, that the first line may retreat through the intervals of the second, the second doubling up its divisions for that purpose, and forming up again in order to check the enemy who may be supposed to have pressed the first line. The Major General would approve also of one division of a battalion attacking in the common open order of two deep, to be supported by the other compact division as a second line, in a charging order of three or four deep. The gaining the flanks also of a supposed enemy, by the quick movements of a division in common open order, while the compact division advances to a charge; and such other evolutions, as may lead the regiments to a custom of depending on and mutually supporting each other; so that should one part be pressed or broken, it may be accustomed to form again without confusion, under the protection of a second line, or any regular formed division." These orders, so proper in themselves, and now peculiarly useful, as no Hessian troops, who usually formed the firm and solid second line to the British, were to embark on the expedition, were not meant to affect the general manoeuvres of the light troops. Lt. Col. Simcoe was permitted to adopt such only as he thought applicable to that service.

The works at Portsmouth being completed, the troops embarked on the 18th of April, and fell down to Hampton road. Gen. Phillips informed the officers commanding corps, in writing, that the first object of the expedition was to surprise, if possible, a body of the enemy stationed at Williamsburgh, at any rate to attack them. At the same time he detailed the plan of operations.

The Rangers were of Gen. Arnold's division, which was destined to land below Williamsburg, and to cooperate with that under Lt. Colonel Abercrombie, which was to land above it. The following orders were more peculiar to the Queen's Rangers: "a detachment of Hessian Yagers will be attached to the light infantry and Queen's Rangers, with which corps they have so often acted, that it is unnecessary to give any directions concerning them; and they will, in course, be always protected by bayonets, both as sentinels and patrols. Should the enemy retreat, upon intelligence of the enterprise against them, or be forced by an attack to retire, Lt. Col. Simcoe will proceed with the utmost diligence to York Town, and there, under every description of caution, endeavour to gain the rear of the enemy's batteries, and of the post; but should he, by certain intelligence and observations, be convinced of there being closed works with troops in them, he is to make an immediate report of it, and not to attack such works without further orders. It is not the intention to risk the loss of men upon any attack at York Town, nor delay by any attack there the progress of the intended expedition. Should, however, Lt. Col. Simcoe gain possession of York Town, he will hoist a red flag, and fire, if possible, signal guns, and at night light two or three fires at different places upon the shore. These are intended to give the *Bonetta* sloop of war notice of York Town being possessed by the King's troops, on which that vessel will move up the river; and Lt. Col. Simcoe will, in that case, consult with Capt Dundass, the commander of the *Bonetta*, how it may be best to act for destroying the armed and other vessels in that river, and also take every means for putting the enemy's cannon at York Town into that armed vessel. It is to be wished that this detailed operation may not take up more than forty eight hours."

The troops arrived off Burrell's ferry on the 19th; Lt. Col. Simcoe was directed to land in such manner as he thought proper. The enemy had thrown up entrenchments to secure the landing, and these appeared to be fully manned. The boats were assembled at the small vessel on board which Lt. Col. Simcoe was, which was anchored about two miles from the shore. Near a mile below the ferry was a small creek which ran a little way into the land, from James river; and at the point formed by this separation, it was determined to land. Capt. Ewald being disabled by his wound from accompanying the expedition. The Yagers were divided between the Queen's Rangers and light infantry; Capt Althause's company of riflemen was also under the command of Lt. Col. Simcoe.

The boats, preceded by the gun-boat, moved directly towards Burrell's ferry. On a signal given, they all, except the gun-boat, turned and rowed rapidly towards the point, where the landing was to take place, assisted by the wind and tide; Major Armstrong, who commanded it, was desired to keep out of the reach of musket shot, and to fire his six pounder at the entrenchments, and particularly to scour a gully on the left, which the enemy must pass if they meant any opposition.

The troops disembarked as intended. Capt M'Kay with a detachment of the Queen's Rangers and Yagers, landing below the inlet, to beat up any party who might be in ambuscade there, and to give greater security to the right flank in case the enemy should attack the corps. Lieut. Col. Simcoe met no opposition in his march to Burrell's ferry, from whence the enemy fled with precipitation, and where Gen. Phillips with the army immediately landed.

Fifty-six horses of the Queen's Rangers had been embarked, those of officers included. The dismounted men brought with them their saddles and accoutrements. Gen. Phillips ordered Lt. Col. Simcoe to proceed to York Town, where, it was understood, there were only the artillery-men, who superintended the battery, and a few militia. He marched accordingly with forty cavalry, accompanied by Major Darner, who acted as Adjutant General to Gen. Phillips: the infantry of the Queen's Rangers proceeded with the army to Williamsburg.

The night was uncommonly dark and tempestuous, and Lt. Col. Simcoe found himself under the necessity of halting at a farmhouse, during its continuance. In the morning he galloped into the town, surprised and secured a few of the artillery-men, the others made off in a boat He directed the guns of the batteries, already loaded, to be fired, as a signal to the *Bonetta* sloop, which sailed up and anchored off the town; and he burnt a range of the rebel barracks.

Upon the hearing of cannon at Williamsburg, the party returned thither; and it appeared, that there had only been a skirmish at the outpost of that place, where the troops had arrived the preceding evening without molestation. Quarter-Master M'Gill, with some of the huzzars of the Queen's Rangers, having charged and dispersed the only patrol of the enemy who had appeared in the front. General Phillips asked Lt. Col. Simcoe, when he waited upon him to make his report, how many men would it require to defend York Town? And on his hesitating, with great quickness, said "Four hundred, five hundred, a thousand," and seemed greatly surprised when he replied two thousand. This was the only conversation that passed between them on the subject.

Lt. Col. Simcoe had no order to reconnoitre the ground, and what he did observe was merely for his own information; and the number of troops necessary for its defence against the American forces, he guessed at, on the supposition of its being properly fortified, and above all made bomb proof, without which he knew all fortifications to be useless, and which he had stated, at a period in which there was not a bomb proof in any of the British fortifications, as absolutely necessary in his plan for the occupation of Billingsport.

The army marched to Barret's ferry, near the Chickahominy, and embarked immediately, the Queen's Rangers excepted, who formed the rear guard and lay on shore the whole night, in a position which a little labour rendered unassailable. Gen. Phillips here gave out the strictest orders to prevent privateers, the bane and disgrace of the country which employs them, from preceding the fleet, and being found upon any of the rivers marauding or plundering. He also explained the second object of the expedition, which was to obtain possession of Hood's battery, now reported to be closed, without unnecessary risk; to open all obstructions on the James river, and to seize the arms said to be at Prince George Court house.

The Major General issued the following excellent order: "Commanding officers of corps, and those detached are to keep regular journals during their absence, which, upon their return, they will give in, with their reports, when called upon." There never was a regulation better calculated to do justice to the active and deserving officer, in every rank and station. It at once established a method, by which it became the duty of officers to detail their own professional skill, and that of those subordinate to them, with the result of it to the Commander in Chief, without wounding modest merit with the necessity of self commendation. At the same time, should any man be so base as to arrogate to himself services which he had never performed, and which

185

sooner or later cannot fail of being divulged, this order would subject the offender to the penalty as well as the disgrace of making a false report.

The troops finding no opposition at Hood's, or on the James river, proceeded without delay up the river. Off Westover Major Gen. Phillips issued the following orders: "A third object of the present expedition is to gain Petersburg for the purpose of destroying the enemy's stores at that place, and it is public stores alone that are intended to be seized; for private property and the persons of individuals, not taken in arms, are to be under the protection of the troops; and Major Gen. Phillips depends on the activity and zeal of the troops on this occasion. The movement from City point to Petersburg, will be made by land; and it is apprehended, the boats will not be able to follow till the shores are cleared of the enemy. The march will be conducted with the greatest caution, and the soldiers will pay the strictest obedience to orders: the conduct of the officers is not to be doubted. When the troops form it is to be done in the following manner: the infantry and huzzars of the Queen's Rangers, with a detachment of Yagers and Althause's rifle company, form the advanced guard, under Lt. Col. Simcoe. The first line to be composed of the light infantry; the second to be composed of the 80th and 76th regiments, who will form three deep, and in compact order. The grenadiers and light infantry of the 80th, with the American legion, to form the reserve under Major Gordon. The cavalry of the Queen's Rangers, to form with the reserve, till such time as they may be called upon the wing, of the first or second line. As the present movements will be made in a difficult country, it becomes necessary that officers leading columns and commanding corps, should use and exert the intelligence of their own minds, joined to the knowledge of the service, in times of an attack, when

they cannot immediately receive the orders of the Brigadier General, or Major General. Should the particular difficulty of the country, occasion the first line to take up new
ground toward the rear, it may not be improper, perhaps, to
do so by becoming a second line in the rear of the 76th and
80th, who will form openings, if necessary, for the purpose.
It is to be observed, that the reserve is to be the point of assembly, for the troops upon any difficult occasion. The impression made upon an attack, by the advanced corps and
light infantry, will be supported in firm order by the second
line; and the cavalry will watch the moment for charging
a broken enemy. The artillery attached to the several corps,
will be under the command of Capt. Fage, who, with the
participation of the commanding officers, or those bearing
the orders, of the General Officers, will exert their utmost
endeavours to co-operate with the rest of the troops."

On the 24th the troops landed, and passed the night at
City point, and on the 25th marched towards Petersburg.
The report of the forces collected at that place varied; but it
was apparent, that they rather distrusted their own strength,
or were miserably commanded, as no shadow of opposition
was made at some passes which were very difficult, and
which would have delayed or embarrassed the army.

Within two miles of Petersburg, the wood ending in a
plain, the army halted until the troops in the rear had closed
to the front. The enemy appeared at a distance, and the
troops advanced. At a gully in front some firing took place
from a party of the enemy, which was posted on the opposite bank; they killed a Yager and fled. A sergeant, who had
been detached with a party of Yagers to the right, by means
of an orchard, got upon the enemy's left flank undiscovered,
and fired with great effect upon them as they retreated.

The ground was divided by small enclosures, with houses on each side of the road, which, through a narrow pass

in front, led to Petersburg. On the right of it were small eminences, terminating at the Appomattox river, and on the left, hilly ground covered with wood, at the foot of which was an old mill stream. The troops halted, and Lt. Col. Simcoe accompanied Gen. Phillips to the right, where, at the distance of a quarter of a mile, he could see the enemy drawn up. Gen. Phillips soon selected a spot to which he ordered the artillery to be brought, and it arrived undiscovered; he then directed it to fire, and ordered Lieut. Col. Abercrombie to march towards the enemy in front, Lieut. Col. Simcoe with the Rangers to pass through the wood to the left to turn the enemy's right flank, and Capt. Boyd with the second battalion of light infantry to support him, as the rest of the troops did Lieut. Col. Abercrombie.

Lt. Col. Simcoe, on emerging from the wood, found a high woody ridge, immediately on his left. He desired Capt. Boyd would attend to it, who sent flanking parties thither. Lieut. Col. Abercrombie pushing forward his battalion, the enemy's first line quitted their station in confusion; but it appeared to Lieut. Col. Simcoe, that they had a second line posted, probably to secure the retreat of the first, and that this party, who seemed totally occupied with what was doing in the front, had no out flankers, but that those of the first line had fallen back upon the main body. His aim was to get as much upon their flank as possible, attack them, and pass the bridge over the Appomattox with them. On the opposite side of this bridge, upon the heights, were troops and cannon, but the banks were-so steep that their fire could do but little injury to an active assailant.

The enemy, still pressed in front by Lieut. Col. Abercrombie, fled so rapidly that the Queen's Rangers had no opportunity of closing with them, though, from their dress, they had marched a considerable way unnoticed. The enemy's cannon began to fire grape at the light infantry, who had reached the town of Blandford, and destroyed the bridge. Lt. Col. Simcoe thought it advisable to try whether there was not a ford, as was rumoured, at Bannister's mills, for the attempt at least would make the enemy draw off their cannon.

A party of horsemen appeared upon the heights near Bannister's house: they galloped off on the approach of the troops, and proved to have been people of the country, who came as spectators of the encounter. The enemy now fired round shot, but ineffectually, at the Queen's Rangers. A party at the same time marched, on the opposite side of the river, towards the mills, but it was soon called off, and the whole of the enemy's corps, supposed to be commanded by Baron Steuben, marched off. The disposition of the enemy was not such as marked any ability in those who made it. By their cannon being placed on the opposite side of the Appomattox, it was evident, that the corps which was stationed at the extremity of Blandford, was merely intended to fire and to retreat; but their very position counteracted their design, as the deep defile would of itself enforce caution in those who were to pass it; the previous skirmish had prevented their making use of an ambuscade, and their right being open, exposed them to what they narrowly escaped, the being cut off from the bridge.

The plan of the ground, which Lt. Spencer took upon the spot, will show, to the military observer, many positions which might have been taken by the enemy to better effect. They were said to have lost near an hundred men killed and wounded, while that of the British was only one man killed, and ten wounded of the light infantry.

The bridge being easily repaired, Lt. Col. Abercrombie with the light infantry and Queen's Rangers, passed over the next day and occupied the heights. The army proceeded towards Osborne's on the 27th, early in the morning:

the bridge at Randal's mills had been taken up, but was presently re-laid. Gen. Phillips, with one division of the army, went to Chesterfield Court house, while the 80th and 76th regiments, with the Queen's Rangers, under Gen. Arnold, marched to Osborne's, where a number of the enemy's shipping was stationed.

Care had been taken that no information of the approach of the troops could reach them; and there was no doubt but that the fire of the cannon would have given the first notice of the arrival of the army. In this situation Gen. Arnold sent a flag of truce to the enemy, offering half the contents of their cargoes in case they did not destroy any part; the enemy answered, That they "were determined and ready to defend their ships, and would sink in them rather than surrender."

The troops marched on: Gen. Arnold stationed Lt. Rogers with two three pounders near the stern of a large ship, which had springs upon her cable. With difficulty she brought her broadside to bear, and returned a smart fire, when Capt. Fage, with two six pounders, opened from an unexpected quarter, with great effect.

Lt. Col. Simcoe placed the Queen's Rangers out of the line of fire, and directed Lt. Spencer, who had been sent to reconnoitre the left, to conduct some Yagers by a route partly covered by ditches, within thirty yards of her stern. Luckily she had loaded her guns only with round shot, expecting that the principal attack would have been made by water; grape shot must inevitably have killed or driven the artillery from their guns. Gen. Arnold sent orders to Lt. Col. Simcoe to march the Queen's Rangers to the shore, and to fire musketry at the ship: he was preparing to execute this order, when, what he shall ever esteem as a most fortunate shot, cut a spring cable and threw the ship round.

In this situation, the crew, exposed to the raking of Lt. Rogers' cannon, and whoever appeared upon deck to the fire of the Yagers, and despairing of assistance from the remainder of the ill-stationed fleet, were frightened and took to their boat to escape: the Yagers beginning a severe fire on them, some jumped overboard. Lt. Spencer, with difficulty, stopped the firing, and partying with the boat's crew, they surrendered, and as they were directed, rowed to the shore in possession of the King's troops.

Lt. Fitzpatrick, with volunteer Armstrong, and twelve of the Queen's Rangers, leaped into the boat and rowed on board the ship. He then sent another boat on shore, and, with great judgment and spirit proceeded towards the furthermost ship in the fleet. The Highland company embarked on board the captured frigate, and a scene of singular confusion ensued. The enemy had scuttled several of their ships, which were now sinking; others, boarded by the intrepid Lt. Fitzpatrick were on fire; and although cannon and musketry from the opposite shore kept up a smart fire on him, that active officer rowed on. He put three men on board one ship, and cut her cable, and he left volunteer Armstrong with three more in another, and attained himself the headmost, whose guns he immediately turned upon the enemy.

A ship, which was blown up near the Tempest, the State frigate, which had been the first taken, in its explosion, lodged some fire on her top gallant and fore stay-sail, which now blazed out. Capt M'Kay, with the Highlanders had cut her cable to avoid the danger, and she now drifted; but the current running easterly, luckily drove her near the shore, occupied by the King's troops, and, by the exertion of the Highlanders, whom their many sea voyages had made active and experienced in such dangers, the flames were extinguished, and the prize effectually secured.

To add to the horror, volunteer Armstrong finding the ship he was on board of in flames, beyond his power to master, had swam on shore to procure a boat to bring off the men he had with him; and the only one in the possession of the troops, was despatched for that purpose. He had just time to save his men, when the vessel blew up. The whole of the fleet, consisting of two ships of twenty guns, a brig of sixteen, and several other armed vessels, were either taken or destroyed. One twenty gun ship, a brig of sixteen guns, two lesser and a sloop, were brought down and safely moored, after a firing which lasted above two hours. Lt. Fitzpatrick brought off that which he was on board of, deliberately closing the rear.

The troops remained in this vicinity till the 29th, when they proceeded towards Manchester.

The bridge at Robert's mills, which had been destroyed, was repaired, and the army encamped near Cary's house. Next morning they marched to Manchester, from whence they had a view of M. Fayette's army, encamped on the heights of Richmond. On the evening they returned to Cary's. Lt. Col. Simcoe, with the rear guard, had orders to destroy a large quantity of flour in Cary's mills; but on his representing to Gen. Phillips, that this duty of fatigue could not be finished in the time allotted for the purpose, he was directed to burn them, which was accordingly done. This flour was destined for the Spaniards, but probably would have been used as supplies for Fayette's army. The troops proceeded by Osborne's to the Bermuda Hundreds. A quantity of cattle was collected for them, by a detachment of the Queen's Rangers the next day; and the whole army embarked on the evening of the 2nd of May.

The captured ships were conveyed down the river by a detachment of the Queen's Rangers, and not without opposition from the militia, particularly against that commanded by Lt. Allen, which ran on shore; but, by his exertions and bravery, was gotten off without material injury.

CHAPTER 23

The Barefoot Rangers

Gen. Phillips, whilst the army lay at Cary's, had thrown some troops over the opposite side of James river. On the return from Stanford, Lt. Col. Simcoe took occasion to represent to him the possibility of the whole army crossing, and that, while the advance guard moved on towards Richmond and masked the road, the army might turn back two miles from the landing place, and by falling into the bye path which Gen. Arnold had formerly been advised to proceed on, might arrive on the plain ground on the heights of Richmond, most probably on the left flank, if not the rear, of Fayette, who would, as it was reasonable to presume, expect the British troops by the route which Gen. Arnold had so recently taken, and whose gasconading disposition and military ignorance might possibly tempt him to stay too long in the face of troops, his equals in numbers, and superior in every thing else that could form the value of an army. The troops fell down the river in prosecution of such further enterprises as Gen. Phillips had determined upon.

Opposite to James Town, the sloop Lt. Col. Simcoe was in, being one of the headmost of the fleet, ran aground near to a landing place. Some people on horseback were seen reconnoitring the fleet: the bugle horns were sounded, and a boat brought round the vessel towards the shore, and instructions for landing were given in a loud voice. This feint, meant merely for amusement, had its effect, and a messenger was seen to gallop off, and M. Fayette in his dispatches mentions it as a seeming attempt of the enemy to land.

It has since appeared, that M. Fayette, as was predicted, followed the troops down the river, the constant and good policy of the enemy; but which, in this case might have proved fatal to his army, had what at first appeared to be Gen. Phillips' design, been now in his power or instructions to execute; for the vessel was scarcely got off, when the officer, who had led the fleet, returned and hailing Lt. Col. Simcoe, directed him to make the utmost dispatch in following him up the river. This was facilitated by its blowing a hard but fair gale.

The whole fleet anchored off Brandon's house, on the south-side of James river; and the troops immediately landed, on the 7th of May, the light infantry excepted, who proceeded to City point. Had the landing been on the opposite shore, and higher up, as by the fair winds might have been the case, the British army would have been above M. Fayette, and he could not have avoided action.

Lt. Col. Simcoe was informed by Gen. Phillips, that he had received an order from Lord Cornwallis to meet him near Petersburg. To the great concern of his army, Gen. Phillips was taken extremely ill, and to accommodate him, Lt. Col. Simcoe went some miles off and procured a post-chaise. Early the next morning, the army marched to Bland's ordinary, passing a very deep gully. Here it was reported that M. Fayette had crossed the James river and was at Petersburg.

It would have been imprudent, had such been a fact, for the corps at Bland's mill to march thither, until it was joined by the light infantry. While conversation to this pur-

A Rifleman of the Queen's Rangers

pose was held by the principal officers, General Phillips, whose indisposition rapidly increased, awakening from his sleep, was made acquainted with the report; and the last material order he gave was that which decided the troops to proceed as quick as possible towards Petersburg, and to order Lt. Col. Simcoe to cross the country, with a party of cavalry to City point, with instructions for Lieutenant Colonel Abercrombie, to march early the next morning to that place, which accordingly was executed, and the whole army united at Petersburg.

Gen. Phillips' army made prisoners some of M. Fayette's suite, who had arrived there to prepare quarters for his army: this was a very fortunate prevention, as the grounds about Petersburg were very strong, if properly occupied, and bridges over the Appomattox would have secured a retreat to the defenders. Lt. Col. Simcoe pressed Gen. Arnold, to let him march towards Halifax, in order to gain information of Lord Cornwallis, from whom no account had arrived; it was not thought prudent to make a detachment while M. Fayette was supposed to be so near: he was, however, sent with the cavalry to destroy Goode's bridge, and to return the next morning.

After proceeding a long way, Lt. Col. Simcoe understood that the bridge was not within the distance which had been apprehended; and Lt. Col. Darner, who had accompanied him, agreeing with him that the enemy might easily throw bridges over the Appomattox much nearer to Petersburg, and would certainly do so if they intended an attack against the troops there, the party returned, and lay a few miles from Petersburg that night, and joined the army the next day.

The enemy sending patrols on the opposite side of the Appomattox, Lt. Spencer had proposed to have swam over with a party, consisting of Lieut. Fitzpatrick and thirty Rangers, and to have laid an ambuscade for them. This officer was perfectly acquainted with the minutest particulars of the ground, having been encamped upon it. In case of the enemy appearing in force, any small gully would have given him a secure retreat to the river, while the cannon and musketry, purposely stationed to protect him, would have prevented the enemy from molesting the party whilst it swam back. This design the patrols to Goode's bridge, had occasioned to be deferred, and it was to have been executed the next morning; but, about the middle of the day, the enemy appeared on the heights, and cannonaded the quarters of the British army, particularly those of Gen. Phillips, whom they knew to be most dangerously ill, by a flag of truce which had been received the day before, and of Lt. Col. Simcoe which was on a height. Some shots being directed at the dragoon horses, then at grass, they set off full gallop towards the ferry, immediately under the enemy's cannon; and had they not fired grape at them, 'tis probable they would have swam to the shore in their possession. Their cannonading had no effect.

Lt. Col. Simcoe went *immediately* to Gen. Arnold, and again applied to march towards Lord Cornwallis, urging that it was apparent, from the discovery which the enemy had made, and their parade of force, that they could mean no serious attempt on the post. The General assented, and the enemy had scarcely drawn off their cannon, when the Queen's Rangers, both cavalry and infantry, marched towards the Nottaway, on the road to Halifax.

M. Fayette gives, as a reason for this cannonade, that he did it in order to cover the march of a detachment which he sent with stores, &c. to South Carolina. A detachment of the Queen's Rangers was more than sufficient to have attacked this convoy, had there been information of it; and it is very probable, in such a case, Gen. Arnold would have sent a party from the light infantry, in pursuit of it; but none of

Mr. Fayette's reasons impress any idea of his military talents. He possibly owed his personal safety to the patrol, which had prevented Lt. Spencer's ambuscade from being carried into execution; and who, not improbably, might have made himself master of his cannon, by rolling them down the steeps of the river, before the escort, which apparently, was left at some distance to avoid the shot of the British guns, could have advanced to their rescue.

Lt. Col. Simcoe proceeded, with the utmost expedition, to the Nottaway river, twenty-seven miles from Petersburg, where he arrived early the next morning. The bridge had been destroyed, which was easily repaired, and Major Armstrong was left with the infantry. The cavalry went on to Col. Gee's, a rebel militia officer. He attempted to escape, but was secured; and refusing to give his parole, was sent prisoner to Major Armstrong.

The cavalry proceeded in the afternoon to Hicks's ford, on the Meherrin, twenty-five miles from the Roanoke. Within a few miles of the river stood Col. Hicks's house. He was deceived, and believed the party to be an advanced guard from M. Fayette's army. From him the first information was received of Earl Cornwallis, and that his Lordship was certainly at Halifax, twenty miles from the Meherrin; and that it was reported his advanced guard had passed that river. Lt. Col. Simcoe's hopes of being in time to facilitate his Lordship's passage were at an end. There was still a probability, if any militia were in his front, of being of service.

Col. Hicks accompanied the party to Hicks's ford, where some militia were assembled. Sergeant Wright, who commanded the advanced guard on the approach to Hicks's, halted and returning to Lt. Col. Simcoe, told him, that he had entered into conversation with one of the sentinels; that the militia consisted of a Captain and thirty men; and that he had passed upon them for their friends. If he, Lt. Col. Simcoe, thought proper, he would relieve the whole party. Wright was directed to execute his intentions. The rebel Colonel was shown, at a sufficient distance, as a friend; and Lt. Col. Simcoe and the militia officers assisting, the whole party was assembled, their sentinels relieved, and their arms piled and secured before they were undeceived: they were then marched into a house, and their paroles given them.

The Captain and others being selected as guides, the party crossed the ford, which had been obstructed by trees felled, as a French officer, who had been that way a few days before, had directed; but which the militia slightly executed. It was understood that Lt. Colonel Tarleton had passed the Roanoke; that a Major of militia, who had commanded the post at Hicks's ford, was gone with a small party to reconnoitre. It was much to be feared, that if Lt. Col. Simcoe should fall in with Lord Cornwallis's advanced guard in the night, the unexpected meeting might occasion great confusion and, perhaps, loss; and it was still probable, that parties of militia might be between them, which, in the dark, it would be impossible to discriminate.

A circuit was therefore taken to the right of the direct road; and, at a situation a few miles from Hicks's ford, the party halted to feed their horses, and to refresh the men who were overcome with fatigue and wanted sleep. They had brought the firearms which had been taken at Hicks's ford, and these were placed along the fence where the men slept. Sergeant Wright was placed in ambuscade, close to the road; and officers, from time to time, visited him, lest that intrepid and vigilant soldier should himself give way to that fatigue which everybody laboured under.

In the middle of the night, Wright brought in an express from a captain who had been detached by M. Fayette for intelligence; he had not time to destroy his despatches, which confirmed the account of Col. Tarleton having passed the Roanoke. He was offered his liberty if he would conduct the party to the place where he had left his captain, the capture of whom would more effectually delay any intelligence which M. Fayette might expect; as it afterwards appeared, by his public letters, was done by this express being made prisoner. After two hours' sleep, the party proceeded and arrived at the place where the captain and his party were reported to have been; but no person was there; nor was it possible to determine whether the prisoner had been faithful to his original trust or his latter promise.

The party soon arrived on the banks of the Roanoke, and sending forward to prevent any errors, joined Lord Cornwallis's army. His Lordship being on the opposite side of the river, Lt. Col. Simcoe passed over to him; and a spy from Gen. Phillips had reached him a few hours before. It was Lt. Col. Simcoe's melancholy office to add to his Lordship's public anxieties, the intelligence of the irrecoverable state of health in which Gen. Phillips lay.

The cavalry refreshed themselves at Jones's house. His Lordship passed the river that evening, and Lt. Col. Simcoe set out on his return. He marched by the direct road to Hicks's ford, where he found Lieut. Col. Tarleton, who had made a circuit to his right from Halifax, and had arrived there a few hours after Lt. Col. Simcoe left it. The rebel Major, who had been to reconnoitre, fell into his hands. As Lt. Col. Tarleton's legion were mostly clothed in white, it was a fortunate circumstance, in making his circuit, he had not marched on the road Lt. Col. Simcoe had taken. The party halted that night at Col. Hicks's.

Lt. Col. Tarleton marched the next morning and proceeded to Colonel Tree's plantation. Soon after the Queen's

201

Rangers marched and rejoined their infantry at Nottaway bridge, where they passed the night in great and necessary security: Lt. Col. Simcoe, with a few dragoons, returning to Petersburg.

From the representations which he had made of Gen. Arnold, and Lt. Col. Abercrombie concurring in opinion that Fayette might possibly attack them, and therefore had deferred his necessary march to Earl Cornwallis, till such time, as by Fayette's cannonade, it was evident he could mean nothing serious, Gen. Arnold was directed to march to the Nottaway. That officer being of opinion, that it was no longer necessary to do so, went himself only, the next morning, with Lieut. Col. Simcoe, to the Nottaway, where he met Earl Cornwallis.

The Queen's Rangers returned to Petersburg that evening; and his Lordship's whole army arrived there the next day, the 20th of May. They marched opposite to Westover, and passed the James river on the 24th.

Lt. Col. Simcoe, while at Westover, received a letter from Gen. Lee, with whom he had been acquainted whilst that gentleman was prisoner in the Jersies, pointing out the enormities committed by the privateers. The proper representation was made to Earl Cornwallis, who took measures to prevent the future misconduct of these licensed miscreants, by representing them to Sir Henry Clinton.

The army marched towards the Chickahominy, and arrived at Bottom bridge on the 28th. Lt. Col. Sim-coe, with his cavalry, by a circuit, passed the Chickahominy, and patrolled to New-Castle, where he seized some rebel officers; and on his return, imposed upon and took several Virginia gentlemen, who were watching the motions of Earl Cornwallis. In the evening his Lordship marched; and Lt. Col. Simcoe halted during the night, and then followed the army; perhaps not without utility, as the rear was uncommonly long, and the road running, in many places, through thickets, patrols of the enemy might easily have taken a great many stragglers. He divided his cavalry into small parties, left them at different distances, and collected the tired men as well as possible, which was not in the power of the infantry, that formed the rear guard, to effect.

Capt Cooke's troop joined the Queen's Rangers, from New York, but without a single cavalry, appointment, or arms.

The army halted near New-Castle on the 29th, and marched to Hanover Court-house the next day, where some large brass cannon, without carriages, were found, and attempted to be destroyed. The Queen's Rangers had advanced to South Anna bridge, and chased and took a patrol of the enemy. The next day they crossed the North Anna, patrolled for intelligence, and took a militia gentleman on his return from Fayette's army. The army proceeded to Tile's ordinary, on the 1st of June.

Lt. Col. Simcoe crossed the North Anna, with his cavalry, with orders to get intelligence of Fayette's march; and Capt. Dundas, of the guards, with the light company, was sent to a strong post, a few miles over the river, to support and cover his retreat. A rebel Commissary was chased and taken; and, after a long patrol, full information was obtained of Fayette's march, and the party returned.

On Lt. Col. Simcoe's arrival at headquarters, he found that two of the Queen's Rangers had committed a robbery and a rape. Lord Cornwallis directed him to enquire into the matter, which was done by the Captains of the corps; and the robbery being fully proved, his Lordship ordered the men, agreeable to Lt. Col. Simcoe's desire, to be executed the next day.

Early the next morning, Lt. Col. Simcoe marched towards the Baron Steuben, who was reported to be at the point of Fork, the head of James river. Lord Cornwallis informed him, that Steuben's force consisted of three or four hundred men; and as the Queen's Rangers were so debilitated by the fatigues of the climate, &c. as to have scarcely more than two hundred infantry and one hundred cavalry, fit for duty, his Lordship ordered the 71st regiment, under Capt Hutchinson, consisting of two hundred rank and file, to join him. At Lt. Col. Simcoe's particular request, a three pounder was annexed.

The incessant marches of the Rangers, and their distance from their stores, had so worn out their shoes, that, on Lt. Colonel Simcoe's calling for a return, it appeared that near fifty men were absolutely barefooted. Upon assembling them, when they were informed that they were wanted for active employment, and that those who chose to stay with the army might do so, there was not a man who would remain behind the corps. Lord Cornwallis ordered him, on his return, to join the army at Goochland Court-house, whither he should march to receive his detachment, and that of Lt. Col. Tarleton, which was to endeavour to seize on the assembly at Charlottesville; and then, if circumstances admitted of it, to fall back by the point of Fork.

Lt. Spencer, with twenty huzzars, formed the advance guard, these were chosen men, and mounted on the fleetest horses. Capt Stevenson, with the light infantry company, and the Hessian riflemen, under Lt. Beikel, followed. The 71st succeeded with the cannon, followed by Capt Althause with his riflemen, and those of the Queen's Rangers. The infantry and Capt Shank, with the cavalry of the Rangers, closed the rear.

In case of attack, the battalion in front (and the two battalions marched there alternately) was directed to form in line; that which followed, to close up into column ready to march to whichever flank it was ordered, as the cavalry under Capt Shank was to the other. The whole of the cavalry preceded the march, till the detachment crossed the bridge over the South Anna. Lt. Col. Simcoe then proceeded with the utmost despatch, by Bird's ordinary, towards Napier's ford, the second ford on the Rivana, above the Fluvana, the junction of which rivers, at the point of Fork, forms the James river. Not a person escaped who was in sight, and the advanced cavalry were so managed as totally to conceal the advance of the infantry.

At night the corps lay upon their arms, in the strongest position which could be conveniently found, on the principle of making a front each way; and having a strong reserve of infantry, as well as cavalry, within the circle, ready to support any part which might be attacked, and to sally from it if ordered. The guards and sentinels were, as usual, in ambuscade.

After two days' march, as the party approached Napier's ford, some prisoners and letters were taken, and other intelligence obtained, by which it appeared, that the march had been hitherto undiscovered, and that Lt. Col. Tarleton's detachment alone had been heard of; that Baron Steuben was about to march to oppose a patrol of Earl Cornwallis' army, or, more probably, deceived in his intelligence of a detachment that had never been made; and, that the Baron's force consisted of nine hundred effective men, exclusive of the militia who were assembling to join him.

The troops had already marched that day nearly twenty miles, and the two preceding days not less than thirty each, when this intelligence was accumulated. Lt. Spencer was directed to proceed cautiously, gaining what intelligence he could, to Napier's house, which stood on a high and commanding ground; near which it was intended to halt during the night and to ambuscade the ford, it being the purpose to attack the enemy by daybreak the next morning.

Lt. Spencer went to the house of a Colonel Thompson, which was surrounded with very high fences, and, alighting from his horse, approached that gentleman, who was accompanied by four of the militia, asking, in a familiar manner, the road to the Baron's camp. Col. Thompson, suspecting his errand, though armed, retreated precipitately and made his escape, with three of his men; the fourth, seeing that two huzzars, who had accompanied Lt. Spencer, could not get over the fence, or assist him, presented a double barrel piece within five yards of his breast. Lt. Spencer, with great presence of mind, immediately threatened to have him flogged on his arrival at the Baron's camp, and, pulling some papers from his pocket, told him, that they were his despatches from M. Fayette. At the same time he moved gently towards him, intending, if possible, to seize the muzzle of his firelock, but, as the one advanced, the other retreated, keeping his piece still presented, until, getting over a fence at the back of the house, he ran towards the river. At this moment, Lt. Spencer could have shot him with a pocket pistol; but having received intimation from Lt. Col. Simcoe, that it was expected the enemy had a post at Napier's ford, two miles lower, he prudently permitted him to escape, rather than make an alarm. These people left five good horses behind them.

He then proceeded to Napier's ford, and leaving his party unseen, at a proper distance, he crossed the river with three men. On the opposite side were two militia men well mounted, from whom he learnt that Baron Steuben was at the point of Fork; that he had sent the greatest part of his stores, and some troops, on the south side the river, and was superintending the transportation of the remainder with the greatest despatch. Lt. Spencer completely imposed on their credulity; they suffered him to relieve them with two of his own men, and accompanied him to Col. Napier's house, whom he took prisoner.

On this intelligence, Lt. Col. Simcoe determined to march, with the utmost celerity, towards Baron Steuben, hoping to cut off his rear guard. Lt. Spencer preceded and occupied the road, and every point from whence the troops could be seen, as they forded the river; and, in order to prevent any intelligence from Col. Thompson. Within two miles of Baron Steuben's encampment, a patrol of dragoons appeared; they were chased and taken. It consisted of a French officer and four of Armand's corps. They confirmed Lt. Col. Simcoe in his belief, that Baron Steuben was ignorant of his approach, as they were destined to patrol twenty miles from the point of Fork to the place where, it afterwards appeared, Earl Cornwallis's army had arrived the preceding night, and they were to have passed the Rivana at its lowest ford, Lt. Col. Simcoe's circuitous march, to cross at the upper, having answered the expected purpose.

The advanced men of the huzzars changed clothes with the prisoners, and dispositions were now made for the attack. The huzzars in the enemy's clothing, were directed to gallop to the only house on the point, and where it was understood Baron Steuben was, at once to dismount and, if possible, to seize him. They were to be supported by a detachment of cavalry, the light infantry company and the cannon. Captain Stevenson was intended to fortify the house, and to place the cannon there as a point of reserve; Captain Hutchinson was to form the Highlanders, on the left; and Lt. Col. Simcoe meant to occupy the wood on the right of the house.

The order was about to be given for the men to lay down their knapsacks, when the advance guard brought in Mr. Farley, Baron Steuben's Aid de Camp. He mistook them for the patrol which had been just taken, and came to see whether it had set off. Sergeant Wright being near the size and appearance of Mr. Farley, was directed to exchange clothes with him, to mount his horse, and lead the advance guard; when that officer assured Lieut. Col. Simcoe, that he had seen every man over the Fluvana, before he left the point of Fork. This was confirmed by some waggoners, who, with their teams, were now taken.

The cavalry immediately advanced, and the enemy being plainly seen on the opposite side, nothing remained but to stop some boats, which were putting off from the extreme point. This Capt. Shank effected, and took about thirty people who were on the banks, from which the embarkation had proceeded.

Every method was now taken to persuade the enemy, that the party was Earl Cornwallis's army, that they might leave the opposite shore, which was covered with arms and stores. Capt. Hutchinson, with the 71st regiment, clothed in red, was directed to advance as near to the banks of the Fluvana as he could with perfect safety, and without the hazard of a single man, from the enemy's shot, who had lined the opposite shore. The baggage and women halted among the woods, on the summit of the hill, and, in that position, made the appearance of a numerous corps. The three-pounder was carried down, the artillery men being positively ordered to fire but one shot and to take the best aim possible, which they performed, killing the horse of one of Baron Steuben's orderly dragoons.

The troops occupied the heights which covered the neck of the point, and their numbers were concealed in the wood. Baron Steuben was encamped on the heights on the opposite side of the river, about three quarters of a mile from its banks. The prisoners, and observation confirmed the information which had been received of his numbers.

As night approached, and the men were somewhat refreshed, every precaution was taken to prevent any surprise
which the number, and the character of the enemy's general, might lead them to attempt Lt. Col. Simcoe who, from
his childhood, had been taught to consider the military
as the most extensive and profound of sciences, had no
apprehension from the talents of such men as had been
educated in different professions, and whom accident had
placed at the head of armies; and he had always asserted it as
a principle, that, from the superiority of the King's troops,
and of the officers who led them, if he should ever have a
command, in which he should be superior in one species
of troops, whether cavalry or infantry, he would be totally
unconcerned for the event of any action he might have
with the enemy.

Baron Steuben had no cavalry, yet, in the present situation, there was great room for anxiety, since the immediate
ground of encampment was not favourable for the exertions of his few, but well trained, well officered, and invincible body of cavalry; and the enemy were led by a Prus-
sian officer. The very military instructions of his king were
capable of forming better officers than any other theory
could possibly do, or probably could be effected by the
experience of ten campaigns under incompetent masters.
In the exercise also which he had given the rebel army, the
Baron Steuben had shown himself an able officer, and that
he well knew how to adapt the science of war to the people whom he was to instruct, and to the country in which
he was to act.

He had passed the Fluvana; but he had done this in consequence of his orders to join General Green's army. An
express sent to countermand this order, Lt. Col. Simcoe
knew had been taken a few days before by Lt. Col. Tarleton;
and it was fair to suppose, that he might now have further

intelligence; that he might be perfectly acquainted with the numbers of his opponents, and might possibly determine to attack Lt. Col. Simcoe, as well as the detachment which the intercepted letter mentioned, that he was preparing to meet. Lt. Col. Simcoe was therefore apprehensive, lest Baron Steuben, having secured his stores which were of great value, over a broad and unfordable river, and, being in possession of all the boats, should re-pass his troops in the night, higher up the river, and fall on him, so that, if the British troops should be beaten, they would have no retreat, being shut up between two rivers, while those of the Americans, should they be repulsed, were preserved from the pursuit of the cavalry by the thick woods, which came close to their encampment, and, from that of the infantry, by the fatigues they had undergone in a march of nearly forty miles the preceding morning.

These ideas occupied the mind of Lt. Col. Simcoe, and he would have quitted his camp had he not thought the troops too much fatigued, to search for a more favourable position, which was not to be attained for some miles; and, partly, had he not hoped that Steuben would believe him to be the advance of Earl Cornwallis' army, particularly, as the light troops had no soldiers among them clothed like the 71st regiment, in red. That regiment, and the Queen's Rangers, occupied the roads, with rail fletches and other defences.

Capt. Althause, with his company and the Yagers, were posted on a knoll, among the woods, between the main body and the Fluvana, the cavalry lay in the rear of the Queen's Rangers, and small posts were extended so as to form a chain between the rivers. Capt. Shank had orders to send continual patrols of cavalry from river to river, about half a mile in front of the infantry; and the troops were acquainted with the probability of an attack, and were perfectly prepared for it.

At night, the enemy were heard destroying their boats, with great noise. At midnight, Capt. Shank informed Lt. Col. Simcoe, that they were making up their fires, and that he supposed they were moving; with which he perfectly agreed, when it was seen that they were *uniformly* refreshed throughout their camp. Soon after, a deserter and a little drummer boy came from the enemy in a canoe, and gave information that Steuben had marched off on the road by Cumberland Court-house, towards North Carolina. It is remarkable this boy belonged to the 71st regiment. He had been taken prisoner at the Cow-pens, enlisted with the enemy, and now, making his escape, was received by the piquet which his father commanded.

When daylight appeared, there was not an enemy to be seen. Sergeant John M'Donald, of the Highland company of the Queen's Rangers, swam over to the enemy's shore, and brought off a large canoe; two or three smaller ones were found on the Rivana. The cannon and riflemen were sent down to line the bushes on the banks of the Fluvana; and, under their protection, Captain Stevenson, with twenty of the light infantry, passed over to the opposite banks, which he found covered with the enemy's stores. Cornet Wolsey was then sent over with four huzzars, with their saddles. He was directed to get some of the straggling horses which had been left by the enemy, to post himself upon the road on the summit of the hill, and then, if he should meet with an enemy's patrol, to make a great shout and every demonstration of pursuing them, to impress them with an idea that the whole corps had passed. Capt. Stevenson was employed in sending off such things as might be useful to the troops, and destroying the remainder.

As the detachment met with plenty of provisions and forage at the point of Fork, Lt. Col. Simcoe determined to halt there the whole of the day; but, that his return to

Earl Cornwallis' army might not be in the least delayed, he was attentive to the building of a float, by which he might pass the Rivana at its confluence with the South Anna, this would save him a day's march, which he must have made in case he should re-pass it at the nearest ford. He also meant to use this float in carrying down the cannon and mortars which the enemy had left, to Earl Cornwallis, at Goochland Court-house.

In the middle of the day a patrol from Lt. Col. Tarleton, who was on the opposite side of the Rivana, communicated with him. The float was completed and launched towards noon, and Capt Stevenson, having effectually done his business, returned in the evening. Cornet Wolsey had very fortunately executed his orders, for a patrol of the enemy had approached to the place where he was posted, and, on perceiving him, fled with the utmost speed. It was afterwards understood, that on this patrol joining Baron Steuben, in consequence of their report, be immediately proceeded twenty miles farther, though he had already marched thirty miles from the point of Fork. He must have believed that the whole of Earl Cornwallis's army were in pursuit of him, or he would have scarcely abandoned such a quantity of stores. A guard of twenty or thirty men would have effectually prevented the Rangers from destroying them, and they would have been in perfect safety in that case, had Earl Corwallis adhered to his first intention, of halting at Goochland Court-house.

The army arriving near the point of Fork on the 7th of June, Lt. Col. Simcoe passed the Rivana, and rejoined it. The Fluvana being a larger river than the Rivana, at its confluence forces back the latter and it becomes as still as a mill pond. The water was fenced, as it were, with spars and canoes, so as to make a lane, and the horses swam over between them. The infantry passed on the float, which held, with ease, a hundred and thirty men, and had been made in four hours; and the artillery, some of which had been brought over from the opposite shore in a smaller boat, made by the junction of two canoes, were carried over on it, and put into empty wagons sent by Earl Cornwallis for that purpose.

There were destroyed at the point of Fork, two thousand five hundred stand of arms, a large quantity of gunpowder, case shot, &c, several casks of saltpetre, sulphur, and brimstone, and upwards of sixty hogsheads of rum and brandy, several chests of carpenters' tools, and upwards of four hundred entrenching tools, with casks of flints, sail cloth and wagons, and a great variety of small stores, necessary for the equipment of cavalry and infantry. Such linen and necessaries, as would be of immediate service, were divided among the captors. There were taken off, a thirteen-inch mortar, five brass eight-inch howitzers, and four long brass nine pounders, mounted afterwards at York Town, all French pieces and in excellent order.

Lieut. Col. Simcoe, on the 9th of June, was detached with his cavalry to destroy some tobacco in the warehouses on the northern bank of the Fluvana. He passed at the lowest ford, and proceeding to the Seven islands, destroyed one hundred and fifty barrels of gunpowder, and burnt all the tobacco in the warehouses on the river side, returning with some rebel militia whom he had surprised and made prisoners.

The army remained in this district till the 13th of June; and the cavalry of the Queen's Rangers made several patrols, particularly one to Bird's ordinary, at midnight, where, it was understood, the Marquis de la Fayette, with his forces, had arrived. It appeared, however, that they were at a great distance, so that the army moved towards Richmond, the Queen's Rangers forming the rear guard.

The 71st regiment here left the Rangers; the two corps had acted with the utmost harmony together, and Lt. Col. Simcoe remembers, with great satisfaction, the expressions of good will and regret which both the officers and soldiers of that distinguished regiment made use of, when they quitted his command.

CHAPTER 24

Williamsburg

Earl Cornwallis arrived at Richmond the 16th of June.

On the 17th, Lt. Col. Simcoe was detached with some infantry and his cavalry, to pass the James river, near Henrico Court-house; which he did the next morning, to facilitate the passage of the boats with convalescents up to Richmond, and to clear the southern banks of the James river of any parties of militia who might be stationed to annoy them. The detachment re-crossed the river on the night of the 19th, from Manchester to Richmond, and Captain Ewald, with the Yagers, joined the Queen's Rangers.

On the 20th it being reported that the enemy had a flying corps, all mounted, under Gen. Muhlenberg, and consisting of twelve hundred men, Lt. Col. Simcoe was directed to patrol for intelligence. He marched with forty cavalry, but, considering this a service of particular danger, with the utmost caution. He quitted the road and marched through the woods, as nearly parallel to it as the enclosures, which had been cleared, would admit.

After a march of a few miles, to his great satisfaction, he discovered a flag of truce, of the enemy; and he was certain, that according to their custom, some of them would be found in its rear. Lt. Spencer was therefore detached with a small party to get beyond them upon the road, which he effected, and found himself in the rear of a party of twenty men; but the woods on his right being open, though Lt. Lawler supported him in front, one officer and two or three men only were taken.

Lt. Col. Simcoe immediately returned, having procured from the prisoners every requisite intelligence.

The army marched, on the 21st of June, to Bottom-bridge, and on the 22nd to New Kent Court-house. The Queen's Rangers, who made the rear with the Yagers, lay near two miles on the left of the army. Lt. Col. Simcoe was ordered to march the next day towards the Chicka-hominy, where it was supposed there was a foundry, and some boats. These he was to destroy, to collect all the cattle he could find in the country, and proceed to Wil-liamsburg; and Lord Cornwallis expressly told him, that he might, in these operations, safely stay two or three days behind the army, who were to be at Williamsburg on the 25th of June.

Lt. Col. Simcoe marched early in the morning of the 24th, consuming a quantity of Indian corn, which had been collected by the enemy's commissary, at the house where he quartered. He found little or nothing to destroy on the Chickahominy, and halted that night at Dandrige's, as Earl Cornwallis did in the neighbourhood of Bird's ordinary.

The bridge over the Diesckung creek (a branch of the Chickahominy) had been broken down. This was three miles in the rear of the detachment, and Lt. Col. Simcoe would have passed it that night, so diffident was he of his security, had not the men been too much fatigued with their march, to be employed in so laborious a task as the repair of this bridge was understood to be. The next morn-ing, at daybreak, the detachment arrived there. It had been carelessly destroyed, and was, by anxious and laborious exertion, repaired sufficiently to pass over. Lt. Col. Simcoe then destroyed it most effectually, and marched on to Cooper's mills on the 25th, near twenty miles from Williamsburg, where Earl Cornwallis arrived in the course of the day. Lord Cornwallis's wagons had been at the mills the day before, and taken from thence all the flour they contained, so that it was difficult to get subsistence.

Lt. Col. Simcoe felt his situation to be a very anxious one. He had not the smallest information of the enemy's movements, whom he knew to be active and enterprising; to have been lately joined by Gen. Wayne; and, that it was their obvious policy, to follow Earl Cornwallis as far towards the neck of Williamsburg as with safety they could, and to take any little advantage which they could magnify in their newspapers. He had received no advices from Earl Cornwallis, whose general intelligence he knew to be very bad; and he and Major Armstrong agreed with Capt Ewald, that the slightest reliance was not to be placed on any patrols from his Lordship's army.

The next advantage, to receiving good intelligence, is to deceive the enemy with that which is false. Lt. Col. Simcoe could not procure any confidential person to go to M. de la Fayette's camp; he therefore promised a great reward to a man, whom he knew to be a rebel, to go thither, with express injunctions to return to him by six or seven o'clock, at the farthest, the next morning, at which time he said he should march. The man accordingly set out towards night; and, at two o'clock in the morning, Major Armstrong with the Yagers, infantry and cannon, was on his march to Spencer's ordinary, on the forks of the road between Williamsburg and Jamestown. There he was to halt till the cavalry joined him, and then the whole, with the convoy of cattle, which Capt. Branson, with some North Carolina loyalists, had been employed to collect, was to proceed to Williamsburg.

Lt. Col. Simcoe, with the cavalry, was under arms at the time his infantry marched, and ready to proceed whenever Captain Branson thought there was light sufficient to drive the cattle, and to collect whatever might be met with on the road. The cavalry did not leave their camp till three o'clock.

On approaching Spencer's ordinary, Lieut. Col. Simcoe ordered the fences to be thrown down, and rode into the open ground upon the right, observing it, as was his custom, and remarking, to the officers with him, "that it was an admirable place for the chicanery of action."

Lt. Lawler had been previously sent to direct the infantry to move onward to Williamsburg, when Major Armstrong returning with him, informed Lt. Col. Simcoe that there were near an hundred head of cattle in the neighbourhood; but that he waited till the drivers arrived to spare the infantry from that fatigue. Capt Branson, with his people, went to collect them; and Capt Shank, who commanded the cavalry, was directed to feed his horses at Lee's farm, and Lt. Col. Simcoe accompanied Major Armstrong to the infantry.

The Highland Company of the Queen's Rangers had been posted in the wood, by the side of the road, as a piquet. A shot or two from their sentinels gave an alarm, and Lt. Col. Simcoe galloping across the field, towards the wood, saw Capt Shank in pursuit of the enemy's cavalry. They had passed through the fences which had been pulled down, as before-mentioned, so that, unperceived by the Highlanders, they arrived at Lee's farm, in pursuit of the people who were collecting the cattle. Trumpeter Barney, who had been stationed as a vidette, gave the alarm, and galloped off so as not to lead the enemy directly to where the cavalry were collecting their forage and watering, and, with great address, got to them unperceived by the enemy, calling out "draw your swords Rangers, the rebels are coming."

Capt Shank, who was at Lee's farm waiting the return of the troops with their forage, in order to post them, immediately joined, and led them to the charge on the enemy's flank, which was somewhat exposed, while some of them were engaged in securing the bat-horses at the back of Lee's farm; he broke them entirely. Sergeant Wright dashed Major Macpherson, who commanded them, from his horse; but, leaving him in pursuit of others, that officer crept into a swamp, lay there unperceived during the action, and when it was over got off. Trumpeter Barney dismounted and took a French officer, who commanded one of the divisions.

The enemy's cavalry were so totally scattered, that they appeared no more. Many of them were dismounted, and the whole would have been taken, had not a heavy fire out of the wood, from whence the Highland company were now driven, protected them.

At this moment Lt. Col. Simcoe arrived. He had, at the first shot, ordered the infantry to march in column into the road towards the enemy, the light infantry company and Capt Ewald's detachment excepted, which, being on the right, were moving straight to their own front to gain the wood. Collecting from the prisoners, that the enemy were in force, and that M. de la Fayette, and Generals Wayne and Steuben were at no great distance, the line was directed to be formed, spreading itself with wide intervals, and covering a great space of ground between the road on its left and Capt. Ewald on the right; and, when formed, it was directed to advance to gain the wood, as it was his idea, to outflank the enemy by the length of the line.

The principle which Lieut. Col. Simcoe always inculcated and acted on against the riflemen, (whom he judged to be in the advanced corps of M. Fayette's army,) was to rush upon them; when, if each separate company kept itself compact, there was little danger, even should it be surrounded, from troops who were without bayonets, and whose object it was to fire a single shot with effect. The position of an advancing soldier was calculated to lessen the true aim of the first shot, and his rapidity to prevent the rifleman, who requires some time to load, from giving a second; or at least to render his aim uncertain, and his fire by no means formidable.

Lieut. Col. Simcoe had withdrawn the cavalry from the fire of the enemy, and directed Capt Althause, whose rifle company had been mounted, to dismount and to check them, if they sallied from the wood in pursuit of the cavalry, or for the purpose of reconnoitring; and this he executed very effectually.

Captain Branson had distinguished himself in the charge on the enemy's cavalry, and being dressed in red, he became a marked object to them. He was now ordered with the drivers and the cattle, to proceed to Williamsburg; expresses were sent to Lord Cornwallis; and Lt. Allen, who acted as Quarter-Master, carried off the baggage that road, was directed to cut down trees, and to barricade the first pass for the corps to rally, in case of necessity. The fences were pulled down on the Jamestown road, in the rear of the cavalry, that the retreat might be made that way, if, which was every moment to be expected, the enemy should have occupied the Williamsburg road in the rear.

Lt. Col. Simcoe moved with the cavalry out of sight of the enemy, down the hill towards Jamestown road, and re-ascending at Lee's farm, there made a display of the whole force; then fell back again behind the hill, leaving only the front, a detachment of huzzars, both to prevent the left from being turned without notice, and to deceive the enemy into a belief that the whole cavalry, whose force they had already felt, were behind the eminences, waiting for an opportunity to fall upon their right flank.

He returned rapidly with the rest of the cavalry undiscovered to the road, and formed them out of sight and out of reach of the enemy, partly in the road and partly on its left. Beyond Captain Ewald's flank there was open ground, which could easily be seen from the eminence on which Lieut. Col. Simcoe was, and (by the turn of the Williamsburg road) the cavalry would have had quick access to it, had the enemy appeared there. By the position of the cavalry, it was also ready, in case the infantry had given way to flank the enemy, if they should issue from the wood in pursuit of it; the best substitute for want of the reserve, which from the extent of the woods and the enemy's numbers, had been thrown into the line.

Upon the left of the road the three pounder was placed, the amuzette having broken down: there too the Highland company had retired. The enemy now appeared in great force, lining the fences on the edge of the wood (which separated it from the open ground) in front of the infantry; and refusing their right upon the open ground, by echelons; probably deceived by the appearance of the cavalry at Lee's farm: to add to their reasons for not advancing, one cannon shot, and no more, was ordered to be fired at the body, which appeared to be at the greatest distance. The infantry was now in line, but with intervals between the companies, advancing as fast as the ploughed fields they had to cross would admit.

Lt. Col. Simcoe did not expect victory, but he was determined to try for it; his best hopes were to obtain and line the wood, checking the enemy's advance, till such times as the convoy was in security, and then to retreat. He had the most general and particular confidence in the officers and soldiers of his corps, who were *disciplined enthusiasts* in the *cause* of their *country,* and who, having been ever victorious, thought it impossible to suffer defeat; nor had he less reliance on the acknowledged military talents of his friend Ewald, and the cool and tried courage of his Yagers. The event fully justified the expression which he used in the beginning of the action, "I will take care of the left; while Ewald lives, the right flank will never be turned".

Fortune now decided in favour of the British troops. The road from Norwal's mills was enclosed with high and strong fences; a considerable body of the enemy being on the right of the road, and, seeing the infantry advancing, faced and were crossing these fences to flank them. They did not observe the cavalry, which, while they were in this disorder, lost not the moment; but, led by Capt Shank, charged them up the road, and upon its left, entirely broke and totally dispersed them.

The infantry were ordered to advance, and they rushed on with the greatest rapidity; the enemy's fire was in vain, they were driven from the fences and the wood. Capt Ewald turned their left flank, and gave them a severe fire as they fled in the utmost confusion. Could he have been supported as he wished, by a very small body of fresh bayonet men, such was the advantage of the ground, that the enemy, in confusion, and panic stricken, would have received a very severe blow, before it could have been possible for them to rally.

Cornet Jones, who led the first division of cavalry, was unfortunately killed. He was an active, sensible, promising officer. The mounted riflemen of the Queen's Rangers charged with Capt. Shank.

The gallant Sergeant M'Pherson, who led them, was mortally wounded. Two of the men of this detachment were carried away by their impetuosity so far as to pass beyond the enemy, and their horses were killed: they, however, secreted themselves in the wood under some fallen logs, and, when the enemy fled from that spot, they returned in safety to the corps.

By a mistake, scarcely avoidable in the tumult of action, Capt. Shank was not supported, as was intended, by the whole of his cavalry, by which fewer prisoners were taken than might have been. That valuable officer was in the most imminent danger, in fighting his way back through the enemy, who fired upon him, and wounded the Trumpeter Barney and killed some of the huzzars, who attended him.

The grenadier company, commanded by Capt. M'Gill, signalized by their gallantry as well as by their dress, lost several valuable men. Capt. Stevenson was distinguished as usual. His chosen and well trained light infantry were obstinately opposed; but they carried their point with the loss of a fourth of their numbers, killed and wounded.

An affair of this nature necessarily afforded a great variety of gallant actions in individuals. Capt. M'Rae reported to Lt. Col. Simcoe, that his subaltern, Lt. Charles Dunlop, who had served in the Queen's Rangers from thirteen years of age, led on his division on horseback, without suffering a man to fire, watching the enemy, and giving a signal to his men to lay down whenever a party of their's was about to fire. He arrived at the fence where the enemy had been posted with his arms loaded, a conduct that might have been decisive of the action. Fortunately he escaped unhurt.

The whole of the loss of the Queen's Rangers amounted to ten killed, and twenty-three wounded; among the latter was Lt. Swift Armstrong, and Ensign Jarvis, acting with the grenadiers. The Yagers had two or three men wounded and one killed. It may be supposed, in the course of so long a service, there was scarcely a man of them, whose death did not call forth a variety of situations, in which his courage had been distinguished, or his value exemplified; and it seemed to everyone, as if the flower of the regiment had been cut off.

As the whole series of the service of light troops gives the greatest latitude for the exertion of individual talents, and of individual courage, so did the present situation require the most perfect combination of them. Every division, every officer, every soldier had his share in the merit of the action; mistake in the one might have brought on cowardice in the other, and a single panic stricken soldier would probably have infected a platoon, and led to the utmost confusion and ruin; so that Lt. Col. Simcoe has ever considered this action as the climax of a campaign of five years, as the result of true discipline acquired in that space by unremitted diligence, toil, and danger, as an honourable victory earned by veteran intrepidity.

The instant Lt. Col. Simcoe could draw off and collect his force, and had communicated with Capt Ewald, it was thought proper to retreat; the information obtained from two and thirty prisoners, many of them officers and of different corps, making it expedient so to do.

The wounded men were collected into Spencer's ordinary, there being no wagons with the detachment, and they were left there with the surgeon's mate, and a flag of truce. The infantry filed off to the right, and the cavalry closed the rear. The party soon arrived at a brook, on the opposite and commanding side of which Lt. Allen, with the pioneers, had cut down some trees, and was proceeding to give it such defences as it was capable of receiving.

In less than two miles, Lt. Col. Simcoe met Earl Cornwallis, and the advance of his army, and returned with them towards Spencer's ordinary. He reported to his Lordship what he had learned from an examination of the rebel prisoners, and by his own and his officers' observations; that the enemy were, at the least, twelve hundred strong in action, above three times the numbers of his corps; that Fayette's army was at no great distance; that they had marched twenty-eight miles, and had no provisions. Lt. Col. Simcoe added, that he had effectually destroyed the Diesckung bridge. Earl Cornwallis examined the prisoners, and observed to Lt. Col. Simcoe, that it was a march of great hazard in Fayette, as on the least previous intimation he must have been cut off.

On the approach to Spencer's; Lt. Col. Simcoe galloped forward, and was very happy to find, that his wounded men were not prisoners, none of the enemy having approached them; and he found a foraging party of Earl Cornwallis's army, with the wagons on which the wounded and the dead were placed.

So little idea was there entertained of Fayette's move, that this foraging party had proceeded some miles on the Williamsburg road, and would have been certainly taken, had it not been for the action at Spencer's. It was reported, and not without probability, that a patrol of the enemy met with this party on the road, where it was natural to expect Lord Cornwallis' army, and took it for his advance guard, and that this belief prevented them from renewing the attack.

Lt. Col. Tarleton soon after arrived at Spencer's. He had advanced up the Williamsburg road, and in the wood in front of Spencer's, met with a great number of arms, thrown away, and other symptoms of the confusion in which the enemy had fled.

The army returned to Williamsburg, and the Queen's Rangers were hutted on the right at Queen's creek. At the commencement of the action, the bat-men and their horses, feeding at Lee's farm, were taken; they were all rescued, Lt. Col. Simcoe's groom excepted, the only prisoner the enemy carried off.

It was generally reported, that the person who had been sent to Fayette's camp, from Cooper's mills, conducted Gen. Wayne thither, about four o'clock in the morning, who, with a large force, charged with fixed bayonets, the fires which the Queen's Rangers had but just quitted. M. Fayette, in his public letters, stated the loss of the British at one hundred and fifty killed and wounded, and attributed it to the skill of his riflemen; his own he diminished, recapitulating that only of the continental troops, and taking no notice of the militia. It is certain they had a great many killed and wounded, exclusive of the prisoners. The riflemen, however dexterous in the use of their arms, were by no means the most formidable of the rebel troops; their not being armed with bayonets, permitted their opponents to take liberties with them which otherwise would have been highly improper.

Cornet Jones was buried at Williamsburg the next day, with military honours.

It was given out in the public orders, at Williamsburg, on the 28th of June, that "Lord Cornwallis desires Lieut. Col. Simcoe will accept of his warmest acknowledgments for his spirited and judicious conduct in the action of the 26th instant, when he repulsed and defeated so superior a force of the enemy. He likewise desires that Lt. Col. Simcoe will communicate his thanks to the officers and soldiers of the Queen's Rangers, and to Captain Ewald and the detachment of Yagers."

Earl Cornwallis visiting York Town on the 28th of June, Lt. Col. Simcoe, with the cavalry, escorted him thither; his Lordship disapproving of it as a post, Lt. Col. Simcoe observed to him, that if any of the points below it, and one was then in their view, would be more favourable for such a garrison as his Lordship intended, that it would be easy to remove York Town to it. His Lordship assented, and personally made the necessary enquiry; but the water was not sufficiently deep to harbour ships of war. The enemy fired a random shot or two, from Gloucester, at the escort when it marched into York Town, and were prepared to repeat it on its return; but this was avoided by keeping on the heights and Earl Cornwallis returned in the evening.

The Queen's Rangers made two patrols during the continuance of the army at Williamsburg: the first was with the design of ascertaining the enemy's post. Lt. Col. Simcoe left the infantry in ambuscade, about five miles from Williamsburg, and proceeding seven or eight miles further, drove in the enemy's advance guard.

The second patrol was made to the same spot, and for the same purpose, Earl Cornwallis understanding the enemy had left it. The peninsula was intersected with roads, full of small woods, and the enemy were in force. Lt. Col. Simcoe expected to be ambuscaded; so that he marched only with his cavalry, and through bye-paths and the woods.

In approaching the post; he left the party with orders for them to *retreat* whensoever the bugle-horns sounded the *advance,* and proceeded himself with a small escort, some officers and the bugle-horns. Being mounted on a tall horse, a matter of great utility in all reconnoitring parties, he saw the heads of some people in ambuscade, before they could stoop from notice on his approach, and another party was plainly discovered on their march to get behind him on the Williamsburg road. The horns sounded, the alarm was given, and the party retreated by the ways they came, unmolested, to Williamsburg.

Chapter 25

Leslie's Expedition

On the 4th of July the army marched to Jamestown, for the purpose of crossing the river at that place, and proceeding to Portsmouth. The Queen's Rangers crossed the river that evening, and took post to cover the baggage, which was passing over as expeditiously as possible.

On the evening of the 6th, as Earl Cornwallis had predicted, M. de la Fayette attacked his army, mistaking it for the rear guard only. The affair was almost confined to the 80th and 76th regiments, under the command of Lt. Col. Dundas, whose good conduct and gallantry was conspicuously displayed on that occasion. M. de la Fayette was convinced of his error, by being instantly repulsed, and losing what cannon he had brought with him.

The army having been passed over, marched on the 9th towards Portsmouth. On its halting at Suffolk, the Queen's Rangers being ordered for embarkation, proceeded to the vicinity of Portsmouth on the 14th, and embarked on the 20th. The embarkation of which, the Queen's Rangers made a part, was supposed to be intended to cooperate in an attack on Philadelphia. It was countermanded, and the troops, sailing up the river, landed at York Town on the 2nd of August, the Rangers being of the first disembarkation, under Lt. Col. Abercrombie.

Several patrols were made from York Town to Williamsburg, by the cavalry of the Queen's Rangers, latterly under the command of Capt. Shank, the health of Lt. Col. Simcoe being much impaired.

This journal, hastening to a conclusion, it is proper that it may be completed, to take notice of Capt. Saunders, and the officers, and chosen men, whom he had taken with him, in order to complete his troop, on General Leslie's expedition; and this cannot be better accomplished than by extracts from a letter which that officer wrote to Lt. Col. Simcoe.

Agreeable to your desire, I now detail some anecdotes of the detachment which was sent under my command with Gen. Leslie.

On the evening of the arrival of the fleet in Lynnhaven bay, I was ordered by Gen. Leslie to land with a detachment, consisting of a subaltern's command of the guards, and the officers and twelve men of my troop, and to march through Princess Ann, for the purpose of taking some of the most violent leaders of the rebels, in that county; but the great swell of the sea obliging me to land in a different place from which I had intended, I was, in consequence, constrained to cross the Lynnhaven inlet, which was unfordable. Knowing that there was a canoe about half a mile on the other side, I asked if anyone would volunteer the service of fetching it. Sergeant Burt instantly offered himself, and, with his sword in his mouth, plunged into the water, swam over and brought the canoe, in which we crossed, and this he did although, on our arrival at the inlet, we had observed a man on horseback, who appeared from the precipitancy with which he had rode off, to have been placed there as a vidette.

A few days after this, I was sent with a detachment, under the orders of Col. Schutz, to Suffolk, by Sleepy-hole ferry. We crossed the ferry at night, and by preceding (under cover of the darkness) with my troop, the rest of the detachment, I collected a sufficient number of horses to mount both men and officers. From Suffolk we returned to Portsmouth, when I requested General Leslie to permit me to occupy the post at Kemp's landing, with the two officers and the non-commissioned officers, and twelve private dragoons of my troop, which he granted, after I had explained to him my intimate knowledge of the people, and of the country. With this force I remained there until the General was obliged to embark for South Carolina.

On our arrival at Charles Town, Colonel Balfour ordered my officers and men up to George Town; and, as he told me that he had not authority to permit the return of myself and party to the regiment, I found it necessary to go to Wynnesburg (180 miles) where Lord Cornwallis was encamped, to solicit his leave. He granted it. I returned to Charles Town, and had the men in the boat, to embark in the *Romulus*, when the arrival of the express with Tarleton's disaster at the Cowpens, induced Col. Balfour to countermand the embarkation, and to detain us till the impression made by this unfortunate event should be done away. He ordered me and my troop to George Town, promising not only to explain to you the necessity of my detention, but also that it should not be long: I went there, and soon after obtained the command of that post. But before I mention what happened under my orders, I shall premise the behaviour of the troop, prior to this, when Lieut. Wilson had the command of it.

On the 25th December, 1780, being the day after Lieut. Wilson's arrival at George Town, he and his party made a patrol, under the command of Col. Campbell of Fanning's corps, when they fell in with a party of above fifty mounted rebels, which they were ordered to charge. They immediately did it, and with effect, defeating them and taking one of their officers prisoner. The others owed their escape to the speed of their horses, and the thickness of the wood. Lieut. Wilson was wounded; he received the thanks of Col. Campbell for his conduct in the following words: "It is with pleasure that the Commanding Officer observes the spirit and gallantry of the troops in general, but is infinitely obliged to Capt. Blucke and Lieut. Wilson, for their distinguished gallantry and behaviour this day. Laments much the wound received by the latter, as it may for a few days deprive him of the services of a good officer."

On the 6th January following, Lt. Col. Campbell having marched some distance into the country, saw about a dozen mounted men in the road: he ordered Lieut. Wilson with his party to charge them. They instantly went to the right about, and retreated with precipitation within a corps which had dismounted and taken a strong and advantageous post in a swampy thick wood on each side of the road. Lt. Wilson and his party received a heavy and unexpected fire from this ambuscade, but impelled by their wonted spirit and intrepidity, and unaccustomed to defeat, they continued the charge and obliged the rebels to betake themselves to their horses, and to flight. Sergeants Burt and Hudgins, having charged through them, were carried off by them; Corporal Hudgins was killed, covered with wounds; two or three of the men were wounded, and three horses killed.

Among a variety of other parties sent into the country by me, in order to prevent, as much as possible, depredation and violence by small bodies of rebels, who occasionally infested the vicinity of George Town, Lt. Wilson was ordered, about the middle of February, 1781, to go about forty miles up the Waccama river, with a detachment of between thirty and forty men, in order to take Capt. Clarke, a very active officer, prisoner, who was said to have a small party with him, for the purpose of protecting himself and oppressing the inhabitants on Waccama neck; he was ordered also, to mount his party, if possible, and to return by land. He set out in the evening with the first of the tide, and would have reached Clarke's house before day had it not been for a heavy fall of rain up the country, which checked the tide with such force, that, notwithstanding every effort, he found at daylight that he had not proceeded above half way. He therefore landed, sent back the boats, and lay concealed in a house till evening, keeping every passenger prisoner. He then marched to Clarke's house, which he reached before daylight, took him prisoner, but found none of his party then with him; took horses sufficient to mount his party, and returned, without loss, to George Town.

In the latter end of February, Cornet Merrit was ordered, with a party of a sergeant and ten dragoons, to cover some negroes who were sent to the neighbouring plantations to search for and bring in some cattle that had escaped from us. He, from his great zeal and anxiety to accomplish this service, was led rather farther than was intended, when he unexpectedly fell in with a corps of the rebels, much superior to his both in the number and the goodness of their horses.

A Light Infantryman and Hussar of the Queen's Rangers

He retreated, in good order, for some distance, but, finding himself much harassed from the fire of their advance, and seeing that it would be impracticable to get off without giving them a check, he determined on charging them, which he did several times, and with such vigour that he always repulsed them. He thus alternately charged and retreated, till having had two horses killed under him, he was so stunned by the fall of the last, that he was left for dead. The rebels were so awed by their repeated repulses, that they suffered his party to escape into the woods, when, by dismounting and concealing themselves in the thick savannahs, most of them got safe into the post. The sergeant was killed, and four men were wounded; several horses killed. Merrit, being supposed to be dead, was fortunate enough, after having recovered his senses, to get to the fort with the loss of his boots, helmet, and arms.

Cornet Merrit having been sent, about the beginning of March, with a flag, to carry a letter to Gen. Marion, by order of Col. Balfour, was detained a prisoner to retaliate for the detention of one Capt. Postell, who, after the surrender of Charles Town, had taken a protection and the oaths to us; and had, notwithstanding again taken up arms, and had the impudence to come to George Town, with a flag of truce, where I detained him. They crammed Merrit, with about twenty others, Sergeants and privates of different British regiments, in a small, nasty, dark place, made of logs, called a bull-pen; but he was not long here before he determined to extricate himself and his fellow prisoners, which he thus effected. After having communicated his intention to them, and found them ready to support him, he pitched upon the strongest and most daring soldier, and having waited some days for a favourable opportunity, he observed that his guards (militia) were much alarmed, which he found was occasioned by a party of British having come into that neighbourhood. He then ordered this soldier to seize the sentry, who was posted at a small square hole cut through the logs, and which singly served the double purposes of door and window, which he instantly executed, drawing the astonished sentry to this hole with one hand, and threatening to cut his throat with a large knife which he held in the other, if he made the smallest resistance, or out-cry. Then Cornet Merrit, and the whole party, crawled out the one after the other, undiscovered by the guard, though it was in the day time, until the whole had got out. He then drew them up, which the officer of the guard observing, got his men under arms, as fast as he could, and threatened to fire on them if they attempted to go off. Merrit replied, that if he dared to fire a single shot at him, that he would cut the whole of his guard to pieces, (having concerted with his men in such a case, to rush upon the enemy and tear their arms out of their hands,) which so intimidated him, that, although Merrit's party was armed only with the spoils of the sentry and with clubs, he yet permitted them to march off, unmolested, to a river at some distance, where Cornet Merrit knew, from conversation which he had had with the sentries, that there was a large rice-boat, in which he embarked and brought his party through a country of above fifty miles safe into George Town.

To you the undaunted spirit and bravery of this young man, is not unknown; they obtained for him in his distress your friendship and protection. Col. Balfour was pleased to approve his conduct, and in a letter to me, dated Charles Town 2nd April, 1781, expresses it then: "I rejoice most sincerely that your Cornet has escaped, his conduct and resolution does him great credit, and I wish I had it in my power to show him my sense of it by more substantial marks than this testimony; but the only mode I have is by offering him a Lieutenancy of a provincial troop." This Cornet Merrit declined.

Lt. Wilson was sent, on the 2nd of April, with twenty men, attended by a galley, to cover a party sent to load some flats with forage, at a plantation on Black river. He debarked and remained on shore several hours before he saw a single rebel; but when he had nearly completed his business, he was attacked by above sixty of them, under the command of a Major Benson. He repulsed them in two attempts that they made to get within the place where he had posted himself; he then charged and drove them off. A rebel Lieutenant was mortally wounded, several others slightly; Lt. Wilson and five of his men were wounded. Col. Balfour expressed his approbation of Wilson's conduct in this affair.

I shall conclude this detail with mentioning one more instance of the gallant behaviour of Merrit, which it would be injustice to omit. Being obliged in an attack I made, on the rebel partisan Snipe, to approach the house in which he had his party, through a narrow lane, terminated within half musket shot of the house by a strong gate, which, I expected, would detain us some time to open; when it was probable their guard would fire on us; and, as I was particularly anxious to prevent any kind of check with the troops I then had with me, I picked out Merrit, Corporal Franks, and four men of my troop to proceed and make an opening for the detachment, which he effected with such readiness and spirit, that the passage was cleared by the time that the detachment could get up, although, for that purpose, he had been obliged to dismount his party under the fire from their guard, and that the gate and fence, on each side of it, had been secured and strengthened, with an unexpected degree of care and attention. Col. Balfour writing to me in the month of April, when I commanded at George Town, says:"being empowered by Lord Cornwallis to raise a troop of Provincial light dragoons, I have, for some time, wished to try your Lt. Wilson as Captain, and this gentleman as Lieutenant, (meaning Cornet Merrit,) they have been both recommended as good and active officers, and, if you agree with me in opinion that a troop could be raised in or near George Town, I should have no hesitation in making the appointment."

Thus I have mentioned to you a few of the many meritorious services performed by the officers and men of my troop, when in Virginia and South Carolina. I regret much at my not having kept a journal during that time, as it would now enable me to do more ample justice to those whose zeal, bravery and good conduct, entitle them to my fullest and fairest report.

It is to be lamented that Capt. Saunders did not keep a regular journal, as it would have related a series of gallant and active services, which he performed when in the command at George Town, and afterwards at Dorchester, and which strongly characterize in that officer the same boldness and prudence with which he maintained himself with his small party in his native country, where his decisive character had its due weight and superiority.

Chapter 26

Defeated but Unbowed

On the 12th of August the Rangers passed to Gloucester, to cover the foraging in front of that post, which the
80th and the Hessian regiment of Prince Hereditaire garrisoned, under the command of Lieut. Col. Dundas.

The climate, the sickly state and condition of the corps,
as more fully detailed in the appendix, and what was reasonably to be apprehended from the militia of the enemy,
now assembling in numbers, rendered this a service of great
fatigue and danger: the troops were generally employed on
it twelve hours in the twenty-four. The infantry, to secure
them from the intense heat, were ambuscaded as much as
possible in the woods, and the cavalry patrolled in their
front, or on their flanks.

Lt. Col. Simcoe, on his return one day from Abington
church, was informed that Weeks, now styled Major, with a
party of the enemy, had just arrived within a few miles. He
instantly pressed on with the cavalry to attack him, ordering Capt. Ewald to proceed to his support as fast as possible
with the Yagers and infantry. On his arrival near the post,
he had the good fortune to push a patrol, which came from
it, so rapidly as to follow it into the house where Weeks
lay, who, with his men, escaped in great confusion into the
woods, leaving their dinner behind them. An officer and

some men were made prisoners, and this check, together with the country being constantly ambuscaded, prevented the foragers from receiving the least interruption.

One morning as the foragers were at some distance from Gloucester, they were surprised at hearing a considerable firing of musketry, between them and the garrison. It was suspected that some party of the enemy might have stolen through the woods; but on a detachment falling back to procure certain intelligence, it appeared, that some men on a predatory party had landed from the shipping, and, being panic-struck, had fired at a wood where they fancied they saw the enemy. Sergeant Ritchie, of the grenadiers of the Rangers, who with the other convalescents had been left in the camp at Gloucester, on hearing the firing, supposed that the regiment was engaged, and assembling such men as were able to move, to the amount of thirty or more, he marched forward, and took up a piece of ground that would have been highly advantageous in case of real action. So spirited were the soldiers, so able were the non-commissioned officers become, by perpetual service and experience!

On the 31st of August, the advance ships of the French fleet blocked up the York river. The cavalry of the Queen's Rangers had been regularly instructed in wheeling and forming in the closest order possible, and they were disciplined in everything that might enable them to maintain that superiority which they had hitherto acquired over all their opponents. It being of the utmost consequence to prevent the enemy gaining any information from deserters, the out sentries were constantly composed of a cavalry and infantry man.

Earl Cornwallis, in a conversation with Lieut.-Col. Simcoe, asked him whether he "thought that he could escape with the cavalry?"

He answered his Lordship, "Without the smallest doubt."

Gen. Washington invested York Town on the 23rd of September; when the blockade of Gloucester was formed by one thousand one hundred French troops, joined with the rebel militia, under the command of Mons. de Choisy, so well known for his surprisal of Cracow. Captain Shank, with thirty huzzars, retreated before them as they advanced, and close to the Duke of Lauzun's legion.

The French ships that blocked the mouth of York river were driven from their station, and narrowly escaped being destroyed by fire-ships, commanded by Capt. Palmer of the navy. This gallant officer would have probably burnt a man of war which was driven ashore, but he was prevented by the misbehaviour of a master of a privateer, who, as might be expected from people of his vile trade, prematurely set on fire one of the small vessels which he had volunteered the direction of and which were to accompany the King's ship, at such a distance as could neither endanger the enemy, or himself.

The out piquet which the Queen's Rangers occupied was on a high bank on the left, close to the York river, which in front was almost inaccessible from a cove into which the tide flowed. This post was maintained at night on the commencement of the blockade; but it was soon attempted to be carried off. Captain Shaw, who commanded, overheard the enemy on their approach, and withdrawing his sentinels and party to a bank in its rear, let them without molestation possess themselves of his fires, when, giving them an unexpected discharge, they fled in great confusion, and with every appearance of several of them being wounded, leaving firearms, caps, and accoutrements behind them. Captain Shaw then resumed his post, which was constantly occupied in the day, and frequently at night, without any further attempt being made upon it.

The health of Lieut. Col. Simcoe began now totally to fail under the incessant fatigues, both of body and mind, which for years he had undergone.

Lt. Col. Tarleton with his cavalry passed over from York to Gloucester.

Lt. Col. Simcoe observed, in conversation with Col. Dundas, that as Capt Shank had faced the Duke of Lauzun with the cavalry of the Rangers the preceding day, it was probable the Duke would not hesitate to attack them, being acquainted with the inferiority of their numbers, when, if Lt. Col. Tarleton's corps, of whose arrival he must be ignorant, should be placed in ambuscade, the Duke's legion might be swept off and totally ruined.

Lt. Col. Tarleton marched out with the cavalry the next morning, Col. Dundas accompanying him; and about mid-day firing was heard, and some people galloped in in great confusion. One of the forage-masters saying Col. Tarleton was defeated, Lt. Col. Simcoe sent him to Earl Cornwallis, ordered the troops to their post, and, being carried from his bed to his horse, went himself to the redoubt occupied by the Rangers.

Capt Shank, on his return, reported to Lt. Col. Simcoe, that being on the left when the line was formed he had received no orders; but when the right, composed of the legion, advanced to charge, he did the same, in close order, but necessarily not in equal front. On the legion giving way, the Rangers followed, quitting the field the last, and in such order as prevented a rapid pursuit, and returned to the charge with Lt. Col. Tarleton, when he, having again offered the enemy combat, which they declined, remained master of the field.

Lt. Col. Dundas being ordered to York Town, Lt. Col. Simcoe, on whom the command of Gloucester devolved, was obliged from total want of health, to give up its duties to Lt. Col. Tarleton.

The most disagreeable that could befall an officer now drew nigh. The works at York Town were rendered untenable by the superior fire of the French artillery, and Earl Cornwallis determined to attempt to escape with the best part of his troops by the way of Gloucester. A principal part of his force was sent over to that place, and Lt. Col. Simcoe was informed that his Lordship meant to attack Mons. de Choisy the next morning. There was every probability of surprising that officer, as he in some measure depended upon the vigilance of the militia joined with him; and a spy, who came into Gloucester almost to the very day of its surrender, could have conducted the Queen's Rangers by the secret path which he made use of, to the rear of the enemy's post.

It was not improbable that his Lordship, on viewing the advantageous position which might be occupied in front of Gloucester, would have been of opinion that the post might at the least have been defended for ten days, if the provisions would last, against any force the enemy could combine to attack it within that period. A violent storm arising, prevented the succeeding division of the garrison of York from passing over; that which had arrived returned early in the morning, and the firing soon after ceasing, it was understood that Earl Cornwallis had proposed a cessation of hostilities, for the purpose of settling the terms on which the posts of York and Gloucester were to be surrendered.

On the first confirmation of this supposition, Lt. Col. Simcoe sent Lt. Spencer to his Lordship, to request that as his corps consisted of loyalists, the objects of the enemy's civil persecution, and deserters, if the treaty was not finally concluded, that he would permit him to endeavour to escape with them in some of those boats which Gen. Arnold had built; and that his intention was to cross the

Chesapeake and land in Maryland, when, from his knowledge of the inhabitants of the country and other favourable circumstances, he made no doubt of being able to save the greatest part of the corps and carry them into New York.

His Lordship was pleased to express himself favourably in regard to the scheme, but said he could not permit it to be undertaken, for that the whole of the army must share one fate.

The capitulation was signed on the 19th of October.

Earl Cornwallis, on account of Lieut. Col. Simcoe's dangerous state of health, permitted him to sail for New York in the *Bonetta*, which by an article in the capitulation was to be left at his disposal, a sea-voyage being the only chance, in the opinion of the physicians, by which he could save his life.

On board of this vessel sailed as many of the Rangers, and of other corps, deserters from the enemy, as she could possibly hold; they were to be exchanged as prisoners of war, and the remainder of Earl Cornwall's army were marched prisoners into the country.

Lt. Col. Simcoe, on his arrival at New York, was permitted by Sir Henry Clinton to return to England; and his Majesty, on the 19th December, 1781, was graciously pleased to confer upon him the rank of Lieutenant-Colonel in the army, the duties and title of which he had enjoyed from the year 1777, and which had been made permanent to him in America in 1779.

Capt. Saunders arriving from Charles Town, took the command of that part of the corps which had come to New York in the *Bonetta*. Many of the soldiers, who were prisoners in the country, were seized as deserters from Mr. Washington's army, several enlisted in it to facilitate their escape, and, being caught in the attempt, were executed. A greater number got safe to New York, and, had the war continued, there was little doubt but the corps would have been re-assembled in detail. The Rangers were so daring and active in their attempts to escape, that, latterly, they were confined in gaol; Capt Whitlock, who commanded them while prisoners in the country, was one of the Captains who drew lots with Captain Asgil to suffer for Huddy's death.

Capt Saunders, and the officers who were with him, had to experience severe mortifications. Sir Henry Clinton, the Commander in Chief, who knew their services, had returned to England, and was succeeded by Sir Guy Carleton. It being apparent that the American war was to be abandoned, they had no longer the certainty of recommending themselves by their services to the protection of the new General. On the 31st of March, 1783, the following order was transmitted from the Adjutant-General's Office, to the officer who commanded the regiment: as it is presumed to be a singular event in military history, it is here published, verbatim, and with no other comment than that which accompanied it as it was transmitted to Lt. Col. Simcoe, then in England:

Adjutant-General's Office
March 31, 1783

Sir—Lt. Col. Thompson having received orders to complete the regiment under his command by volunteers from the different Provincial corps, and to raise in like manner four additional companies of light infantry, for a particular service; the Commander in Chief desires you would give all possible assistance to Lt. Col. Thompson and those concerned with him in the execution of this business, by encouraging the men belonging to the corps under your command to engage in this service, and his Excellency directs me to assure you that neither the officers nor others who may remain with you in the corps shall suffer any loss or any injury to their pretensions by the diminution of your numbers arising from the volunteers who may join the corps under the command of Lieut. Col. Thompson. It is to be understood, that though the men wanted for this service are to engage as soon as possible, yet they are not to quit the regiments to which they at present belong, till further orders.

(Signed) *Ol. Delancy*, &c.

I will only say that though as military men they could not publicly reprobate and counteract this unjust, humiliating, and disgraceful order, yet conscious of their superiority both in rank, in life, and in military service to the person whom it was meant to aggrandise, they could not but sensibly feel it. I am sorry to say that some of the Rangers, being made drunk, were induced to volunteer it. The arrival of the last packet, as it took away the pretence of their being for "some particular service," has put a total stop to this business. The warrant, I am told, specified that when this corps was completed and embarked, they were from that time to be on the British establishment.

The officers of the Queen's Rangers had prided themselves, and justly, in preventing, as much as officers by precept, example, and authority could do, plundering and marauding. Being cantoned with other corps on Long Island, the depredations which were committed, drew upon the Queen's Rangers the displeasure of Sir Guy Carleton, and the denunciation of his precluding the officers from their just promotion. Capt Saunders, who then commanded them, conscious that they were innocent, as became his character and station, addressed the following letter to the Commander in Chief:

Sir—I take the liberty, as commanding officer of that part of the Queen's Rangers at Huntingdon, to address your Excellency. A letter received from Col. de Wurmb, containing your very severe reprehension of their conduct, in consequence of representations made to your Excellency of their frequent depredations, is the cause.

Myself and officers, conscious of the falsehood and malevolence of those representations, feel ourselves highly injured, and as the charge materially affects the honour and reputation of the corps, we hope and request that your Excellency will be pleased to order an enquiry into this matter, so that we may have an opportunity of meeting our accusers face to face, and of removing from your Excellency's breast the impression that has been made so disadvantageous to us.

No answer was returned to this application, and a very young officer who had not seen any service, was promoted from another corps to a troop vacant in the Queen's Rangers.

Soon after the above-mentioned letter was written it was proved before a court martial, that those depredations, which had drawn down upon the Rangers the Commander in Chief's indignation, had been committed by men of the legion and for which they suffered.

Everything now tended to the American colonies being declared independent of Great Britain, and the officers of the Queen's Rangers seem to have been oppressed with every circumstance that could wound the hearts of men who were soldiers on the best principles, except the consciousness of not having deserved it; but this cloud was soon to pass away.

General Conway was Commander in Chief of his Majesty's forces, and Sir H. Clinton had arrived in England; Sir

Charles Grey was appointed to succeed Sir Guy Carleton, Lieut. Col. Simcoe, whose exchange Government had procured from Dr. Franklin, was to have accompanied him as secretary to his commission, a post that he hoped to fill to the approbation of that General, who was ready, had it been necessary, to have supported those claims of the Queen's Rangers for British rank and establishment, which Sir H. Clinton had personally recommended to the protection of General Conway, and this he had done in the strongest manner, not only as due to the fidelity and actions of a corps which he had been an eye-witness of, but " in justice to his country," as he was pleased to express himself, "that, in case of future war, it might not be deprived of the services of such a number of excellent officers."

These representations had their due effect, and on the 25th of December, 1782, his Majesty was graciously pleased to make that rank universally permanent which they had hitherto only held in the scene of action, America—and the Queen's Rangers, cavalry and infantry, were honourably enrolled in the British army. The corps was disbanded at the ensuing peace, and many of the officers, and most of the soldiers, settled on the lands to which they had a claim in Nova Scotia.

Thus concludes the principal events in a journal of a corps of light troops, whose services care best be estimated by observing, that for years in the field, to use the language of a former age, they were the *forlorn of the armies in which they served,* and that even in *winter quarters,* when in common wars troops are permitted to seek repose, few hours can be selected in which the Queen's Rangers had not to guard against the attacks of a skilful and enterprising enemy.

Appendix of Such Letters, Papers and Observations as are Necessary to Illustrate this Journal

WHEN SIR WILLIAM HOWE QUITTED THE COMMAND
OF THE ARMY MAJOR SIMCOE LAID THE FOLLOWING
MEMORIAL BEFORE HIM, WHICH HE PROMISED
TO SUPPORT ON HIS RETURN TO ENGLAND

Your memorialists, with all submission and respect, beg leave to entreat your Excellency will lay them at his Majesty's feet, humbly soliciting that he, in his gracious favour, will be pleased to establish them in the rank of the army, as has been given to the regiments now raising in Great Britain.

The generality of the officers, who now request your Excellency's countenance, at the breaking out of the present rebellion; left their estates and settlements in Virginia, joined his Excellency Lord Dunmore, and underwent with him all the vicissitudes of service, till his junction with the army at Staten Island. The Queen's Rangers being intended for active employ, your Excellency was pleased to appoint your memorialists, on account of their being more experienced in actual service, to supersede the generality of those who were its officers: how far your Excellency's favourable opinion of them has been justified, the subsequent behaviour of the corps in the Jersies, at the battle of Brandywine, and during a variety of fatiguing and detail services on which they have been employed in the course of the late winter, must testify.

Attached to his Majesty and the cause of their country, from the purest motives, habituated to the fatigues of war, and ambitious of exerting themselves in it, confident that the men they command are disciplined equal to the important service of the light troops with whom they have constantly served, and conscious that, should they obtain their desired rank, their conduct will neither disgrace it as Gentlemen and as Officers; your memorialists humbly hope that your Excellency will patronize their request, and that your intercession will induce his Majesty to look favourably on their petition, and to mark his approbation of their services by conferring on them the honour of enrolling with the army.

A GENERAL PLAN OF DEFENCE WAS CALCULATED FOR THE WHOLE, THE GENERAL ORDERS WERE, IN CASE OF ALARM, THE FOLLOWING ARE TO BE THE POSTS OF THE DIFFERENT COMPANIES

Captains M'Rae and Kerr's companies (supposed to be the right) to maintain their barrack, Capt. M'Rae's above and Capt. Kerr's below stairs.

Capt Dunlop's company to occupy the right hand sunken fleche, Capt. Saunders the left; whichever of those companies gains its post first, to be divided and occupy both fleches, till the arrival of the other: Captain Smith's to occupy the sunken work in front of the Artillery barrack. The huzzars will be provided with arms, and are to gain the fleche on the left of Capt Smith's, nor are they to think of their horses till ordered to get them by a field officer, or the senior officer within the second abatis, who commands the whole of the out-works and redoubt.

Captains Stevenson and Shank's companies to retreat on the heights to the one tree hill, and to act according to emergency, retreating from if attacked, recoiling on the enemy. if they retreat, and falling on their rear if they attempt to force the redoubt.

The grenadiers, the highlanders, and the piquet of cavalry, to join the light infantry at their barracks.

The guards to retreat and join the first company under arms; if attacked to keep up a galling fire.

All soldiers, whether officers' servants or others, whom their commanding officers permit to lie out of their barracks, are to have their arms with them, and to join the first party under arms that they meet The most profound silence to be kept, and the Lt. Colonel recommends it to the officers not to fire if possible; but of the necessity they must judge themselves: whatever quarter is attacked, must be defended. The first officer that gets to his company, to march to its post Every quarter will be fortified as soon as possible: every soldier must have his post in it: their arms must be arranged, and bayonets always fixed, and the doors barricaded; when the barracks are finished, the commanding officers must report to the Lt. Colonel, who will inspect them. The officer in the redoubt, in case from necessity or intention the regiment shall not join him, must maintain his post. If he cannot keep the platforms, he is to dismount his cannon, and bring them into his guard-house, which he is to defend, unless attacked by cannon, with his life.

The officers commanding companies will copy such orders as relate to themselves only, and inform their subalterns of them; and it is their duty to ask for an explanation of such parts as they do not perfectly understand, both in this and all other situations—no soldier, or non-commissioned officer, to be acquainted with these orders.

ON LT. COL. SIMCOE'S
CAPTURE AND IMPRISONMENT

Lt. Col. Simcoe had many providential escapes. Marrener prevented a boy from bayoneting him, as he lay senseless on the ground, saying "let him alone the rascal is dead enough;"

and another person regretted that he had not shot him through the head, which he would have done had he known him to be a Colonel, but he thought "all Colonels wore lace." The sensations which he felt. as he gradually awakened into recollection, and heard distant shouts and scattered firing, and saw what hands he had fallen into; and, when recovering more perfectly, his situation, and all his professional hopes rushed at once upon his mind, are better felt than described. He had other dangers to surmount, the populace were driven to fury by the death of Capt. Vorhees; and he was shown a letter from a field officer of the Jersey militia, in which was the following paragraph: "It was intended to bring Col. Simcoe to Captain Vorhees' grave, to show him the cruelty of his people, but I could not answer it."

The soldiers, who had been taken, were with difficulty preserved by Mr. Clarkson, Mr. Morris (who bled Lt. Col. Simcoe) and other gentlemen, from assassination: and Governor Livingston, after making "a little harangue," as he termed it, to the populace, thought it necessary to give to Lt. Col. Simcoe the following written protection:

> The Governor being informed, that some people have a design to abuse and insult Lt. Colonel Simcoe, a British captive, and wounded in a skirmish that happened this day, between our militia and the British horse: though the Governor is not inclined to believe a report that would infer so great a disgrace upon the people of this state, as that of the least inclination of revenge against a wounded enemy in our power; yet to prevent the execution of any such attempt, it is his express orders to treat the said officer according to the rules of war, known and practised among all civilised nations; and as it is his desire to be carried to Brunswick, it is his further orders, that no molestation be given to him in his being carried thither, and that,

while there, he be treated with that humanity which the United States of America have always observed towards their prisoners.

William Livingston

Brunswick Landing, 2nd Oct. 1779

N. B. Mr. Alexander Kellock having come with a flag, as a surgeon, to take care of Colonel Simcoe and a Sergeant, and also Edward Heifernon, his servant, are to attend him unmolested. *William Livingston.*

It would be unjust not to mention that some people of Brunswick, to whom Lt. Col. Simcoe, when Captain of grenadiers, had it in his power to be of service, remembered the protection and in arms volunteered to assist Major Navios in preserving him from insult. It is with great pleasure Lt. Col. Simcoe has preserved the following letter, which he received from Lt. Wilson:

Richmond, Oct 28, 1779

Yesterday, and part of the day before, there was nothing but the picture of distress in every countenance; but this morning the soldiers are shouting "the father of the Rangers is alive." In short, nothing can exceed the joy which appears in the countenance of officers and soldiers, and prayers for your speedy recovery; but none can possibly be more sincere than those of, &c.

J. Wilson

On the 26th Lt. Col. Simcoe was removed on parole to Borden Town, to a tavern kept by Col. Hoogland of the Jersey militia, by whom he was treated with great civility. The principal people of Borden Town were very violent, in particular Messrs. Borden and Kirkbride. Lt. Col. Simcoe, in the son of the former, recollected the officer whose life he had probably saved; and the circumstances were so well known that the fact was acknowledged; but this did not contribute to lessen the illiberal treatment he met with, and the umbrage which the inhabitants took at seeing him and Mr. Kellock walk about was such, that he soon confined himself to the house.

Col. Lee had written to offer Lt. Col. Simcoe pecuniary assistance; as Lt. Campbell, of the 74th regiment, who was on parole at Prince Town, had kindly supplied him, he had declined the acceptance of Col. Lee's civility.

During his captivity here were many reports spread of Lt. Col. Simcoe's cruelties; and some rebel justices were anxious for affidavits to support them; but the direct contrary was the case; many of their party in Pennsylvania offering to give ample testimony of Lt. Col. Simcoe's humanity, and speaking most favourably of his conduct, while in that province.

On the 6th of November he received the following letter from Col. Lee:

Monmouth, 6th Nov. 1779

Sir,—I am happy to hear by your polite reply, to an offer dictated by the feelings of man for man, that you had already been supplied in cash by the friendship of a brother officer; should you hereafter stand in need of that article. I assure myself, you will not suffer your want to continue long. From some insinuations I have heard, and from a paragraph in the last Trenton Gazette, I apprehend your local situation not the most agreeable—perhaps you may wish a remove; of course must address the Governor; being employed in a similar line by our respective Generals; it may not be amiss to appeal to me, should his Excellency require contradiction to the reports propagated prejudicial to your character. I am a stranger to what officer the barbarities exercised on some captured militia in Bucks county, Pennsylvania, can be truly attributed. I have never heard yourself declared as the author, and am led to believe you was not present: the unhappy sacrifice of Captain Vorhees in the late enterprise, I am told, took place after you fell.

Your treatment of one of my dragoons, who fell into your hands last campaign, was truly generous, and then made an impression on my mind which it still retains. Anxious to prevent injustice being done to the unfortunate, I have been particular in this letter, though I please myself in presuming that it will be unnecessary. Your most obedient humble servant,

H. Lee, Jun.

Lt. Col. Simcoe made his acknowledgments to Col. Lee, and in regard to the affair at the Billet, informed him, that he planned the attack on General Lacy; but that no cruelties whatever were committed by the Queen's Rangers.

On the 7th of November, Governor Livingston came to Borden Town; from his conversation Lt. Col. Simcoe had hopes of an immediate exchange: he was therefore much surprised the next evening, on the arrival of a militia party conducting Col. Billop of the Loyal militia of Staten Island, to be accosted by the Sergeant who commanded it, and informed that he was a prisoner, and must be confined, and marched the next morning to Burlington jail. Col. Hoogland with great humanity interfered, and, upon their paroles, carried Cols. Billop and Simcoe in his own light wagon to Burlington the next morning. Mr. Kellock, who accompanied them thither, returned, as he must have also been confined, which Lt. Col. Simcoe by no means would permit. Lt. Col. Simcoe, his servant and M'Gill, who had come from Staten Island, were confined, and no person was admitted to speak to them.

Col. Billop was treated as the following mittimus directed, and received at the same time a letter from Boudinot, the Commissary of Prisoners.

To the Keeper of the Common Jail for the county of Burlington

Greeting—You are hereby commanded to receive into your custody, the body of Col. Christopher Billop, prisoner of war, herewith delivered to you, and having put irons on his hands and feet, you are to chain him down to the floor in a close room, in the said jail; and there so detain him, giving him bread and water only for his food, until you receive further orders from me, or the commissary of Prisoners for the State of New Jersey, for the time being.

Given under my hand at Elizabeth Town, this 6th day of Nov. 1779

Elisha Boudinot

Com. Pris. New Jersey

Sir,—Sorry I am that I have been put under the disagreeable necessity of a treatment towards your person that will prove so irksome to you; but retaliation is directed, and it will, I most sincerely hope, be in your power to relieve yourself from the situation by writing to New York, to procure the relaxation of the sufferings of John Leshier, and Capt. Nathaniel Randal. It seems, nothing short of retaliation will teach Britons to act like men of humanity.

I am, sir, your most humble servant,

Elisha Boudinot

Com. S. Pris. Elizabeth Town, Nov. 6, 1779

Col. Christopher Billop, Burlington

John Leshier had murdered a Loyalist, whom he had waylaid, and, in the room of being instantly executed as a murderer, and as he deserved, was confined in irons. Nathaniel Randal was the skipper of a vessel, being a private militia man he was not permitted his parole, which indulgence is only extended to officers. Col. Billop, who was to retaliate for these people, was a gentleman of most excellent character, and considerable property; who, in the House of Assembly, where he had a seat, had uniformly opposed those measures which led to a rupture with Great Britain; and, on the breaking out of the war, had accepted of the commission of Colonel of the Staten Island militia: so that nothing could possibly suggest to Boudinot the reflection he made on the national humanity, but that he could do it with impunity; and that it did not misbecome his birth and extraction, being the son of a low Frenchman, who kept an ale-house at Prince Town. His brother has been President of Congress.

There were two soldiers of the guards in Burlington jail, they had been taken prisoners in Pennsylvania, and confined in Fort Frederick, from whence they had made their escape; but being re-taken, were imprisoned. They had no provisions allowed them, but depended upon the precarious charity of a few friends for subsistence. Lt. Col. Simcoe represented their situation to the sheriff, which their emaciated appearance fully confirmed; in consequence, they were shortly after removed from Burlington.

Col. Lee still continued his generous attention; and to the utmost of his power supported the request which Lt. Col. Simcoe had made, to be permitted to go on parole to Staten Island, as the following letter will evince.

Monmouth, 14th Nov. 1779

Sir,—I have received an answer from Gov. Livingston, to my letter of request, in your behalf. I was very particular in my address, and, although I cannot congratulate myself on its full success, I flatter myself it will lead to the completion of your wishes. The following is an extract from the Governor's letter:

> Col. Simcoe's treatment by this state is not founded on his character. We think it our indispensable duty to retaliate the enemy's severity to some of our citizens in New York; but that such treatment should, however, happen to be exercised on a person of whom you entertain so favourable an opinion, (besides the disagreeableness of such measures at any time,) is particularly afflictive to, &c. &c. &c.

From the above declaration I presume, that your parole may be procured, in a few days, if any expectation can be held out to the executive power of the State, tending to a liberation of any one of her citizens in New York.

Perhaps your presence with Sir Henry Clinton might affect an alteration in the measures complained of, and a system of perfect liberality might be established in future: if you will permit me to declare your determination on this point, and, if it answers my expectation, I will do myself the pleasure of waiting on the Governor in person, to attempt the full settlement of the unhappy business. I have, as yet, no reply from Mr. Boudinot, though his station does not promise much service, and therefore his opinion will be very unimportant. I have the honour to be, &c.

H. Lee, Jun.

Lt. Col. Simcoe answered Col. Lee's letter, and in that part which referred to the liberation of Randal, or Fitzrandolph, he assured Col. Lee, "that if that person had acted without a commission, as it was reported, and his opinion was asked by Sir Henry Clinton, it would be immediately to execute him, though he, on his return from Staten Island, should suffer the same fate by a retaliation, to use the Governor's phrase."

Gov. Livingston gave the following answer to Lt. Col. Simcoe's letter, demanding to know what persons would be received in exchange for him, and requesting his parole to Staten Island.

Mount Holly, Nov. 10th, 1779

Sir,—I have received your letter, without date. Your confinement, and the order relative to Col. Billop, is in consequence of the advice of the Privy Council; till they rescind their resolve, I am not at liberty to deviate from it; I hope, however, that you will not be disagreeably situated, except as to the confinement. The exchange proposed for you and Col. Billop (which is Col. Reynolds, Mr. Fitzrandolph, Leshier, and Jackson, and as many other privates as will make it equal) has, I suppose, before this time reached New York. If you are not soon released, it will be the fault of the British. For my part, I heartily wish it may be effected in the speediest manner, and not only for the sake of our citizens in captivity at New York, but also from sentiments of humanity towards Col. Billop and yourself, as I am not gratified by the sufferings of any man; and I am sure the Governor does not, and fully pursuaded the Council do not harbour any personal resentment against Col. Billop. Unfortunately for that gentleman, the treatment of some of our citizens in New York, has induced this State to consider retaliation their indispensable duty, and it is his particular misfortune to be in our possession at this melancholy juncture.

Respecting your request of going to Staten Island on your parole, I hope your exchange will be negotiated without it; and, for that purpose, any of your letters on that subject shall be cheerfully transmitted to New York, by Sir, your humble servant,

William Livingston

P. S. In answer to Dr. Kellock's letter, desiring to attend you as Surgeon, I have acquainted him that there is no objection, provided he consents to be confined with you.

Sir—I have just now the honour of receiving your letter; I am sorry you will not permit me to go to Staten Island, to negotiate mine and Col. Billop's exchange.

I shall embrace an opportunity of writing to New York; but I must first beg to be acquainted, whether Mr. Randolph is or is not a Captain? He being styled such in M. Boudinot's letter to Col. Billop.

I am also to beg, you will please to inform me for whom I am to retaliate, or for what I am confined? Such usage being most unprecedented.

As you are pleased to observe that no private resentment is harboured against Col. Billop, I wish to know whether there be any against me.

I should be happy to have an early answer, and am, sir, your humble servant,

J. G. Simcoe

Burlington Goal, Nov. 10th, 1779

P. S. I am not well acquainted with these matters, but I conceive the present proposition to be what last year Gen. Washington refused to exchange Gen. Burgoyne's army on when made by Sir Henry Clinton; and I should be glad to know the ranks of those people, with the number of privates, necessary to complete them to Col. Billop's rank.

Mount Holly, 11thNovember, 1779

Sir,—I have just now received your letter of yesterday's date.

As the particular mode of exchanging American for British prisoners will, I presume, not be insisted upon by Sir Henry Clinton in the present case; I hope no difference about his Excellency Gen. Washington and him will retard the effect of the present proposition, and it was for that very reason, if I rightly apprehended you, that you preferred your being considered as a prisoner to this state.

Mr. Fitzrandolph is no officer in our militia, but, nevertheless, of so respectable a character that we are universally solicitous for his release; and, though a gentleman of the strictest honour, has been treated with the greatest indignity by your superiors.

The rest of the persons proposed for exchange, save Col. Reynolds, are also privates. As to the additional number of privates necessary to make the exchange equal in consideration of your and Col. Billop's rank, it must be determined by military usage; which it will be easy for the two Commissaries to adjust, and no reasonable cause of obstruction will, I hope, originate from that source.

You also ask me for whom you are retaliated upon, and for what you are confined? Such usage being, as you are pleased to observe, most unprecedented. Considering, sir, that the confinement of our citizens, both officers and privates, when prisoners with the enemy, has been as uniformly directed as if it had been a matter of course, it ought not to appear wonderful, should we adopt the same mode of treatment, even without any view to retaliate; the precedent being set by our adversaries without the least pretence on their part of retaliating upon us. But when such measures are ordered by us for the express and sole purpose of relieving our suffering subjects, the impartial world must approve, and humanity itself, from their tendency to procure milder treatment, in the final result, be constrained to applaud them. Superadd to this, your counteracting the express terms of your parole at Borden Town, (I would wish to believe rather from your misconstruction than determinate design to violate it,) and your having been heard to say, that whenever you should apprehend yourself in danger of being insulted by the people, you should think yourself at liberty to effect your escape, (of which danger you doubtless intended to be judge,) not to mention that your present situation is your best security against all popular violence, in case there were any grounds for such apprehension; and, I doubt not, you will, on cooler reflection, find no reason to charge the step in question with any unnecessary severity.

To your question, whether private resentment is harboured against you? I answer, sir, that public bodies are not actuated by private resentment; but the actions of individuals of a public nature, such as cruelty to prisoners, may nevertheless properly occasion towards such individuals a line of conduct, very different from what is observed towards those of an opposite character, and this, with as little colour for complaining of personal resentment as of the civil magistrates punishing a public offender; but as no such charge has been proved, (though many have been alleged against you,) I have no reason to think that such reports have influenced this Government in the measures hitherto directed, concerning you.

The negotiating the exchange of prisoners being, by

our law, entirely committed to the Commissary, (though the Governor is authorised to superintend their treatment,) you will be pleased, sir, in your future correspondence on that subject to be referred to him; I do not mean by this to discourage you from making any necessary application, to, sir, your most humble servant,

William Livingston

Sir,—I must beg of you to forward the enclosed packet to Sir Henry Clinton.

I was pleased that I had fallen into the hands of the state of New Jersey, rather than into that of the Continental army, solely from the reliance I had on the assurances you gave me, that I probably should be exchanged in a few days, naming to me Colonels Reynolds or Hendrickson, as the likely persons.

I never heard of a Lt. Colonel's being taken from his parole, and confined in a common goal, because a private sentinel was imprisoned; and am at a loss, in such treatment, to find the meaning of retaliation.

You cannot force yourself to believe, sir, that I ever harboured a thought of violating my parole; although the principle of honour be very imperfectly felt among common people, no man, even in that class, would break his word, or suspect that a British officer dare do it, were he not himself divested of all probity.

I conceived at Borden Town, that I was at liberty to walk in its environs, according to military usage, for my health: Col. Hoogland, whom I consulted, was of the same opinion; I never exceeded a mile, and confined myself to my house when I found it was disagreeable. There being some difficulty in procuring a guard for my protection when at Rariton landing, I publicly told Major Navius, that *if my life was attacked* and I was not protected, I should think myself at liberty to escape, in the propriety of which he acquiesced: I never mentioned, sir, nor meant, in case I was insulted; many insults I have met with, which, as they deserved, I have treated with contempt. I should not have asked whether private resentment was harboured against me, had not you written, sir, that neither you or the council harboured any personal resentment against Colonel Billop; that gentleman's sufferings, and my own confinement, I must still conceive to be most severe and unprecedented. I am to observe, sir, that I never complained of personal resentment; I was far from thinking I had any reason to apprehend it; but it is my duty to obtain as explicit reasons as you choose to give, for my superiors to judge why I am treated contrary to the laws of arms and humanity.

In regard to the newspaper, and popular fabrications of cruelty alleged against me, I should treat them with contempt, had not you been pleased to take notice of them: such imputations, sir, will not fasten on me; my character is not in the power of those who wish to injure it, and the most unexceptionable evidence is necessary to prove, that the characteristic of cowardice distinguishes my conduct. My employment gave me the cursory possession, the momentary charge of prisoners; and cruelty is contrary to my nature, my education, and my obedience to my orders. My private affairs calling me to Staten Island, my application was made to you, sir, on that consideration.

I still trust you will intercede to obtain me that permission; and, if I do not effect my exchange, I shall return to prison with the satisfaction of having settled my private business.

I have the honour to be, sir, &c.

   J. G. Simcoe

Lt. Col. Simcoe enclosed the correspondence he had held with Governor Livingston to Sir Henry Clinton in the following letter, which was open and forwarded by the Governor to New York:

Sir,—Governor Livingston having promised me to forward to your Excellency my letters; I take the earliest opportunity of acquainting you with my late and present situation.

The result of my incursion your Excellency is acquainted with, and I have only to observe, that it was neither the valour of my enemies, or the least inattention of my party, that occasioned my being made a prisoner; but it is to be attributed to the most uncommon and malicious fortune.

My life was preserved by the eagerness with which, as I have been informed, I was plundered when in a state of insensibility, and afterwards by the humanity of Mr. Morris.

A Capt. Vorhees was killed by the detachment in its return, after I was taken; his relations seemed to the Governor so determined to revenge his death by my destruction, that he gave me a written protection; and afterwards directed Major Navius, who treated me with great humanity, personally to prevent any injuries that might be offered to me. I was removed to Borden Town on my parole, until the 9th, when I was taken from it, and close confined in Burlington goal.

As my commitment expressed no reason for this treatment, I wrote to Governor Livingston on the subject, and enclose to your Excellency the correspondence.

I look upon my present situation as most particularly unfortunate.

My private affairs called for my greatest attention,

and having procured your Excellency's leave, I had great prospect of success in them.

I trust, sir, that having obtained your recommendation near a twelve month since for promotion, you will still patronise the application you then honoured with your approbation.

My fair fame has been struck at, and cruelty, the attribute of fear, has been imputed to me in the public prints, and industriously propagated by ignorant, designing, and cowardly people.

My honest ambition has been most severely disappointed; and I am doomed to pass the flower of my youth in a goal with criminals, when my state of health, affected by my fall, leads to an imbecility of mind, that will not permit to me the consolations resulting from my liberal education: yet, should I even be doomed obscurely to perish in the quicksand of deceit and calumny, with which I am now surrounded, it is my duty to expect, that no further ungenerous advantage may be permitted to the adversary, who, trampling on the respect due to his own adherents, and presuming on the attention your Excellency may be inclined to pay to my situation, may think to offer, without impunity, some further insult to the British service, the liberal customs of war, and to the honour of my country.

Of my proposed exchange you, sir, are the best judge.

Governor Livingston observed to me, that I was the more likely to be immediately exchanged by being a prisoner of the state of New Jersey, than if I had been taken by the Continental army. I acquiesced in his opinion; not then conceiving how much the field officers, who fight under the banners of this state, are depreciated in its estimation.

There is one hope near, very near to my heart, which is, that your Excellency will patronise my corps, and employ it in the same line as if I was present; its reputation would be the greatest comfort I could receive in a situation that excludes me from participating in its danger and its glory.

Colonel Billop was confined, from his parole given to the Continental army, the same day with me; and that most respectable and amiable gentleman suffers according to the enclosed mittimus—I subjoin to your Excellency his parole, and M. Boudinot's letter to him on his confinement.

For my own part, sir, I wish for no retaliation that may affect the rights which the custom of war allows to individuals of rank, in order to soften the horrors of it. I am obliged to write at intervals; or I should, before now, have sought an opportunity of transmitting an account of my situation to your Excellency, of wishing you every personal and public success you can desire, and of subscribing myself your most obedient, and most humble servant,

J. G. *Simcoe*

In the preceding letter Lt. Col. Simcoe made the fullest display possible of his miserable situation, purposely to give greater force to his contempt of all personal consequences. At this period he had been informed, by some friends who were anxious for his safety, that if Lt. Hele, of the navy, (who was then at Philadelphia a prisoner, in order to undergo whatsoever might befall Cunningham, imprisoned for piracy in England,) should die, and he was dangerously ill, Lt. Col. Simcoe was talked of by the rebels as a proper substitute for that officer: and this information was, in some measure, confirmed by the little attention which the Governor and Council paid to the pressing application of the friends of those officers of the Jersey militia, who were prisoners in New York, and whose exchange was reasonably supposed to depend upon that of Colonels Billop and Simcoe.

A few days after these letters had been forwarded to Sir Henry Clinton, Lt. Col. Simcoe was removed from the room he had hitherto inhabited, at midnight, into that of the felons: he then determined, in case of any intelligence of Cunningham's execution arriving at Philadelphia, instantly to make his escape; and he had found means to have received the earliest notice of this event.

There were many British soldiers, prisoners of war, at work in the neighbourhood; his idea was to get eight or ten of them to assemble at a given place; M'Gill had already conferred with a Sergeant of the 17th infantry, to whom the highest offers would have been held out in case of necessity. The carbines of Col. Lee's dragoons and their ammunition were in the goal—there was confined, a bold and daring man of the name of Bloxam; he had been the armourer of one of his Majesty's ships. M'Gill got an impression of the key of the room where Lee's arms were, and, with the aid of Bloxam, a false one was made of pewter: with this, as soon as Lt. Col. Simcoe was let out of his room, the gaoler one morning entrusting M'Gill with that office, being himself indisposed, they opened the armoury, saw the carbines, and that they were fit for service, and locked the door, when the key broke in it.

These were the most anxious moments Lt. Col. Simcoe ever underwent; if the gaoler had come upstairs, it is probable Bloxam or M'Gill would have been executed; and a party of Col. Lee's were every moment expected to visit the storeroom; Bloxam, with great ingenuity, cut the key, so that it dropped undiscovered into the lock; and Col. Lee's people, on their arrival, found no difficulty in opening it.

Another key was made, and the escape was determined on, and probably would have taken place if necessary. The plan was to surprise a party of Col. Lee's, who lay about ten miles off and to take their horses and proceed to Sandy Hook; and this, it was hoped, might have been effected by stealth rather than violence. M'Gill offered to personate Lt. Col. Simcoe and remain behind in his bed, if it could facilitate his escape.

Lt. Col. Simcoe enclosed to Governor Livingston a letter he received from Major Andre, proposing his being admitted on his parole to New York, the same indulgence being granted the rebel Colonel Baylor to Virginia; Lt. Col. Simcoe informed the Governor that "he had received this proposal, General Sir Henry Clinton supposing that he was on his parole, and not knowing that he was treated as a criminal." To this Governor Livingston returned the following answer.

Mount Holly, Nov. 29th, 1780

Sir,—I received your letter without date last night; this is the second time I have remarked that omission. What you mean by being used like a criminal, I am at a loss to determine, if you refer to your imprisonment; our own people have received similar treatment from the British in numerous instances; Mr. Fitzrandolph, one of our citizens, who is proposed to be exchanged for you and Col. Billop, is at this very time used in the same manner, and is no more a criminal than any man that is not so.

If Sir Henry Clinton will agree to any exchange, I cannot see why he should object to the one proposed; and, considering that one of those we want to have liberated is in gaol, and that the other has been chained to the floor for above four months, there is the highest reason for this State to insist upon it, if he is against all exchange whatsoever, to him, sir, you must ascribe the prolongation of your durance.

That we consider your reputation with the British troops and your intended voyage to Europe, as two circumstances that will probably expedite the relief of our suffering citizens, you will be pleased to impute (though you may regret, as I really do myself, your personal disappointment) to my fidelity to those for whose liberty it is my duty to be anxious. Considering that they, though for many months in captivity, have never been indulged to return home on parole to procure their final release; and that we cannot conceive, how your going to New York should facilitate General Clinton's acceding to our proposal, there is no probability of the Council's adopting that measure. I am, sir, your most humble servant,

William Livingston

Sir,—I have received your letter of the 29th of November, and am to apologize to you for the unpolite, though accidental omission, of my not dating the letter which it answers.

I conceive myself treated as a criminal; the custom of civilized nations allows a parole of honour to officers, but not to private sentinels: as such Mr. Fitzrandolph's confinement is an usual matter, therefore it does not confer any disgrace or hardship upon him, but what was incident to his employment; his station is allowed by yourself in the claim you make for mine and Col. Billop's release.

I do conceive, sir, that when it was proposed that Col. Billop and I should be exchanged for Lt. Col. Reynolds, and as many privates as make up the difference of rank between a Colonel and a private sentinel, that neither did you or the Council seriously imagine it could be accepted of.

I know of no officer in the British army who, consistent with his duty, could apply, or wish for, so disproportionate a mode of exchange; the proposal is ungenerous to your prisoners, nor do I conceive that your own field officers, or those whom you rank equal with them, will consider it as intended to expedite their return from captivity. My state of health and expectations of returning to Europe, I presumed might have some little weight with my enemy, if he was a generous one; it never entered into my thoughts, that these matters of mere private concern could be swollen into a public one, or becoming such, could be supposed in the least particular to influence my conduct.

The reputation, you are pleased to observe, that I have with the British troops, I hope you will do me the justice to believe, it has been my endeavour to acquire by doing my duty to the best of my power; the principle of which is still the same, whether I am actively employed in the field, or suffering an ungenerous and unmerited confinement in prison. My going to New York would most certainly not in the least facilitate Sir Henry Clinton's acceding to a proposal, that was it in his power to agree to, it would never be in my inclination to solicit: the exchange I mentioned would, I thought, if accepted of, answer every purpose that you have held out as your intentions. The indulgence of my parole to New York, is what has been extended to Cols. Reynolds, Potter, &c. your prisoners.

Agreeable to my duty I shall forward Major Andre's letter, and make application to General Washington.

I have the honour to be your most obedient humble servant,

J. G. Simcoe

As soon as I can find a proper convenience I shall, by your leave, send to procure winter clothing, wine, &c. from Staten Island, if I am not permitted to go there.

Lt. Col. Simcoe had forwarded to Gov. Livingston a proposal for exchange of prisoners with the state of New Jersey, although all exchange between the British and Continental troops was totally at a stand; this proposal was formed on the usual principle of rank for rank, and kindly permitted by Sir Henry Clinton to expedite Lt. Col. Simcoe's exchange.

Lt. Col. Simcoe enclosed copies of the preceding letters to Major Andre, and observed in a letter to him, "a few evenings ago I was taken from my bed, and moved into a room which had been occupied by felons for months, and placed among their filth, and closely locked up; this was by order of Mr. Read, Secretary to the Council, and at a time when the Governor held out to me a prospect of exchange, which, till that moment, I did not suspect to be delusory."

These letters were sent unsealed, to be forwarded by Gov. Livingston.

The proposal Gov. Livingston alluded to, he knew had never been made; in pursuance of his plan Lt. Col. Simcoe addressed himself to General Washington in the following letter, preparatory to an application which he meant, in case it should pass unnoticed, to prefer to the Congress.

To General Washington

Sir,—I am induced to lay myself before you, from what I conceive to be a principle of duty, and that not merely personal.

You may, perhaps, have heard, sir, of the uncommon fortune that threw me into the hands of the Jersey militia.

Gov. Livingston told me I was a prisoner of the State, a distinction I never till then was acquainted with, and observed, that it was probable I should be soon exchanged as such, naming to me officers of similar rank as the likely persons.

I was allowed my parole, was taken from it the 9th, and have ever since been confined a close prisoner in Burlington goal, with Col. Billop, who is in irons and chained to the floor, to retaliate for F. Randolph and Leshier, the latter of whom is (said to be) confined in the same manner in New York: my mittimus hath not expressed what I am imprisoned for; but, by the tenor of Governor Livingston's letters, I suppose it is to retaliate for the former of those citizens, whom he allows to be a private soldier, and who is simply confined as such.

Colonel Billop joins me in my application, sir, to you for redress from our unparalleled usage.

I apply to you, sir, either as a prisoner of war, or as appealing to you from an unjustifiable stretch of power without precedent or generosity.

I am led to consider myself as a prisoner of war under your authority, from Governor Livingston's doubts expressed to me of his having the disposal of me; from his correspondence with Gen. Robertson, published in the newspapers, where he submits Gen. Dickinson's prisoners to your disposal, and from Col. Billop, my fellow prisoner, being taken by a party of Continental troops, receiving his parole from Mr. Beaty, and living under it, till he was taken from it by a party of militia, and by M. Boudinot's order confined in Burlington gaol.

He claims the protection that was first extended to him from the Continental Commissary of prisoners.

I hope, sir, you will make use of the power that I conceive enabled you to transfer Col. Billop to the state of New Jersey, in extending to me the rights allowed by civilized nations, and which, without a given reason, I have been deprived of.

If, by any law I am unacquainted with, I am in the power and disposal of Governor Livingston, &c, I think myself entitled to appeal to you, sir, from the injustice used towards me, as I cannot suppose there is no application for redress in a case, which, if drawn into a precedent, most confound every distinction of rank, and will operate in a wider circle than that of the state of New Jersey.

Governor Livingston has offered, as he has written to me, to exchange me for Lt. Col. Reynolds, and Col. Billop for as many privates as make up his rank, naming among them the people for whom Col. Billop is avowedly retaliating. This proposition, I conceive, it never was supposed Gen. Sir Henry Clinton could comply with.

I hope, sir, you will do me the honour of early to this letter; if Col. Billop only should be claimed by those whose prisoner he unquestionably appears to be, I should look upon it as a fortunate event, though I should be doomed to wear his ignominious chains.

I have the honour to be, sir,

Your most obedient and humble servant,

J. G. Simcoe

I beg leave to enclose to you Major Andre's letter, though Governor Livingston, to whom I addressed it, has passed it by without notice; I hope it will be the means of my obtaining my parole to New York.

General Washington never answered this letter, but in a very few days Colonels Billop and Simcoe were exchanged; and it is to be remarked, that soon after Congress passed an act, declaring that all prisoners whatsoever, whether taken by the Continental army or *militia*, should be absolutely at the disposal of their Commander in Chief, General Washington, and not of the Governors of the different provinces.

Col. Hendrickson, who was in the British Commissary's proposals to be exchanged for Col. Billop, and had his parole to give effect to it, arrived at Burlington on the 26th of December, and brought the following letter from Boudinot to Lt. Col. Simcoe:

Elizabeth Town, 23rd Dec. 1779

Sir,—I am happy to inform you, that there is a probability of your being released from your captivity. As your disagreeable confinement was owing entirely to the like treatment of a number of our field officers, prisoners in New York, I doubt not you will endeavour to use that influence which an officer of your abilities must undoubtedly have, to prevent the necessity of my executing orders so repugnant to my feelings as a man.

I am confident your delicacy will be extremely wounded at being called upon for security for the performance of your parole; this, I assure you, is not because your honour is at all questioned, but to follow a late *cruel example* in Col. Hendrickson; perhaps when Mr. Loring sees the consequence of such conduct, he may be led to adopt a practice less destructive of every personal virtue.

I have the honour to be,

E. Boudinot

M. Boudinot does not seem to have known the distinction of field officers, as none of this description were confined at New York; Mr. Loring had insisted on security from Hendrickson, because several of the American militia officers had broken their paroles. Lt. Col. Simcoe told Col. Hendrickson that it was absurd to suppose he could break his parole in passing through the Jersies to Staten Island; but that he had no objection to find surety, provided he, Colonel Hendrickson, would be bound for him.

This officer went to the Governor, and Lt. Col. Simcoe was emancipated on the 27th of December from Burlington gaol; he was still apprehensive of being detained, as it was reported that the person, from whom the paper money had been taken, had applied to the Governor to confine him till the money was returned, he having promised to pay it at Brunswick. The promise of paying any debt, by the laws of New England, rendered the person who gave it liable for the payment; but this custom had never prevailed in the Jersies.

Lt. Col. Simcoe proceeded without molestation, and arrived at Richmond on the 31st: his arrival made a little triumph, and the testimonies of friendship and affection, which he received from his officers, soldiers, and the loyalists, compensated in a moment for all the anxiety which he had undergone.

Many projects, he found, had been in agitation to rescue him from prison; and, particularly, Lt. Wilson had, by the assistance of some loyalists of New Jersey, digested one, which appeared so likely to succeed, that nothing but the daily prospect which had been held out of his being exchanged, had prevented Major Andre, to whom it had been communicated, from adopting it.

Forty friends of Government armed themselves, and had arrived in the neighbourhood of Burlington the day after Lt.

Col. Simcoe was exchanged, for the avowed purpose of rescuing him; they came near two hundred miles, and had provided horses and a proper place for his retreat Their leader, the Prince of the woods, so called from his knowledge of them, which in America are, as it were, another element, had sprained his leg; or the rescue would have taken place, as he afterwards told Lt. Col. Simcoe, ten days before his liberation.

At the time that Lt. Col. Simcoe landed on his incursion, a packet-boat lay at Sandy Hook bound for England; she sailed the next day, when it being generally supposed that he was killed, the Commander in Chief, Sir Henry Clinton, reported his death to the Secretary of State, Lord George Germain: when Lt. Col. Simcoe was at Charles Town, the General showed him the following paragraph in a letter which he had just received from Lord George Germain, in answer to the report which had been made of his expedition and death:

> The loss of so able and gallant an officer as Colonel Simcoe is much to be lamented; but, I hope, his misfortune will not damp the spirit of the brave loyalists he so often led out with success. His last enterprise was certainly a very bold one; and I should be glad he had been in a situation to be informed, that his spirited conduct was approved of by the King.

Bloxam made his escape soon after Lt. Col. Simcoe's exchange, and, after a variety of adventures, when he got into Staten Island, that officer was gone to Charles Town. He worked in New York until his return, when he joined him that very day on which the Queen's Rangers made the advance guard of General Matthews's column in the Jersies; and, at his own request, being furnished with arms he fell in with the Queen's Rangers, and, to Lt. Col. Simcoe's great regret, was killed by a cannon shot when the corps was halted, and he was sleeping.

Lt. Col. Simcoe offered M'Gill an annuity, or to make him Quarter-master of cavalry; the latter he accepted of, as his grandfather had been a Captain in King William's army; and no man ever executed the office with greater integrity, courage and conduct.

In the charge on Brunswick Plains, Hampton, was taken prisoner

Marrener was taken prisoner while Lt. Col. Simcoe was at Charles Town; he was obnoxious to the magistrates of New York, and probably would not have been exchanged; but on Lt. Col. Simcoe's explaining to the Commander in Chief the obligations he was under to him, Sir Henry Clinton was pleased to let him return home on his parole.

Randal, or Fitzrandolph, was included in the exchange with Lt. Colonel Simcoe; he was soon after killed, and probably by the Rangers. On that day the army passed Governor Livingston's house; and Lt. Col. Simcoe, who commanded the rear guard, took the most anxious pains to preserve it from being burnt by any of the exasperated loyalists; and he happily succeeded.

General Stirling's response to Lt. Col. Simcoe's ideas

3 P. M. 31st January, 1780

Dear Sir,—I am favoured with yours; your ideas are great, and would be of importance if fulfilled; as I am confident of your zeal and capacity, I should be sorry to check them, therefore, if you see it clearly, should not stop it.

I have no doubt, myself, of the rebels intending an attack; but I think they can only do it in one place, the other must be a feint I am much of opinion that Richmond should be withdrawn, as it might fall if this does, and the addition of your regiment would be great to us here, &c.,&c.

LT. COL. SIMCOE'S LETTER TO GENERAL TRYON
DETAILING HIS PREPARATIONS

The preparation's are sketched out in the following letter transmitted to Gen. Tryon; to which are added his approbation of the plan, and his good wishes towards the author of it, now rendered doubly valuable, as since the compilation of these memoirs death has deprived his King and country of that officer, so eminently distinguished for private virtues, and for his zeal in the public service.

Sir,—I beg leave to submit to you, and hope that you will communicate to his Excellency General Kniphausen, the service in which I think that the Queen's Rangers may, from their present position, be essentially employed.

I would propose, that I should be immediately furnished with two gun-boats and twenty batteaux, a water force sufficient to transport and to cover the landing of three hundred infantry and sixty horse.

The gun-boats should be supplied with swivels, which might occasionally be transferred to the bows of the batteaux; the small boat already here with a slide or carriage, on which the amuzette of the Queen's Rangers might be mounted; the whole should be most completely equipped, in which state I would always be attentive to preserve them,

I would wish also, for a sloop to carry the lower framework of three small block houses, and occasionally provisions, and other articles: she might be under the protection of the vessel stationed at Billop's point, as the batteaux would under that of Richmond redoubts.

It would be of great service if the batteaux could be mounted on carriages, as it is but two miles and an half from Richmond to the South beach, and by such conveyance the advantage of either tide might be obtained and a movement made, with scarce a possibility of the enemy's being previously acquainted with it; though, I fear, such an operation is not at present in our power, I am not without hopes to be able to furnish the means of it from the enemy's shore.

The block houses would be of essential service in securing an encampment, or strengthening a position on the enemy's shore; they would effectually protect a re-embarkation.

With this force, capable of moving without the obstructions arising from the combination of different services, the delay of waiting for orders, and the want of secrecy, which necessarily attends the protecting of operations, I doubt not but I should be able to protect Staten Island; to keep the enemy in constant alarm from Sandy Hook to Newark bay; to force Mr. Washington to give up the sea coast from Middleton to Brunswick, or to protect it with Continental troops; to encourage desertion at this very critical period, when the rebel army is most seriously discontented; in short, to exemplify and improve the advantages resulting from our situation.

Could more batteaux be spared I should be glad; the cavalry on this island (the best part of which I consider the detachment of the 17th dragoons from their superior discipline to be) being in numbers equal, and in all other respects superior, to the cavalry of Mr. Washington's army between the Delaware and Hudson's river, might from hence, without more risk than becomes the service, be of frequent and most extensive utility. Gen. Stirling highly approves of the plan; there are now at Richmond a gun-boat, and the barge I mentioned to you; the latter I should have sent round by water but had no opportunity. I do myself the honour to enclose to you the deficiencies of each, and should be glad if supplied. I could wish Major Bruen would be so good as to have the barge valued here by some person in his department, and a receipt given to the refugees, if you think proper to have it purchased. I enclose to your Excellency the draught of the gun-boats constructed by Lt. Col. Campbell, at the Savannah; by being covered at the top they were able to pass without injury from the fire of small arms, under the boldest bluffs; the top opened occasionally for refreshment by means of the hinges, as described in the drawing. This addition made to our gun-boats would give them great security.

If by this, or any other mode of operation, I could be of any service to my King and country, I should be most happy: the attempt, I am persuaded, will meet with your Excellency's approbation, which, as I highly value, I shall ever hope to deserve, being, with great respect,

Your Excellency's most obedient and most humble servant,

J. G. Simcoe

New York, 3rd May, 1780

Sir,—I received, with much satisfaction, your letter, delivered me by Capt. Beckwith. My not having the pleasure of seeing you on your departure for the southward, was a disappointment to me. It was much my desire to have testified my readiness to promote those spirited measures you proposed for his Majesty's service; and, though circumstances have deprived me of that gratification, permit me to assure you, I most sincerely wish you, in your career of glory, every honourable success your merit, spirit, and zeal, entitle you to. I am &c, &c,

W. Tryon

Lt. Col. Simcoe

LT. COL. SIMCOE HAD COLLECTED SECRETLY THROUGH THE THICKETS UPON THEIR FLANK

It was at this moment that a guide, as it appears in the proceedings of a court-martial, in the unhappy dispute between two officers of the guards, brought an order to Lt. Col. Simcoe, " to march into the road," from which (by the extending of his line) he was distant three hundred yards; and on his replying, "he could take no orders from a guide," Gen. Matthews sent Col. Howard (now Earl Suffolk) to repeat them. This note is inserted merely to say that it was no pertinacious adherence to form; but his being occupied in the attempt to cut off a party of the enemy, which occasioned Lt. Col. Simcoe's reply to the guide, and which, if an officer had brought the order, he would at once have seen and reported to the General, whom the intervening thickets prevented from the observation of what was transacting on his left.

ON THE EXECUTUON OF MAJOR ANDRE

Upon the first intimation of Major Andre's detention, Lt. Col. Simcoe, by letter, desired Lt. Col. Crosbie to inform the Commander in Chief, "that if there was any possibility of rescuing him, he and the Queen's Rangers were ready to attempt it, not doubting to succeed in whatever a similar force could effect."

At the same time, he sent out persons to watch the road between Washington's camp and Philadelphia; for he reasoned, that without the concurrence of Congress that General would not proceed to extremities, and that probably he would send Major Andre to Philadelphia, in which case he might possibly be retaken upon the road thither.

Lt. Col. Simcoe wrote to Col. Lee, of whose generous temper he had personally received so many proofs, to procure an interview with him, ostensibly for the exchange of prisoners, but really to converse with him relative to Major Andre. That officer penetrated his views and returned the following answer.

Light Camp, Oct. 2nd, 1780

Sir,—I will attend to the release and return of Jeremiah Owens.

Be assured no time will be lost in the transaction of this business.

Our personal feelings are perfectly reciprocal, and I embrace, with peculiar pleasure, the overture of a meeting.

My expectation of moving daily, will not allow me to fix on the time at present.

Our next station, I hope, will be opportune to both of us, when I will do myself the honour of notifying to you my readiness.

Be pleased to accept my best wishes, and for heaven's sake omit in future your expressions of obligations conferred by me; as my knowledge of your character confirms my assurance, that a similar visit of fortune to me, will produce every possible attention from you.

I am happy in telling you, that there is a probability of Major Andre's being restored to his country, and the customs of war being fully satisfied.

I have the honour to be, &c.

Henry Lee

Since writing the foregoing, I find that Sir Henry Clinton's offers have not come up to what was expected, and that this hour is fixed for the execution of the sentence. How cold the friendship of those high in power!

Lt. Col. Simcoe in his answer said:

I am at a loss to express myself on the latter paragraphs of your letter; I have long accustomed myself to be silent, or to speak the language of the heart. The useless murder of Major Andre would almost, was it possible, annihilate that wish which, consentaneous to the ideas of our sovereign, and the government of Great Britain, has ever operated on the officers of the British army, the wish of a reconciliation and speedy reunion with their revolted fellow subjects in America.

Sir Henry Clinton has the warmest feelings for those under his command, and was ready to have granted for Major Andre's exchange, whatever ought to have been asked.

Though every desire that I had formed to think, in some instances, favourably of those who could urge, or of him who could permit the murder of this most virtuous and accomplished gentleman, be now totally eradicated; I must still subscribe myself with great personal respect, sir,

Your most obedient and obliged servant,

J. G. Simcoe

There were no offers whatsoever made by Sir Henry Clinton; amongst some letters which passed on this unfortunate event, a paper was slid in without signature, but in the hand writing of Hamilton, Washington's secretary, saying, "that the only way to save Andre was to give up Arnold."

Major Andre was murdered upon private not public considerations. It bore not with it the stamp of justice; for there was not an officer in the British army whose duty it would not have been, had any of the American Generals offered to quit the service of Congress, to have negotiated to receive them; so that this execution could not, by example, have prevented the repetition of the same offence.

It may appear, that from his change of dress, &c. he came under the description of a spy; but when it shall be considered "against his stipulation, intention and knowledge," he became absolutely a prisoner, and was forced to change his dress for self-preservation, it may safely be asserted, that no European general would on this pretext have had his blood upon his head. He fell a sacrifice to that which was expedient, not to that which was just: what was supposed to be useful superseded what would have been generous; and though, by imprudently carrying papers about him, he gave a colour to those, who endeavoured to separate Great Britain from America, to press for his death; yet an open and elevated mind would have found greater satisfaction in the obligations it might have laid on the army of his opponents, than in carrying into execution a useless and unnecessary vengeance.

It has been said, that not only the French party from their customary policy, but Mr. Washington's personal enemies urged him on, contrary to his inclinations, to render him unpopular if he executed Major Andre, or suspected if he pardoned him.

In the length of the war, for what one generous action has Mr. Washington been celebrated? What honourable sentiment ever fell from his lips which can invalidate the belief, that surrounded with difficulties and ignorant in whom to confide, he meanly sheltered himself under the opinions of his officers and the Congress, in perpetrating his own previous determination? And, in perfect conformity to his interested ambition, which crowned with success beyond human calculation in 1783, to use his own expression, "bid a last farewell to the cares of office, and all the employments of public life," to resume them at this moment (1787) as President of the American Convention?

Had Sir Henry Clinton, whose whole behaviour in his public disappointment, and most afflicting of private situations, united the sensibility of the Friend, with the magnanimity of the General, had he possessed a particle of the malignity which, in this transaction, was exhibited by the American, many of the principal inhabitants of Carolina then in confinement, on the clearest proof for the violation of the law of nations, would have been adjudged to the death they had merited.

The papers which Congress published, relative to Major Andre's death, will remain an eternal monument of the principles of that heroic officer; and, when fortune shall no longer gloss over her fading panegyric, will enable posterity to pass judgment on the character of Washington.

Lt. Col. Simcoe's letter detailing plans for the capture of Billing's Port

The present system of war seems to aim principally at striking at the resources of the rebels, and in consequence by incapacitating them from remitting the produce of their country to foreign markets, to render them a burden to the powers of Europe who are confederate with them against Great Britain.

A post on the Delaware would be of utility to this end; and the situation of Billing's Port, peculiarly adapted for this purpose, strikes me so forcibly that I trust your Excellency will pardon my particularizing some of its features, and a few of its many advantages.

The ground is an entire flat; it is not commanded; the rebels had begun a large work there, which they left unfinished when Sir William Howe took possession of Philadelphia. On our evacuation of that city Mr. Mifflin pointed out to them the necessity of resuming and completing the fortification; the opening of the *chevaux du frize* is made close under the bold bluff, which terminates the *terre-plein* towards the water: this, with the other *chevaux du frize* above, would be turned much to our advantage. A sufficient water force to prevent any shipping or galleys from commanding the river above, and which in some respect should be moveable, would be requisite: perhaps a transport or two on the establishment of the *Margery*, a transport of the garrison armed with cannonades, a few galleys and gun-boats, would accomplish every wished for end.

The work to be erected should be calculated at least for three hundred regular troops to defend, to which should be added three hundred light troops, habituated to make incursions, &c. &c.

It seems probable that an expedition will sooner or later be formed for Virginia; the troops intended for this service might be landed, fortify, and leave a garrison at Billing's Port in a few days, carrying with them frame works for bomb proofs, &c. from New York, which might be given out to be intended for Portsmouth, or some post in Virginia. The advantages resulting from the possession of this port, would be an entire stop of the trade of the Delaware, probably the driving the Congress from Philadelphia, or by a very little exertion of policy, being in early possession of their most secret resolutions and intentions; it would encourage desertion, particularly that of the shipbuilders in Philadelphia.

To besiege this garrison while the river is open will be a matter of great difficulty; the road from Staten Island to Trenton being so much nearer than a retreat from Billing's Port to that pass, and the Delaware being almost everywhere too wide for a bridge of boats, or for batteries raised upon each shore effectually to command a retreat. The place might be invested by the Jersey militia; they are not numerous, or to be feared, and would soon be disarmed by a proper mixture of conciliatory and vigorous measures,

The officer commanding the port should, if it could be contrived, have the command also of the water forces; at least not a boat should be permitted to land without his concurrence. The garrison should purchase what fresh provisions might be allowed them, and should never be placed in a situation to commit unmilitary depredations.

I doubt not but that a thousand advantages and disadvantages resulting from this post must strike your Excellency's comprehensive views, which do not appear to my partial one. If, at any future time, although I am not willing to be wedded to a redoubt, your Excellency should seize on this post, I should be very ready to stake on its defence, or its loss from the most inevitable reasons, every hope that I have of military preferment, and of being esteemed a faithful and honourable servant of my King and Country.

It is probable that had not circumstances prevented Sir Henry Clinton from pursuing the plan of operations which he had intended, in the course of them Billing's Port would have attracted his attention.

CAPT. STEVENSON'S HUMANITY WAS ALARMED
AND THE LETTERS BETWEEN LT. COL. SIMCOE
AND COL. PARKER PREVENTED ALL FURTHER
BAD CONSEQUENCES

Portsmouth, Sunday, March 4,1781

Sir,—I do myself the honour of enclosing to you Captain Stevenson's justification of Mr. Gregory in your service; and am to assure you, what the ties of humanity summon me to declare, that Capt. Stevenson mentioned to me, some hours before it was known that the gun-boat was taken, the fictitious letter you found among his papers; at a distance the matter appeared in a ludicrous light; as it may otherwise probably lead to serious consequences, I solemnly confirm the truth of Capt. Stevenson's explanation of the affair; and add, upon the sacred honour of a soldier and a gentleman, that I have no reason to believe or suspect that Mr. Gregory is otherwise than a firm adherent of the French King, and of the Congress.

I have the honour to be, sir, &c,

J. G. Simcoe

To Col. Parker

Lt. Col. Simcoe

Sir,—The honour of a soldier I ever hold sacred, and am happy that you are called on by motives of humanity to acquit General Gregory. As to my own opinion, I believe you: but as the management of this delicate matter is left to my superiors, I have forwarded the letter you honoured me with to Baron Steuben, who I trust will view it in the same manner I do.

I have the honour to be, sir, &c,

J. Parker, Col.

March 5, 1781

GENERAL PHILLIPS ASKED LT. COL. SIMCOE
HOW MANY MEN IT WOULD REQUIRE
TO DEFEND YORK TOWN?

This conversation is dwelt upon in the journal in order to set in its proper light a passage in a letter from Sir Henry Clinton to Lord Cornwallis—"I confess I could not conceive you would require above four thousand in a station where General Arnold had represented to me, (upon report of Colonel Simcoe,) that two thousand men would be amply sufficient."

General Arnold was second in command, so that no particular report was made to him; but he was present at the conversation which passed between Lt. Col. Simcoe and General Phillips.

A LETTER FROM GENERAL LEE. TO
LT. COL. SIMCOE AT WESTOVER

March 3rd, 1781

Dear Sir,—From the liberality of mind which you are universally allowed to be blessed with, I have little doubt but that what I am about to offer to your consideration will be favourably received—but I must first premise that, whatsoever some flaming zealots in the British army may insist to the contrary, it is very possible that several who embarked on this side in the present contest were very good Englishmen, and I can venture to assert that I am one of this stamp—for I considered, that had the Ministry succeeded in their scheme of establishing the principle of taxing America without her consent, the liberties of Great Britain would that instant have been annihilated in effect, though the form might have remained. For as the pecuniary influence of the Crown was already enormously too great, so prodigious an additional weight thrown into the preponderating scale must sink to utter ruin every part of the Empire—on the other hand I will venture to assert, notwithstanding all that some of the flaming fanatics on this side may please assume, that it is the interest of every good American that Great Britain should ever be a great, powerful, and opulent nation—but the measure she ought to pursue, in my idea, to obtain and secure this power, opulence, and greatness, I cannot at present with propriety explain; but I can with propriety point out some which she ought not to pursue. For instance, her Generals and Commanders ought not to suffer, or connive at by impunity, the little dirty piratical plundering of individuals—such proceedings can only tend to widen the breach already, to the misfortune of both parties, much too wide, by souring men's minds into a state of irreconcilable resentment: in short, it is diametrically repugnant, not only to the honour, but to the true interest and policy of Great Britain, abstracted from all considerations of the cruelty and inhumanity towards very worthy families. But to be just, I really believe that most, if not all of these flagitious scandalous acts are committed unknown to the English General and Commodore, as from the air and garb of the robbers they have not the appearance of being legally commissioned. This, my dear sir, is the main purpose of my letter, which I write as a good Englishman, as a good American, and as a gentleman addressing himself to another of whom he has a very high opinion; and I have no doubt but that you will exert all your power and influence to punish and put an end to such abominable practices.

I have nothing to add, but to entreat that whatever letters I may send in you will convey safely to my relations. There is indeed one other favour I request; which is, that you will by the first opportunity assure Sir Henry Clinton, General Robinson, and General Leslie, of my personal respect and esteem, and I beg you will remember me kindly to General Phillips:—But above all, I entreat you will believe me to be, most sincerely your's,

Charles Lee

LT. COL. SIMCOE'S RESPONSE TO LT. COL. TARLETON'S VIEW

In Col. Tarleton's history of the campaigns in the southern Provinces, published since the completion of this Journal, there is the following paragraph:

If the distance would have allowed Lt. Col. Simcoe to send a small party of huzzars to inform the corps at Charlottesville of the flight of the Americans, Lt. Col. Tarleton might have been in time to harass Baron Steuben's progress, whilst Lt. Col. Simcoe would have pressed him in the rear; and a combination of this sort would, in all probability, have ruined that body of new levies: but the distance of thirty-five miles in an enemy's country, and the uncertainty of Tarleton's success, perhaps represented such a co-operation as too speculative and precarious.

It appears that Lt. Col. Tarleton marched from Charlottesville towards the Point of Fork nearly at the time that Lt. Col.

Simcoe arrived there; had that officer sent a patrol to Lt. Col. Tarleton, the whole of the intelligence it could have conveyed to him would have been, that the Baron Steuben, with a far more considerable force than had been apprehended, had crossed a rapid, broad, unfordable river, was in possession of all the boats, and encamped upon its banks: but Lt. Col. Simcoe most assuredly could not have ordered Lt. Col. Tarleton immediately to join him, to pursue the Baron with any probability of success; and, without an absolute certainty, he could not have taken the liberty of breaking through Earl Cornwallis's express orders of rejoining him, without delay, at Goochland Court-house, and of marching away with all his light troops to a considerable distance. But there was a total impossibility of passing the river; it was not fordable for many miles, and the combination, Lt. Col. Tarleton talks of, was absolutely impracticable. He observes, that the distance from Charlottesville was thirty-five miles, which would have been too great had the river been fordable; but the uncertainty of his success could be no impediment as, at any rate, there was no enemy to oppose him, and his march was easily to be traced; nor could these reasons represent such cooperation as speculative and precarious, at least to Lt. Col. Simcoe, as the idea never once entered his mind, and he was much surprised when he saw it in Lt. Col. Tarleton's campaigns, as till then he never had heard it suggested.

IT WAS REPORTED THAT A PATROL OF THE ENEMY MET WITH THIS PARTY ON THE ROAD, WHERE IT WAS NATURAL TO EXPECT LORD CORNWALLIS' ARMY, AND TOOK IT FOR HIS ADVANCE GUARD

In Lt. Col. Tarleton's history is the following passage:

The movement of Lt. Col. Tarleton from his advance post in the morning was a favourable incident for the Americans; for if the legion foraging party under Capt. Ogilvie, who accidentally approached the flank of the riflemen, could produce hesitation and astonishment, the charge of the whole cavalry, must have considerably assisted Lt. Col. Simcoe, whose judicious conduct obliged Col. Butler to fall back upon Gen. Wayne, before the arrival of the infantry from Williamsburg, or the dragoons from Burrers; the loss in this affair was nearly equal, except that the British took some prisoners.

It is not to be doubted, but that Lt. Col. Simcoe would have been happy to have been assisted by Lt. Col. Tarleton and his cavalry, and would have employed him to the best of his power; but the ground was such that the cavalry could not have been properly risked in an attack, otherwise than what Capt. Shank accomplished, or adventured in the pursuit, as the enemy fled through thick woods which led to a ravine, beyond which M. Fayette's army drew up in force.

The approach of Capt. Ogilvie was not of the least service to the Rangers, as it was at too great a distance to assist their attack; nor could any movement from Williamsburg have been in time sufficient to have preserved the troops under Lt. Col. Simcoe, who owed their preservation as much to their own exertions as if there had not been another British soldier in Virginia. Upon the first repulse of the enemy, it was Lt. Col. Simcoe's business to retire, and this he instantly effected.

Capt. Ewald, who since the war has published some military observations in Germany, has proposed to those who may be in similar circumstances, Lt. Col. Simcoe's conduct as a proper example; he affirms, that had he pursued he would have been cut off.

Infantry might have been of service in following the enemy through the wood, to the brink of the ravine.

Lt. Col. Simcoe's observations on the climate and the sickly state and condition of the corps from a letter to Sir Henry Clinton

I do myself the honour of writing to your Excellency by the present opportunity, and of making such representation of the Queen's Rangers as I think to be my indispensable duty. The infantry are much reduced in numbers by desertion, the consequence of their composition, opportunities, unremitting fatigues, and by death; while those remaining are much shattered in point of constitution: the cavalry are admirably mounted, but more than half are without accoutrements, or any arms, but such as we have taken from an ill-appointed enemy. The arms and accoutrements, which I apprehend had been intended for Capt. Cooke's troop, were sent by the Inspector to Lord Cornwallis, who gave them to the legion, for whom he had made the application. In this situation, without time to discipline, and without proper arms, I am obliged to trust more to fortune than I have ever found necessary, and that against an enemy who is improving every day.

My duty therefore leads me to hope, that, as we have been already embarked for New York, that your Excellency, should any troops be ordered there, will be pleased to direct the Queen's Rangers to be sent among the first, with, or if that cannot be done, without their horses; as that is the only place where the corps can be recruited. Your Excellency will, I am sure, be confident, that no private view dictates this application; and believe, that all climates and services, where I can be useful, are indifferent to me.

Lt. Col. Simcoe had been directed by the Commander in Chief to communicate with him, and to give him such information from time to time as he thought might be for the good of the service, while he was under the command of Gen. Arnold; and he had always most strongly represented the great importance of possessing a small naval force on the Carratuck inlet, both to secure a retreat and to connect the operations of Virginia with those of Carolina: he had been an eyewitness, that the naval force stationed in the Chesapeake bay, by no means blocked it up, or prevented the enemy's vessels from going in or out at their pleasure. In this letter he added:

> I take this opportunity of enclosing to your Excellency two sketches, taken amongst the papers of the Marquis de la Fayette. The road from Philadelphia to Kent island is accurately delineated; and, should your Excellency, as I hope, visit Philadelphia in your way to this colony, points out the facility of crossing the isthmus, and the consequence of Kent Island, where I have long thought a post would be of great effect, to give an asylum to the distressed friends of government, and by the station of a few cruisers effectually to block up the Chesapeake, which cannot or has not hitherto been done.

It was natural for Lt. Col. Simcoe to fix his mind on those operations, which he had reason to expect would be undertaken on the upper part of the Chesapeake; the country of the associated loyalists.

This wish to return to New York was considerably strengthened by the belief, that the sea voyage would greatly amend the health of the soldiers, and by his hopes that they might be of public utility in their convalescent state, if the General and Admiral would have consented to have entrusted his friend, Capt. Thomas Graves and himself with a flying squadron, to have carried on that mode of war which would have been severely felt by the enemy; the keeping their coasts in constant alarm, from Boston to Virginia, and the following and destroying their shipping in their innumerable smaller harbours. The fatal event at York Town terminated these views, and Lt. Col. Simcoe's services. His friend, Capt. Thomas Graves, was more fortunate: he was appointed to the frigate *La Magicienne*, which he manned at a considerable private expense; but with a disinterested spirit truly becoming the British officer, declined taking possession of her, while in the command of a line of battle ship, he thought he could be more useful to his country, and that honourable service was to be met with in the West Indies or America: and when he accepted of the frigate, being employed on convoys, he fell in with the *Sybil* French frigate of superior force to himself, doubly manned, and commanded by an officer of distinguished character. Their engagement was rendered memorable by their being locked close to each other for near two hours, with *every sail set,* by the carnage on board the British ship, exceeding what in similar numbers is to be met with in the annals of the late war, and by the circumstance, that when Capt. Graves had silenced the fire of his opponent, the masts of the *La Magicienne* fell overboard and fortune deprived him of his prize and of all, but the glory of having deserved it.

EARL CORNWALLIS ASKED LT. COL. SIMCOE "WHETHER HE THOUGHT HE COULD ESCAPE WITH THE CAVALRY" HE ANSWERED ,"WITHOUT THE SMALLEST DOUBT."

The great outline which Lt. Col. Simcoe laid down as the means by which he could escape, was to march straight up the country till such time as he had arrived parallel to the fords of the Susquehanna; leaving it uncertain whether he meant to proceed to Carolina or Pennsylvania; he then would have crossed towards the Susquehanna, directing his march so as to endeavour to release the Convention army, or to impress the enemy with a belief that such was his intention, if it should appear impracticable: when, being above the fords of the Delaware, he would have passed that river, and proceeded towards Staten Island or New York; by that route which would have been most feasible.

For some time previous to Earl Cornwallis' question, Lt. Col. Simcoe had formed the idea of escaping with his cavalry, and such men as could have been mounted, in short the whole of his corps; and he had acquired a most perfect knowledge of the different fords, and formed for himself a regular plan. Capt. Ewald saw him one day looking over *Xenophon*, and immediately said, "My Colonel, you are going to retreat; for God's sake do not leave the Yagers behind you."

Those who are not acquainted with the American country and its internal situation, would look upon such an attempt as chimerical; but a consideration of circumstances might alter their opinion. The whole of the enemy's force was concentrated at York Town; their cavalry consisted of the Duke of Lauzun's legion, ill-mounted, few in numbers, and unacquainted with the country and the genius of the war; no serious interruption or pursuit could be expected from them; such a corps as four or five hundred men were exactly calculated for the attempt. A single plantation would have furnished them with sufficient provisions and forage; the rapidity of their march would prevent any determined opposition; and, as the party proceeded, horses could be accumulated to remount those which might be disabled.

The country was sufficiently loyal to give the best intelligence; much could have been procured by means of the negroes, and these people, if properly managed, might have been of infinite service as auxiliaries; they are brave, excellent horsemen, masters of the sword, capable of fatigue and exertion in the hottest weather, and would have been tremendous in a pursuit.

The composition of the Queen's Rangers suited it for any enterprise; the huzzars had been practised in swimming their horses, and the native Americans and emigrants were expert in whatever might facilitate the passage of rivers, or prevent an enemy from effecting it. There were no troops between New York and Virginia, and if the militia were called out to guard the principal fords (as was reported) it was with a view to stop an army, and not a light corps, whose march would be directed far above the line they were destined to occupy, and to points with which they were unacquainted.

His Lordship was pleased to express
himself favourably in regard to the
scheme, but said he could not permit
it to be undertaken, for that the whole
of the army must share one fate

The Rangers from their many voyages, on board of half-manned transports, and from their officers encouraging them to assist in the working of the vessels, were become so ready and expert at sea, that in a periodical production which stated the number of the troops taken at York Town, it was not surprising that the *Queen's Rangers* were remarked as, *all sailors.*

Upon Capt. Palmer's success, Lt. Col. Simcoe had taken the liberty of suggesting, "that by fitting out all the small craft as fire vessels, and driving the French ships from the river in the night, two thousand men, which the boats would carry, might escape to the Maryland shore;" his Lordship replied,"he saw no daylight in that mode of escape."

The duty and consequent principles of a subordinate officer and a commander in chief are as different and distinct as limited views and universal ones can possibly make them: the inferior officer has only to perform any service he may be ordered on, and to be ready for those which are most hazardous, while the commander in chief weighs the propriety of any measure, sees it in all its lights and relations, and determines accordingly; and the greater alacrity which his troops show to execute his designs, the more valuable they become; and cannot fail strongly to interest a noble mind in their preservation. And this principle Earl Cornwallis, when he surrendered York Town to the prodigious superiority of force combined against him, generously expressed in the following terms: "Our numbers had been diminished by the enemy's fire; but particularly by sickness, and the strength and spirits of those in the works were much exhausted by the fatigue of constant watching and unremitting duty. Under all these circumstances, I thought it would have been wanton and inhuman to the last degree, to sacrifice the lives of this small body of gallant soldiers, who had ever behaved with so much fidelity and courage, by exposing them to an assault, which, from the numbers and precautions of the enemy, could not fail to succeed."

BENJAMIN FRANKLIN ARRANGES
LT. COL. SIMCOE'S EXCHANGE

Lieut. Col. Simcoe has always thought himself under the highest obligations to his Majesty's Ministers for this mark of attention; the terms on which he was exchanged are here inserted, verbatim, from Dr. Franklin's discharge:

Being informed by William Hodgson, Esq. Chairman of the Committee of Subscribers for the relief of American Prisoners in England, of the benevolent and humane treatment lately received by the said prisoners in consequence of orders from the present British Ministers; and that the said Ministers earnestly desire, that Lt. Col. Simcoe, a prisoner on parole to the United States of America, should be released from his said parole; and being further of opinion, that meeting the British Government in acts of benevolence, is agreeable to the disposition and intention of the Congress: I do hereby, as far as in my power may lie, absolve the parole of the said Lt. Col. Simcoe; but on this condition, that an order be obtained for the discharge of some officer of equal rank, who being a prisoner to the English in America, shall be named by the Congress, or by Gen. Washington for that purpose, and that three copies of such order be transmitted to me.

Given at Passy, this 14th of January, 1783

B. Franklin

Minister Plenipotentiary from the United States of America at the Court of France

This seems a proper place to relate, that Captain Agnew of the Queen's Rangers, who had been so severely wounded at the battle of Brandywine, as to render him unable to undergo the duties of the corps in the field, had embarked for Virginia, of which he was a native at the time General Leslie went to that province; his father, Mr. Agnew, Chaplain of the Queen's Rangers, Captains Parker and Blair, loyalists, who had joined Earl Dunmore on the first revolt of Virginia, and other gentlemen, sailed on the same expedition. They followed the movements of Gen. Leslie into Carolina; and, Gen. Arnold having taken possession of Portsmouth, were returning to that place on board of the *Romulus*, when that ship was captured by a French squadron.

The following letters will explain their consequent situation; and exemplify some of those acts of benevolence agreeable to the intention and disposition of the Congress, as mentioned by Dr. Franklin in his preceding letter:

Dear Sir—Fortune, I trust, at last has put it in my power to inform you of our unhappy and wretched captivity. You may remember Gen, Washington's visit to the French fleet; it is from that period I date the commencement of our misfortunes last spring; when, being informed of the prisoners taken in the *Romulus*, a distinction was made between the gentlemen of the ship, and the officers passengers for the army in Virginia, viz. Captains James Parker, Blair, Agnew, my father, and Mr. Cramond. Some of the above gentlemen were formerly his old acquaintances. From the knowledge these gentlemen had of the colony, and the French and American operations being so soon to take place there, Mr. Washington's conduct can be easily accounted for; as a demand was soon after made of us, which we were informed of by Congress. The French, either thinking it improper to give up their prisoners to the Americans, or having other views relative to us, refused the demand; but at the same time consented to treat us in the manner I am to inform you of. We were immediately separated from our friends, and embarked on board the frigate *La Hermione*, (as we understood,) for France; having a letter from the Major d'Escadre, informing us we should be sent to France. The *Hermione*, on the contrary, was bound to Boston, where we soon after arrived, and were re-embarked on board *La Concorde*, still thinking ourselves on our way to France; but, to our great surprise, soon learnt that the ship was for St. Domingo, and that we were to be confined there. We arrived the 6th of July; a room in the common prison was prepared for us; but, by the humanity of the Captain of the *La Concorde*, we were prevented going to the prison, and were shut up in an hospital, in hot cells, near four months. As the French and American operations took place in Virginia, so the time of our deliverance approached; and we were (to fulfil the Major's letter) embarked on board of different ships, armed *en Flute*, for France, the 23rd of October. Our passage was dismal. *L'Union*, a 64 gun ship, on board of which was Capt Parker, foundered at sea, the crew being happily saved. *La Sensible*, in which was Mr. Blair, has never been heard of since; the ship, on board of which were my father and myself having lost the use of her rudder in a storm, lay a wreck twenty-four hours. However, sir, we have escaped all, to be more barbarously treated in France. The 6th of December we arrived at Brest; we were landed, and immediately carried to a place of confinement, where we found two officers of the 86th, of the Tobago capitulation. Brest not being a place for keeping prisoners, and the Commandant, probably not knowing of Mr. Blair's absence, sent the next morning an order to conduct the five officers from St Domingo to Dinant Castle. The order being indiscriminate, and the two Tobago gentlemen coming in the same fleet, they were instantly taken and carried off with Capt. Parker, my father, and self, to Dinant. Whether this is a mistake at Brest, or not, I cannot know; for, as the original reason for treating us five with such severity cannot now exist, and having heard we were regarded as hostages for French officers, that were, or had been, in the hands of Admiral Arbuthnot, our present misfortunes may arise from other causes than the primitive, as we are now actually regarded as prisoners of state to France: the above, whether intentional or accidental, had one happy tendency, which is that Mr. Cramond I hope, is, in England. We were put into a large vault or dungeon in Dinant Castle, where we remained in the most wretched situation, until we found means to acquaint the Commandant of Bretagne of our situation, who has been humane enough, for such I must call it, to remove us to St Maloes Castle, where we now are, shut close up as prisoners of state; having seen the orders sent to the Count De Guión for that purpose. I am afraid there is some secret reason for our treatment, that I cannot divine; for no nation, I believe, admires the virtue of loyalty and firmness more than the French. I am indebted to stratagem for the conveyance of this; by the same means, I have written to the Minister, being deprived of pen, ink, and paper, and probably may not have another chance; I trust, should my letter to Lord George Germain miscarry, that Col. Simcoe will use those means his judgment will best point out to inform our friends at home of our situation.

Suffer me, Col. Simcoe, to recommend to your humane and tender sensibility an aged and beloved parent, that, should she stand in need of your kind attention or advice, she may always have it in her power to have recourse to a friend!—But oh God! who knows, perhaps she at this moment, from an independent affluence, is reduced, by the vicissitudes of the times, to penury!—My heart, afflicted with the misfortunes of our family, can no more——

Yours, &c,

Stair Agnew

St. Maloes Castle, 26th Feb. 1782

Caen, 20th August, 1782

My Dear Colonel,—Apprehensive my letters do not reach you, as I have never had the honour of hearing from you since in France, and now having a private opportunity, I send you in part duplicates of those letters which I have wrote you, and which will best tend to inform you of our situation. Your being in England is a circumstance the most happy for us, being convinced at last we have a friend I hope this will not be subjected to any inspection, and consequently shall endeavour to be as particular to you as possible, relative to our present situation.

It is to the Duke of Harcourt, Governor of the province of Normandy, we are indebted for our parole here, and the present indulgences we enjoy; hearing of our situation in the castle of St. Maloes, the victims of policy, he most readily interested himself with the Minister in our behalf, and through his remarkable attention and politeness has much alleviated our misfortunes. He has not been less assiduous in endeavouring to exchange us; but alas, his powers are not equal to his good inclination. Le Marquis de Castries has referred him to the American Minister, and has informed him it was at the instance of America we were detained in France. I have the honour of transmitting to you the letter of Mr. Franklin in answer to the Marquis de Castries on this subject.

Passy, 2nd April, 1782

I have received the letter your Excellency did me the honour of writing to me, relating to Messrs. Agnew, father and son, and Capt. Parker, Englishmen, prisoners taken in America, and brought to France. I know nothing of those persons, or of the circumstances that might induce

307

the Delegates of Virginia to desire their detention, no account of them from that state being come to my hands, nor have I received any orders or instructions from the Congress concerning them. I therefore cannot properly make any opposition to their being permitted to reside at Caen on their parole of honour, or to their being exchanged in pursuance of the cartel, as his Majesty in his wisdom shall think proper.

I am, sir, &c.,

Benjamin Franklin

From this letter we readily concluded that every obstacle was removed; and in consequence the Duke of Harcourt wrote to M. de Castries requesting our exchange, that we might, as British officers, benefit ourselves of the cartel established between the two nations for that express purpose.

The Duke has shown me the answer of M. de Castries to this last letter, and from which it appears determined to keep us in France. He tells him, *«Qu'il ne lui est pas possible d'y condescendre, parceque M. de la Luzerne a mandé à M. de Rochambault que le Congres desiroit qu'ils ne fussent pas échangé, comme étant des Torries dangereux dans le Sud, ou ils servoient trop bien leur Patrie.»*

Such is our situation at present, my dear Colonel; nor have we a hope of relief, but in our country, and your kind endeavours; if we are not demanded, here we remain during the war! Heavens! What a succession of melancholy vicissitudes! I have an aged parent at New York, who, totally dependent on the endeavours of her husband and an only son, perhaps, from a genteel affluence, at this moment is reduced to want! Oh God! what do I say? Perhaps she is no more! Such are the misfortunes attendant on civil war; and shall we, my dear Colonel, who have sacrificed all but a natural and unalienable allegiance, shall we not find friends who dare reclaim us? Who dare insist on our exchange? For what is there a cartel between the two nations? Are we not British officers? Are we not French prisoners? I ever apprehended that the meanest servant was entitled to the protection of the state he served; and shall France, at the instance of America, shut up his Majesty's subjects in her dungeons and castles with impunity? No! Should this happily reach you, I trust such measures will be adopted as to effect our exchange agreeable to the cartel. Surely there are French officers enough in England.

Your's, &c,
Stair Agnew

Lord George Germain had applied to the French Ministry for the release of these officers, previous to the arrival of Lt. Col. Simcoe in England, but with little effect; application was made to the succeeding Secretaries of State. On the approach of peace they were exchanged: it is most probable had the war continued they would have remained prisoners; so faithfully did the Ministers of France serve the American Congress, and maintain the character which that kingdom has acquired for ages, of trampling upon every tie of humanity which interferes with her policy!

The Duke de Lauzun politely offered to procure Lt. Col. Simcoe a passage in the frigate he was to proceed with to France: he received many civilities from the American officers to whom he had been opposed, and Col. Lee, by visiting him, afforded him an opportunity of personally acknowledging the obligation he had been under to that officer. General O'Hara had kindly interested himself in explaining to Earl Cornwallis how necessary it was for him immediately to proceed to New York; and Baron

Steuben desired to procure, through Gen. Washington, a passage for him in the French frigate ready to sail for Europe. Lt. Col. Simcoe had asked Lt. Spencer to acknowledge his sense of the Baron's civilities, and in some trifling points to request his interference; that officer had a long conversation with Baron Steuben, who told him that he had heard of Lt. Col. Tarleton's march to Charlottesville, but not of Lt. Col. Simcoe's to the Point of Fork, and that he took his corps for Earl Cornwallis's army. Lt. Col. Simcoe has often had occasion to mention some of the many, instances of Lt. Spencer's military talents; and the following anecdote will evince the heroic spirit with which he was animated, and on that account be acceptable to the readers of this journal.

At the conclusion of the American war, and previous to the evacuation of New York by the King's troops, Lieut. Spencer of the Queen's Rangers, (who was then at Philadelphia,) received a letter from Major Hanger of the British legion, informing him, that Lieut. H. Paymaster of that regiment had absconded; that he had taken with him five standards which that regiment had in different actions seized from the enemy, and that he was supposed to be in Philadelphia. The Major was pleased to pass some compliments on Lt. Spencer, expressive of the idea he entertained of his integrity and zeal for the service, he desired him to go to Mr. H. well armed, and to force him *at any rate* to deliver up the trophies: indeed he said "I am at ease; for I am sure nothing but the loss of your life in the attempt, can prevent you getting them."

At seven in the evening Lt. Spencer received the Major's letter; without losing a moment he put a pair of pistols in his pockets, went to the sign of the Indian Queen, where he learnt Mr. H. quartered, enquired for his room, and was told by one of the servants that he lodged in such a number, and was at home; he went up, but Mr. H. was not there; he took the liberty however of opening a small trunk he saw in the room; he found the standards, took off his coat, waistcoat and shirt, wrapped them round his body, slit up his waistcoat behind, that he might button it, &c. came out of the house and went to the inn, from which the vehicle set off for New York, which it did that night at 8 o'clock; and the next day he delivered the standards to the Major in New York, who received them with singular marks of joy and proper acknowledgments.

On his road to New York, at Brunswick, Lt. Spencer was insulted by some of the inhabitants; they knew him by his uniform to be one of the cavalry of the Queen's Rangers; of course concluded that he was one of those who had attended Lt. Col. Simcoe in his alert at the time that gentleman was taken prisoner. A singular dislike of the Queen's Rangers had been occasioned by the frequent incursions that corps had made into the Jersies, and particularly by the death of Capt. Vorhees, who was killed on the return of the party under the command of Lt. Col. Simcoe: he was an inhabitant of Brunswick, and was to have been married the day after, if his death had not happened.

The populace assembled (during dinner) round the house, hissing and hooting; and had it not been for the interposition of some American officers, passengers in the same wagon, it is likely they might have proceeded to violent measures had they laid hands on Mr. Spencer, and found the colours as described in his possession: those, only, who are acquainted with the vindictive spirit of the Jersey people can know the fatal consequences.

Lt. Spencer returned immediately to Philadelphia on purpose to give Mr. H. every satisfaction he might require; Mr. H. waited on him and desired immediate redress; Mr.

S. expostulated with him on the impropriety of his conduct; the hour was appointed for the meeting, but Mr. H.
cooled, was sorry for what he had done, and here the matter ended.

****

The following letters will conclude this appendix; they
were sent to Lt. Col. Simcoe soon after the preliminaries of
the peace were divulged in America. The former was written by one of the principals of the associated loyalists on
the upper parts of the Chesapeake, and transmitted to Lt.
Col. Simcoe by Mr. C. Sowers, a loyalist of Pennsylvania. It
is more easy for the reader to imagine than it is for him to
describe the pleasure he has received from these honourable testimonies.

I have the honour in behalf of the deputies of the
associated loyalists in Pennsylvania, Maryland, and the
lower counties on Delaware, by their particular direction, and being fully authorised by them for that purpose, now to express to you the high sense they entertain of your political and military conduct during the
late rebellion in America. They are at a loss whether
most to admire your activity and gallantry in the field,
or your generous and affectionate attachment to his
Majesty's loyal subjects in America, and your unwea-
ried exertions as well to promote their true interest,
as to preserve and protect their property.

As they have with pleasure and satisfaction had
frequent opportunities of seeing your arms crowned
with success, so have they as often experienced the
marks of your favour, attention and protection; these
acts have endeared you to them, and claim their
warmest gratitude.

Your particular countenance to and zeal for the associated loyalists, and your ready concurrence in the

312

measures proposed for their relief, and kind solicitations in their behalf, have made an impression on their minds, words cannot express and time only can erase; and they have exceedingly to regret that the opportunity was not afforded them of evincing to the world, under your command, the sincerity of their professions and their attachment to their sovereign.

They would deem themselves culpable if they did not take this opportunity to mention that your abhorrence of the pillage that too generally took place in this country, and the success that attended your vigilant exertions to prevent it, have marked your character, and insured to you the esteem of all orders and ranks of good men.

Your sudden and unexpected departure from America prevented their paying this tribute of respect to you personally, which they entreat you now to accept, and that you will be assured that under all changes and circumstances your name will be dear to them, and that their wishes and prayers will always be for your prosperity and happiness.

Huntingdon, July 1st, 1783

When we reflect on your military conduct in the course of this war, we, in common with others acquainted with its occurrences, cannot withhold our admiration and respect. But, when you rise to our minds in the relation in which you stand with us, and we view you as our leader and companion, who not only has pointed out to us the road to military reputation, but has shared in common with us its dangers and hardships; when we find, that the whole tenor of your conduct demonstrates the most friendly disposition and attachment to our interests, which, in a particular manner, you have evinced by your unremitted assiduity and zeal, in making known and preferring our pretensions to our Sovereign, which has obtained for us the most gracious marks of his approbation, and the most honourable reward for our services: when these things recur to us, we feel our hearts warmed with the generous glow of gratitude and affection.

We cannot omit observing, with very particular satisfaction, that in the establishment of the corps the whole of the officers are included, and in the ranks they respectively bore.

Wishing you every success in your public pursuits, and the most perfect domestic happiness, we have the honour to be, with the greatest regard, and most perfect esteem,

Yours, &c. &c.

Signed on behalf of the officers of the regiment by

R. Armstrong, Major

John Saunders, Captain

****

A few additions are made to the author's appendix: the extracts have an increased interest in connection with his journal.

THE QUEEN'S RANGERS

Before the command of the Rangers was given to the author, the corps had distinguished itself in the service, and had attracted the attention of the Commander in Chief. In the *Pennsylvania Ledger,* newspaper, of December 3rd, 1777, was printed the following notice:

No regiment in the army has gained more honour this campaign than Major Wemys' (or the Queen's) Rangers; they have been engaged in every principal service, and behaved nobly; indeed most of the officers have been wounded since we took the field in Pennsylvania, General

314

Kniphausen, after the action of the 11th of September, at Brandywine, despatched an aid-de-camp to General Howe with an account of it: what he said concerning it was short, but to the purpose. Tell the General (says he) I must be silent as to the behaviour of the Rangers, for I even want words to express my own astonishment to give him an idea of it. The 13th the following appeared in orders:

> The Commander in Chief desires to convey to the officers and men of the Queen's Rangers his approbation and acknowledgment for their spirited and gallant behaviour in the engagement of the 11th instant, and to assure them how well he is satisfied with their distinguished conduct on that day. His Excellency only regrets their having suffered so much in the gallant execution of their duty.

Captain Saunders patrolling towards Byra Bridge

The New York Commercial Advertiser of October 18th, 1843, contained an article from which an extract may properly be here introduced:

> Whether the imputation upon the honour of Colonel Thomas is true or not, we cannot positively decide. Col. Simcoe, from the bitterness of his prejudices against the Whigs, would of course be disposed to present the case in its worst aspect. It is but just, however, to Col. S. to admit that we have discovered a piece of testimony going directly to maintain what he has said in relation to the violation of his parole by Col. Thomas.
>
> In rummaging one of our drawers of old manuscript collections, on Wednesday, we found a couple of sheets of very interesting reminiscences connected

with the war of the revolution, in New York and its vicinity. Among other matters of curious import, it contains a particular account of the capture of Col. Thomas, of his detention on Long Island, and of his most extraordinary escape; admitting, withal, that he did violate his parole. The good Woman to whom he was in the main indebted for his safety, had probably taken a lesson from the Jewish 'wench' who, under equally emergent circumstances, concealed the messengers conveying to David the state of affairs in Jerusalem, when the unhappy monarch was flying before the legions of his treacherous son.

We regret that we have forgotten to whom we are indebted for this manuscript. If we do not mistake, however, it was handed to us two or three years since, by an elderly gentleman from Long Island. Be that as it may, it comes in very opportunely in connection with the revolutionary recollections revived by the narrative of Col. Simcoe.

THE MANUSCRIPT

Whenever the British army took possession of Long Island, the inhabitants were ordered to appear at Gen. Howe's headquarters, to take the oath of allegiance. Many attended and were sworn, who received a certificate of protection, for which they had to pay a *douceur*. They were then ordered to wear a red band or rag in their hat, as a badge of protection. Whenever it was discovered that a red badge afforded safety and protection to the person who wore it, every white man and negro, with all the boys in the country, mounted a red rag in their hats, which soon caused the abandonment of this badge of slavery. In the year '77, when the Americans had captured many Hessian and British prisoners, and could retaliate on them, for the cruelties which the Americans suffered, the British then relaxed in their severity towards the prisoners of the American army—the officers were removed from the prisons, and paroled to four of the towns of King's county, *viz.* to Flatbush, Flatlands, New Utrecht and Gravesend, where they were billeted on the inhabitants. After the prisoner officers were quartered in those towns, the inhabitants enjoyed peace, preserved the produce of their labour, and became rich; they also received payment for the board of the officers; which many of them never deserved, for the contempt with which the prisoners were treated. The prisoners were strictly forbidden to cross the ridge of hills, or to go to New York; either was deemed a breach of parole. Several broke their parole undiscovered, but several were discovered and remanded to prison. Major Bowne sprang from the custody of the officer who was conducting him to New York, and escaped. Col. Thomas, of West Chester, also escaped from the officer; his case, however, was marked with extreme difficulty, but he succeeded to clear the British in the end.

This officer was surprised in his own house, in West Chester, at daybreak, by a detachment of dragoons. He had gone to his house in the evening, a spy brought the intelligence to the British post, and a detachment of horse was immediately sent to seize him. His house was surrounded before he knew it, when he took his musket and shot a dragoon at his door; he ran up stairs, stepped on a piazza, and sprang over the enemy who were below it; leaped a fence and ran for a piece of woods. Thus the bird would have flown; but one of the officers, who had a fleet horse, leaped the fence and took Thomas, by laying the flat of his sword gently on his head, when Thomas surrendered and was paroled on Long Island.

After he had broken his parole, and escaped from the officer, he returned to New Lotts, where he remained in the woods secretly for several days, and received provisions from his fellow officers, until he got an opportunity to go to New York, where he joined a party of wood-cutters. Thomas was in disguise, and had permitted his beard to grow. The British knew he was in New York, and were searching for him with a negro who knew him well. They came to the house where he was with the wood-cutters. Thomas saw them from a window, when they came to the door, and went in bed; when his face was uncovered, the negro saw him and said, "that is not Thomas."

He then communicated his situation to Mr. John Franklyn, who provided a place for him in the house of a faithful widow. The British suspected that he was concealed in this house, and a party was sent there also to search for him; the widow was apprised of their coming, took Thomas down into the cellar, turned a hogshead over him, and then threw half a bushel of salt on the head of the tub, and left him. The house and cellar were searched, and Thomas escaped by the widow's stratagem. John Franklyn, Henry Ryker, and another person of New York known by No. one, kept a canoe concealed in the barn of No. one, near Greenwich, on the North river; when a favourable opportunity occurred, Franklyn removed Thomas from the widow's house, and No. one conveyed him across the North river to Fort Lee, when he was safe; thus Col. Thomas miraculously escaped.

Lt. Col. Simcoe had information that fifty flat-boats, upon carriages, &c., &c.

The affair narrated in the Journal is told in Lee's Memoirs of the War. Lee's account of the expedition, written in his usual happy manner, is preceded by a handsome compliment to Lieut. Col. Simcoe. The praise awarded to the British officer deserves consideration, coming from the distinguished rebel and gallant young soldier commanding the American Legion, which was a corps similar in most points to Simcoe's, and which, in the defence of the cause of independence, no less distinguished itself.

This officer commanded a legionary corps called the Queen's Rangers, and had during the war signalised himself upon various occasions. He was a man of letters, and like the Romans and Grecians, cultivated science amid the turmoil of camp. He was enterprising, resolute, and persevering; weighing well his project before entered upon, and promptly seizing every advantage which offered in the course of execution. General Washington expecting a French fleet upon our coast in 1779-80, and desirous of being thoroughly prepared for moving upon New York, in case the combined force should warrant it, had made ready a number of boats, which were placed at Middlebrook, a small village up the Raritan river, above Brunswick. Sir Henry Clinton being informed of this preparation, determined to destroy the boats. The enterprise was committed to Lt. Col. Simcoe. He crossed from New York to Elizabethtown Point with his cavalry, and setting out after night, he reached Middlebrook undiscovered and unexpected. Having executed his object, he baffled all our efforts to intercept him on his return, by taking a circuitous route. Instead of turning towards Perth Amboy, which was supposed to be the most probable course, keeping the Raritan on his right, he passed that river, taking the direction towards Monmouth county, leaving Brunswick some miles to his left. Here was stationed a body of militia, who being apprised (it being now day) of the enemy's proximity, made a daring effort to stop him, but failed in the attempt. Simcoe, bringing up the rear, had his horse killed, by which accident he was made prisoner. The cavalry, deprived of their leader, continued to press forward under the second in command, still holding the route to English town. As soon as the militia at Brunswick moved upon the enemy, an express was despatched to Lt. Col. Lee, then posted in the neighbourhood of English town, waiting for the expected arrival of the French fleet, advising him of this extraordinary adventure.

The legion cavalry instantly advanced towards the British horse; but notwithstanding the utmost diligence was used to gain the road leading to South Amboy (which now was plainly the object) before the enemy could reach it, the American cavalry did not effect it. Nevertheless the pursuit was continued, and the legion horse came up with the rear soon after a body of infantry sent over to South Amboy from Staten Island by Sir Henry Clinton to meet Simcoe, had joined, and gave safety to the harassed and successful foe.

This enterprise was considered, by both armies, among the handsomest exploits of the war. Simcoe executed completely his object, then deemed very important; and traversed the country, from Elizabethtown Point to South Amboy, fifty-five miles, in the course of the night and morning; passing through a most hostile region of armed citizens; necessarily skirting Brunswick, a military station; proceeding not more than eight or nine miles from the legion of Lee, his last point of danger, and which became increased from the debilitated condition to which his troops were reduced by previous fatigue. What is very extraordinary, Lt. Col. Simcoe being obliged to feed once in the course of the night, stopped at a depot of forage collected for the Continental army, assumed the character of Lee's cavalry, waked up the commissary about midnight, drew the customary allowance of forage, and gave the usual vouchers, signing the name of the legion Quarter-master, without being discovered by the American forage commissary or his assistants. The dress of both corps was the same, green coatees and leather breeches; yet the success of the stratagem is astonishing.

GENERAL ARNOLD

Extract from Dunlap's History of New York. Vol. II

It appears strange, that Sir Henry Clinton should entrust a traitor with the lives and liberty of armies as he did. But I have been assured by a gentleman of the most unblemished character, now far advanced in years, that when Arnold departed from New York in the command of the army with which he committed depredations in the Chesapeake, 'a dormant commission' was given to Colonels Dundas and Simcoe, jointly, by Sir Henry Clinton, authorising them, if they suspected Arnold of sinister intent, to supersede him, and put him in arrest. This proves that Clinton did not trust him, and we may reasonably suppose that such a watch was set upon his conduct on other occasions.

The gentleman who communicated this fact to me, was in his youth a confidential clerk in Sir Henry Clinton's office, and copied and delivered the dormant commission as directed. This explains a passage in Clinton's letter to his government, in which he says, 'this detachment is under the command of General Arnold, with whom I have thought it right to send Colonels Dundas and Simcoe, as being officers of experience, and much in my confidence.'

M. Fayette, in his public letters, &c., &c.

Extract from *Washington's Writings*, edited by Jared Sparks Vol. VIII

A retreat had been recently commenced by Lord Cornwallis, after pursuing Lafayette to the interior of Virginia. Lafayette said:

The enemy have been so kind as to retire before us. Twice I gave them a chance of fighting, (taking care not to engage farther than I pleased,) but they continued their retrograde motion. Our number is, I think, exaggerated to them, and our seeming boldness confirms the opinion. I thought at first that Lord Cornwallis wanted to get me down as low as possible, and use the cavalry to advantage. But it appears he does not as yet come out, and our position will admit

of partial affairs. His Lordship had (exclusive of the riflemen from Portsmouth, said to be six hundred,) four thousand men, eight hundred of whom were dragoons or mounted infantry. Our force is about equal to his; but only fifteen hundred are regulars, and fifty dragoons. Our little action marks the retreat of the enemy. From the place, at which they first began to retreat, to Williamsburg, is upwards of one hundred miles. His Lordship has done us no harm of any consequence. He has lost a very large part of his former conquests, and has not made any in this state. Gen. Greene demanded of me only to hold my ground in Virginia; but the movements of Lord Cornwallis may answer better purposes than that in the military line.
—*La Fayette's MS. Letter, June 28th.*

In the following letter to the Governor of Virginia of the same date, Lafayette gives an account of the recent action:

Colonel Simcoe was so lucky as to avoid a part of the stroke; but, although the whole of the light corps could not arrive in time, some of them did. Major McPherson having taken up fifty light infantry behind fifty dragoons, overtook Simcoe, and, regardless of numbers, made an immediate charge. He was supported by the riflemen, who behaved most gallantly and did great execution. The alarm-guns were fired at Williamsburg (only six miles distant from the field.) A detachment just then going to Gloucester was recalled, and the whole British army came out to save Simcoe. They retired next morning, when our army got within striking distance.

Our loss is two captains, two lieutenants, ten privates wounded; two lieutenants, one sergeant, six privates killed; one lieutenant, twelve privates, whose fate is not known; one sergeant taken. The enemy had about sixty killed, among whom are several officers, and about one hundred wounded. They acknowledge the action was smart, and Lord Cornwallis was heard to express himself vehemently upon the disproportion between his and our killed, which must be attributed to the great skill of our riflemen. This little success has given great satisfaction to the troops, and increased their ardour. I have put all the riflemen under Campbell. Tomorrow I intend to reconnoitre a position below Byrd's Ordinary. Your return to Richmond, and this little affair, will particularly mark his Lordship's retreat, and the recovery of every part of the state not under naval protection.

— *La Fayette's MS. Letter, June 28th*

THE CAPITULATION AT YORK TOWN

Extract from the general return of officers and privates surrendered prisoners of war, the 19th of October, 1781, to the allied army, under the command of General Washington, taken from the original muster rolls:—

Queen's Rangers—1 lieutenant-colonel, 1 major, 10 captains, 15 lieutenants, 11 cornets, 3 quarter-masters, 2 surgeons, 24 sergeants, 5 trumpeters, 248 rank and file—total 320.

Memoir of the Author

In the church of St. Andrew, town of Cotterstock, North-amptonshire, England, is erected a white marble monument bearing this epitaph:

> To the memory of John Simcoe, Esq., late commander of his Majesty's ship *Pembroke*, who died in the royal service, upon the important expedition against Quebec, in North America, in the year 1759, aged 45 years. He spent the greatest part of his life in the service of his king and country, preferring the good of both to all private views. He was an officer esteemed for his great abilities in naval and military affairs, of unquestioned bravery, and unwearied diligence. He was an indulgent husband, a tender parent, and sincere friend; generous, humane and benevolent to all; so that his loss to the public, as well as to his friends, cannot be too much regretted. This monument was, in honour to his memory, erected by his disconsolate wife, Catharine Simcoe, 1760.

Captain Simcoe, of the navy, was a native of Northamptonshire, and, after a life most honourably employed in the service of his country, closed his career in the profession which seemed to promise him much renown and advancement, leaving a widow and two infant sons, the eldest of whom was John Graves Simcoe, the subject of this memoir, then about seven years of age.

Though bred in the navy, and highly esteemed as an excellent officer, Captain Simcoe was peculiarly partial to the military service, and is said to have left behind him a valuable treatise on tactics in that profession. The most striking occurrence of his life arose however, it is said, from an accident, improved in a manner peculiar to genius and extensive professional knowledge. The story is that he was taken prisoner by the French, in America, and carried up the river St Lawrence. As his character was little known, he was watched only to prevent his escape; but, from his observations in the voyage to Quebec, and the little incidental information he was able to obtain, he constructed a chart of that river, and carried up General Wolfe to his famous attack upon the Canadian capital. He was promoted to a captaincy in 1743, at the age of twenty-nine. Upon the trial of Admiral Byng in 1756-7, he served as a member of the court martial convened for that purpose, and was then aged forty-two years.

The widowed mother with her two sons, soon after their father's death, removed to Exeter, and our author received the first part of his education at the free grammar school of that town. His younger brother was unfortunately drowned in his childhood. The earliest years of the young soldier were rather solid than brilliant, though he possessed both spirit and emulation, and was in the foremost rank among his fellows. But though a school-boy, his acquisitions in some departments of knowledge were of a superior kind. At an early age he had read Homer in Pope's translation; and in his boyish days acted with his companions the scenes of the Illiad. He was not slightly versed in modern history, and already devoured with eagerness every tale of war. At about the age of fourteen, he was removed to Eton school, and from thence in due course to Merton College, Oxford.

But the military ardour of young Simcoe, which so early sparkled, soon blew into a flame, and, at the age of nineteen, he obtained an ensign's commission in the 35th regiment, an event probably hastened by the impending hostilities with America. He did not embark from England with his regiment, but he landed at Boston on the memorable day of the battle of Bunker's Hill. He soon afterwards acted as adjutant of the 35th regiment, but it does not appear that he ever was actually appointed to this office; and at no distant period purchased command of a company in the 40th, which he led at the battle of Brandywine, where he was wounded. Captain Simcoe was always a soldier in his heart, and attentive to every part of his duty. He already saw that regularity in the interior economy of a soldier's life contributed to his health, and estimated the attention of the inferior officers by the strength of a company or a regiment in the field. His ambition invariably led him to aspire at command; and even when the army first landed at Staten Island he went to New York to request the command of the Queen's Rangers, a provincial corps then newly raised, which he did not finally obtain until after the battle of Brandywine, in October, 1777. He knew that common opinion had imprinted on the partisan the most dishonourable stain, and associated the idea with that of dishonesty, rapine, and falsehood. Yet, on the other hand, he also knew that the command of a light corps had been considered as the best source of instruction, as a means of acquiring a habit of self-dependence for resources, and of prompt decision so peculiarly requisite in trusts of importance.

The corps of Rangers claimed all the attention of the now Major-commandant Simcoe, and contributed greatly to lessen his paternal fortune, for though warmly alive to the interests of others, he was always inattentive to his own.

We find in Rivington's Royal Gazette, printed at New York during the presence of the British army in the city, an advertisement for recruits somewhat significant of the care and expense bestowed upon the equipment of this effective band of partisans. It is as follows:

All aspiring heroes have now an opportunity of distinguishing themselves by joining the Queen's Ranger Huzzars, Commanded by Lieutenant-Colonel Simcoe. Any spirited young man will receive every encouragement, be immediately mounted on an elegant horse, and furnished with clothing, accoutrements, &c., to the amount of forty guineas, by applying to Cornet Spencer, at his quarters, No. 1033 Water street, or his rendezvous, Hewitt's Tavern, near the Coffee House, and the defeat at Brandywine, on Golden Hill.

Whoever brings a Recruit shall instantly
receive two guineas.
Vivant Rex et Regina

The Rangers were disciplined, not for parade, but for active service. They were never to march in *slow* time; were directed to fire with precision and steadiness; to wield the bayonet with force and effect; to disperse and rally with rapidity. In short, in the instructions for the management of the corps, its commander seems to have anticipated the more modern tactics of the French army.

The deeds and adventures of Colonel Simcoe and his Rangers during the War of Independence, need not be told here: his journal of their campaigns is before the reader—written, it is said, "with the simplicity of Caesar and Xenophon." Being stationed with his corps at Gloucester Point, opposite York Town, when the latter place was besieged by the allied French and American forces, the

Queen's Rangers and their commander were included in the surrender of the army of Cornwallis. Colonel Simcoe, in ill health, equally the resuLt. of excessive fatigue from his arduous services, and of vexation at the inglorious fate of his cherished soldiers, was sent away in the *Bonetta* sloop of war, which, by an article of the capitulation the British reserved to transport their sick and disabled to New York city, to be exchanged as prisoners of war. The famed Queen's Rangers were never, as their enthusiastic leader had fondly hoped, re-assembled under his command. The officers of the corps were afterwards put on the half-pay list, and their provincial rank was made permanent in the regular British army.

The capture at York Town being essentially an end of the war, Colonel Simcoe returned to England greatly exhausted, and his constitution considerably impaired. He was received with the most gracious attention by the King, by his friends with the most ardent affection, by the companions of his toils and dangers with the sincerest congratulation. The services he had performed being not unknown to his Sovereign he was appointed Lieutenant-Colonel commandant to a corps to be raised in Canada, to which he gave the name of the Queen's Rangers.

The profession of a high principle of soldierly honour, of ardent attachment to military life, and the claim of credit for his Rangers, which occur in the Journal of the brave Simcoe, may be considered fully warrantable. Stedman, a British historian of the War of Independence, who himself served during its campaigns, makes frequent and honourable mention of the corps and its commander. Tarleton, who was engaged in the same kind of service, mostly in the southern department, corroborates whatever of Simcoe's narrative comes within the scope of his own history of the British Legion which he commanded.

Sir Henry Clinton's letter to Lord George Germaine may be quoted as sufficient authority for the value attached to his services by his superiors in rank:

> Lieut. Col. Simcoe has been at the head of a battalion since October, 1777; and since that time has been the perpetual advance of the army. The history of the corps under his command is a series of gallant, skilful, and successful enterprises against the enemy, *without a single reverse.* The Queen's Rangers have killed or taken twice their own numbers. Col. Simcoe himself has been thrice wounded; and I do not scruple to assert, that his successes have been no less the fruit of the most extensive knowledge of his profession which study and the experience within his reach could give him, than of the most watchful attention and shining courage.
>
> Charleston, South Carolina, May 13th, 1780

The leisure of the camp and of winter quarters was by Col. Simcoe filled up with study. Tacitus and Xenophon were his chief companions, and military history claimed a considerable portion of his attention. Few retired scholars read more than the officer on the alert in the advance of the army; and very few read to a better purpose. He saw with clearness, and comprehended with accuracy, every subject in all its varied bearings, and in its most extended relations. His daily improvements must of consequence have been considerable; and though his own profession attracted his principal attention there were few subjects of science not familiar to him.

A life of tranquillity restored the soldier's mind to its former tone, and his constitution to a state of health, which, if not perfect, was apparently so. Not long after retiring from active service he married a Miss Guillim, a near relation of the lady of Admiral Graves, who had commanded at Boston, and who was a distant relation of his own. He was, in 1790, elected a member of Parliament to represent the borough of St Maws', Cornwall, and his name appears in the debates on the bill by which the province of Quebec was divided into Upper and Lower Canada, and each of them placed under the superintend- ence of a Lieutenant-Governor, subject to the authority of the Governor-General of British America. Col. Simcoe was appointed Lieutenant-Governor of Upper Canada, and on his arrival with his family in the province had the country accurately surveyed, and then formed his plans for peopling and improving it.

He first thought of placing the centre of his settlements within the land enclosed by the lakes Ontario, Erie, and Huron, and the Detroit river; but as the Niagara was to be given up to the United States, he altered his plan. York, on the north-west side of Lake Ontario, had been before determined on for the capital, but Governor Simcoe, not approving of that plan, intended to fix it on the banks of the river Thames, between Huron and Ontario. This was also dropped, and York (now Toronto) was made the seat of government. To increase the population was the great and favourite scheme of the new governor, and as he had the allotment of lands vested in him, he was enabled to pro- mote this desirable and useful measure.

The families of American officers and soldiers who ad- hered to the royal cause at the conclusion of the war, ob- tained grants on the British side of the boundary line, as well as many officers and soldiers of the regular forces. The policy of Governor Simcoe was to draw as many emigrants from the American states as he could, and by means of his mild and disinterested government, to promote a love for the national character of Englishmen in those states. To half-pay officers he held out a share of these lands, and he also granted discharges to soldiers serving in the regiments then in Canada, who had been a certain number of years in the country, and allotted settlements to them. In the meantime, that the forces might not be incomplete, he proposed enlisting Americans whom he expected to become soon attached to the service. These military settlers he intended to occupy the lands on the frontiers towards the states, and on the banks of the lakes.

The inland parts he set aside for those who had emigrated, and, in case of their not being zealously attached to the existing government, the military settlers, from their situation, were to act with vigour against them, or in the event of a war with America, which would be contrary to the interest of both nations, defend the frontiers. A militia formed of such settlers might, he thought, in those instances, prove nearly as useful as a regular corps. In pursuance of these plans, Col. Simcoe, on all occasions, gave encouragement and assistance to those who applied for lands, or who were already in possession of them. The whole of his conduct, during the time he enjoyed the government of Upper Canada, was honourable, liberal, and admirably calculated to lay the foundation of private and public prosperity.

After remaining five years in this settlement, Governor Simcoe returned to England, to the great regret of all the inhabitants, who appreciated his many public and private virtues. Governor Simcoe has been charged with unworthy acts towards his American neighbours of the United States. Instigating the savages to hostilities upon our frontiers, that our government might be harrassed with Indian wars; abetting the natives in their claim to territory west and north of the Ohio River; disposing of his military forces, and arranging other matters upon the borders of his province with a direct view to a breach of peace between his nation and the

American states, are alleged to have been practices pursued in a manner confirming the stories of his hatred towards the "Yankees," and his desire to repay them for their unpardoned offence of having recently achieved their independence as a people. Naturally some prejudice would be indulged in by Governor Simcoe towards those with whom he had been actively at war in a civil contest. The cause for such feeling, or proof that it was shown in improper words and acts, need not now be sought. The Governor's kindness and hospitality to some of our official agents, while in his province, it is pleasing to find recorded in the private journal of General Lincoln, kept by him when despatched as one of the Commissioners of the United States to treat with the Indians in 1793. The following passages are, at this day, somewhat curious and interesting:

May 25.—Immediately on my arrival at Niagara, Governor Simcoe sent for me; the other Commissioners were with him; he showed me my room. We remained with him a number of days; but knowing that we occupied a large proportion of his house, and that Mrs. Simcoe was absent, and so probably on our account, we contemplated a removal, and of encamping at the landing, six miles from this place. But when the Governor was informed of our intentions he barred a removal. His politeness and hospitality, of which he has a large share, prevented our executing the designs we had formed.

June 24.—The King's birthday.—At eleven o'clock the Governor had a levee at his house, at which the officers of government, the members of the legislature, the officers of the army, and a number of strangers attended. At one o'clock there was firing from the troops, the battery, and from the ship in the harbour. In the evening there was quite a splendid ball, about twenty well dressed handsome ladies, and about three times that number of gentlemen present. They danced from seven o'clock to eleven. Supper was then announced, where we found everything good and in pretty taste. The music and dancing were good, and everything was conducted with propriety. What excited the best feelings of my heart was the ease and affection with which the ladies met each other; although there were a number present whose mothers sprang from the aborigines of the country. They appeared as well dressed as the company in general, and intermixed with them in a manner which evinced at once the dignity of their own minds and the good sense of others. These ladies possess great ingenuity and industry, and have great merit; for the education which they have acquired is owing principally to their own industry, as their father, Sir William Johnson, was dead, and the mother retained the dress and manners of her tribe.

Governor Simcoe is exceedingly attentive to these public assemblies, and makes it his study to reconcile the inhabitants, who have tasted the pleasures of society, to their present situation, in an infant province. He intends the next winter to have concerts and assemblies very frequently. Hereby he at once evinces a regard to the happiness of the people and his knowledge of the world; for while the people are allured to become settlers in this country, from the richness of the soil, and the clemency of the seasons, it is important to make their situation as flattering as possible.

The Duke de la Rochefoucault Liancourt speaks at great length of Governor Simcoe and his Canadian policy. He says:

But for this inveterate hatred against the United States, which he too loudly professes, and which carries him too far, General Simcoe appears in the most advantageous light. He is just, active, enlightened, brave, frank, and possesses the confidence of the country, of the troops, and of all those who join him in the administration of public affairs. To these he attends with the closest application; he preserves all the old friends of his King, and neglects no means to procure him new ones. He unites, in my judgment, all the qualities which his station requires, to maintain the important possession of Canada, if it be possible that England can long retain it.

In his private life, Governor Simcoe is simple, plain and obliging. He lives in a noble and hospitable manner, without pride; his mind is enlightened; his character mild and obliging; he discourses with much good sense on all subjects, but his favourite topics are his projects and war, which seem to be the objects of his leading passions. He is acquainted with the military history of all countries; no hillock catches his eye without exciting in his mind the idea of a fort, which might be constructed on the spot; and with the construction of this fort he associates the plan of operations for a campaign, especially of that which is to lead him to Philadelphia.

Mrs. Simcoe is a lady of thirty-six years of age. She is timid, and speaks little; but she is a woman of sense, handsome and amiable, and fulfils all the duties of mother and wife with the most scrupulous exactness. The performance of the latter she carries so far as to be of great assistance to her husband by her talents for drawing, the practice of which confined to maps and plans, enables her to be extremely useful to the Governor.

An anecdote, related by the Duke, is worth quoting as a curious illustration of Simcoe's wish to gain the favour of the savages:

> The Governor is very anxious to oblige and please the Indians; his only son, a child four years old, is dressed as an Indian, and called Tioga, which name has been given him by the Mohawks. This harmless farce may be of use in the intercourse with the Indians."

In October, 1794, Colonel Simcoe was promoted to the rank of Major-General, and a new field was soon opened for the exercise of his abilities in the Island of St. Domingo, which in 1793 had been taken possession of by the troops from Jamaica, and now required a person of talents to take the command of it, as civil governor and commander in chief, in the room of Sir Adam Williamson. As there was none more deserving of so important a station, Major-General Simcoe was appointed, with the local rank of Lieutenant-General, on the 3rd of December, 1796. The nomination of this officer was very acceptable to all ranks in the island, in which he arrived during February of the following year. But the colony was soon deprived of its valued governor, who returned to England in the month of July, in the same year. Short, however, as was his stay, he did more than any former general, in conciliating the native inhabitants to the British government.

On the 3rd of October, 1798, he was made a Lieutenant-General in the British army. In 1801, when the French invasion of England was threatened, the important command of the town of Plymouth, the county of Devon, &c, was entrusted to him, and from his uncommon exertions in discipling the volunteers, and in other preparations, it was thought that the enemy, in any attempt to land in that part of the country, would have received a severe check.

The suspected design of France to invade Portugal, in 1806, directed the anxious attention of the British government towards the critical situation of that country, and the first care of the ministry was promptly to provide the only remaining ally of England upon the continent with the assistance of forces proportioned to the magnitude of the threatened and imminent danger. Lieutenant-General Simcoe and the Earl of Rosslyn, with their staff, were immediately sent to join Lord St. Vincent, who was with a fleet in the Tagus, and to open, in conjunction with him, such a communication with the Court of Lisbon, as might at once lead to a full understanding of the extent of the threatened danger, the means of resisting it, and the best mode of co-operating for that purpose.

General Simcoe was taken ill on the voyage, and his malady increased so rapidly after his arrival, that he was under the necessity of speedily returning to England, where he died a few hours after he landed.

The appointment to the chief command of the British forces in India had been conferred upon General Simcoe as successor to Lord Lake, and his lady was in London making the necessary preparations for the voyage when she received the melancholy intelligence of his death, shortly after his arrival at Torbay in Devonshire.

Thus died Lieutenant-General John Graves Simcoe at the age of fifty-four years, a soldier, a gentleman, and a scholar. The glory, the titles, and the preferments seeming to await his career in India were by an overruling Providence not permitted to be attained by him. Nature made him one of her noblemen, and by inheritance likewise the title was his. Fortune has given him a space moderate indeed in history. But for his untimely end, however, no complaint probably would have been made that he did not reach the goal of his highest ambition as a soldier, to wear his honours in their newest gloss at least, if, in death, he had cast them aside too soon.

His country was deprived of an accomplished and skilful officer, and his widow and children of an excellent husband and father. As a military man General Simcoe was often consulted by those high in office, and was a member of every board of general officers ordered by the King after his promotion made him eligible. In fact few gentlemen in the service were more capable of deciding on professional affairs, whether respecting discipline, or interior economy. He was also highly esteemed by a numerous circle of friends of the first respectability, and his opinion and advice were taken in matters of the most interesting nature, for which he was eminently qualified, by his good sense and knowledge of the world.

LEONAUR

ALSO FROM LEONAUR
AVAILABLE IN SOFTCOVER OR HARDCOVER WITH DUST JACKET

THE COMPLEAT RIFLEMAN HARRIS *by Benjamin Harris as told to & transcribed by Captain Henry Curling*—The adventures of a soldier of the 95th (Rifles) during the Peninsular Campaign of the Napoleonic Wars

WITH WELLINGTON'S LIGHT CAVALRY *by William Tomkinson*—The Experiences of an officer of the 16th Light Dragoons in the Peninsular and Waterloo campaigns of the Napoleonic Wars.

SERGEANT BOURGOGNE *by Adrien Bourgogne*—With Napoleon's Imperial Guard in the Russian Campaign and on the Retreat from Moscow 1812 - 13.

SWORDS OF HONOUR *by Henry Newbolt & Stanley L. Wood*—The Careers of Six Outstanding Officers from the Napoleonic Wars, the Wars for India and the American Civil War, with dozens of illustrations by Stanley L. Wood.

SURTEES OF THE RIFLES *by William Surtees*—A Soldier of the 95th (Rifles) in the Peninsular campaign of the Napoleonic Wars.

ENSIGN BELL IN THE PENINSULAR WAR *by George Bell*—The Experiences of a young British Soldier of the 34th Regiment 'The Cumberland Gentlemen' in the Napoleonic wars.

HUSSAR IN WINTER *by Alexander Gordon*—A British Cavalry Officer during the retreat to Corunna in the Peninsular campaign of the Napoleonic Wars.

NAPOLEONIC WAR STORIES *by Sir Arthur Quiller-Couch*—Tales of soldiers, spies, battles & sieges from the Peninsular & Waterloo campaingns.

JOURNALS OF ROBERT ROGERS OF THE RANGERS *by Robert Rogers*—The exploits of Rogers & the Rangers in his own words during 1755-1761 in the French & Indian War.

KERSHAW'S BRIGADE VOLUME 1 *by D. Augustus Dickert*—Manassas, Seven Pines, Sharpsburg (Antietam), Fredricksburg, Chancellorsville, Gettysburg, Chickamauga, Chattanooga, Fort Sanders & Bean Station..

KERSHAW'S BRIGADE VOLUME 2 *by D. Augustus Dickert*—At the wilderness, Cold Harbour, Petersburg, The Shenandoah Valley and Cedar Creek.

A TIGER ON HORSEBACK *by L. March Phillips*—The Experiences of a Trooper & Officer of Rimington's Guides - The Tigers - during the Anglo-Boer war 1899 - 1902.

LEONAUR

ALSO FROM LEONAUR
AVAILABLE IN SOFTCOVER OR HARDCOVER WITH DUST JACKET

SEPOYS, SIEGE & STORM *by Charles John Griffiths*—The Experiences of a young officer of H.M.'s 61st Regiment at Ferozepore, Delhi ridge and at the fall of Delhi during the Indian mutiny 1857.

CAMPAIGNING IN ZULULAND *by W. E. Montague*—Experiences on campaign during the Zulu war of 1879 with the 94th Regiment.

THE STORY OF THE GUIDES *by G. J. Younghusband*—The Exploits of the Soldiers of the famous Indian Army Regiment from the northwest frontier 1847 - 1900..

ZULU: 1879 *by D.C.F. Moodie & the Leonaur Editors*—The Anglo-Zulu War of 1879 from contemporary sources: First Hand Accounts, Interviews, Dispatches, Official Documents & Newspaper Reports.

THE RECOLLECTIONS OF SKINNER OF SKINNER'S HORSE *by James Skinner*—James Skinner and his 'Yellow Boys' Irregular cavalry in the wars of India between the British, Mahratta, Rajput, Mogul, Sikh & Pindarree Forces.

TOMMY ATKINS' WAR STORIES 14 FIRST HAND ACCOUNTS—Fourteen first hand accounts from the ranks of the British Army during Queen Victoria's Empire Original & True Battle Stories Recollections of the Indian Mutiny With the 49th in the Crimea With the Guards in Egypt The Charge of the Six Hundred With Wolseley in Ashanti Alma, Inkermann and Magdala With the Gunners at Tel-el-Kebir Russian Guns and Indian Rebels Rough Work in the Crimea In the Maori Rising Facing the Zulus From Sebastopol to Lucknow Sent to Save Gordon On the March to Chitral Tommy by Rudyard Kipling

CHASSEUR OF 1914 *by Marcel Dupont*—Experiences of the twilight of the French Light Cavalry by a young officer during the early battles of the great war in Europe.

TROOP HORSE & TRENCH *by R. A. Lloyd*—The experiences of a British Lifeguardsman of the household cavalry fighting on the western front during the First World War 1914-18.

THE EAST AFRICAN MOUNTED RIFLES *by C. J. Wilson*—Experiences of the campaign in the East African bush during the First World War.

THE FIGHTING CAMELIERS *by Frank Reid*—The exploits of the Imperial Camel Corps in the desert and Palestine campaigns of the First World War.

LEONAUR

ALSO FROM LEONAUR
AVAILABLE IN SOFTCOVER OR HARDCOVER WITH DUST JACKET

CAPTAIN OF THE 95th (Rifles) *by Jonathan Leach*—An officer of Wellington's Sharpshooters during the Peninsular, South of France and Waterloo Campaigns of the Napoleonic Wars.

THE KHAKEE RESSALAH *by Robert Henry Wallace Dunlop*—Service & adventure with the Meerut volunteer horse during the Indian mutiny 1857-1858

BUGLER AND OFFICER OF THE RIFLES *by William Green & Harry Smith* With the 95th (Rifles) during the Peninsular & Waterloo Campaigns of the Napoleonic Wars

BAYONETS, BUGLES AND BONNETS *by James 'Thomas' Todd*—Experiences of hard soldiering with the 71st Foot - the Highland Light Infantry - through many battles of the Napoleonic wars including the Peninsular & Waterloo Campaigns

A NORFOLK SOLDIER IN THE FIRST SIKH WAR *by J W Baldwin*—Experiences of a private of H.M. 9th Regiment of Foot in the battles for the Punjab, India 1845-46

A CAVALRY OFFICER DURING THE SEPOY REVOLT *by A.R.D. Mackenzie*—Experiences with the 3rd Bengal Light Cavalry, the Guides and Sikh Irregular Cavalry from the outbreak to Delhi and Lucknow

THE ADVENTURES OF A LIGHT DRAGOON *by George Farmer & G.R. Gleig*—A cavalryman during the Peninsular & Waterloo Campaigns, in captivity & at the siege of Bhurtpore, India

THE COMPLEAT RIFLEMAN HARRIS *by Benjamin Harris as told to & transcribed by Captain Henry Curling*—The adventures of a soldier of the 95th (Rifles) during the Peninsular Campaign of the Napoleonic Wars

THE RED DRAGOON *by W.J. Adams*—With the 7th Dragoon Guards in the Cape of Good Hope against the Boers & the Kaffir tribes during the 'war of the axe' 1843-48

THE LIFE OF THE REAL BRIGADIER GERARD - Volume 1 - THE YOUNG HUSSAR 1782 - 1807 *by Jean-Baptiste De Marbot*—A French Cavalryman Of the Napoleonic Wars at Marengo, Austerlitz, Jena, Eylau & Friedland

THE LIFE OF THE REAL BRIGADIER GERARD Volume 2 IMPERIAL AIDE-DE-CAMP 1807 - 1811 *by Jean-Baptiste De Marbot*—A French Cavalryman of the Napoleonic Wars at Saragossa, Landshut, Eckmuhl, Ratisbon, Aspern-Essling, Wagram, Busaco & Torres Vedras

ALSO FROM LEONAUR
AVAILABLE IN SOFTCOVER OR HARDCOVER WITH DUST JACKET

EW2 EYEWITNESS TO WAR SERIES
CAPTAIN OF THE 95th (Rifles) *by Jonathan Leach*

An officer of Wellington's Sharpshooters during the
Peninsular, South of France and Waterloo Campaigns
of the Napoleonic Wars.

SOFTCOVER : **ISBN 1-84677-001-7**
HARDCOVER : **ISBN 1-84677-016-5**

WFI THE WARFARE FICTION SERIES
NAPOLEONIC WAR STORIES
by Sir Arthur Quiller-Couch

Tales of soldiers, spies, battles & Sieges from the
Peninsular & Waterloo campaigns

SOFTCOVER : **ISBN 1-84677-003-3**
HARDCOVER : **ISBN 1-84677-014-9**

EWI EYEWITNESS TO WAR SERIES
RIFLEMAN COSTELLO *by Edward Costello*

The adventures of a soldier of the 95th (Rifles) in the
Peninsular & Waterloo Campaigns of the Napoleonic wars.

SOFTCOVER : **ISBN 1-84677-000-9**
HARDCOVER : **ISBN 1-84677-018-1**

MCI THE MILITARY COMMANDERS SERIES
**JOURNALS OF ROBERT ROGERS OF THE
RANGERS** *by Robert Rogers*

The exploits of Rogers & the Rangers in his own words
during 1755-1761 in the French & Indian War.

SOFTCOVER : **ISBN 1-84677-002-5**
HARDCOVER : **ISBN 1-84677-010-6**

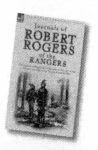

CPSIA information can be obtained at www.ICGtesting.com
Printed in the USA
BVOW08s0016290715

410876BV00001B/49/P